Los Gatos High School

THUNDERHEAD UNDERGROUND FALLS

by

Joel Orff

ALTERNATIVE   COMICS

Thunderhead Underground Falls

First printing, May 2007

Published by Alternative Comics
503 NW 37th Avenue
Gainesville, FL 32609-2204
(352) 373-6336
email: jmason@indyworld.com
website: www.indyworld.com/altcomics

joelorff@yahoo.com   www.jorff.com

Publisher: Jeff Mason

Thanks to Tony, Andrea and Lynn for
the indispensable help and advice, and to
the 'mad poets' for braving the coldest night
of the year in Duluth and providing the
original inspiration for this book.

Printed in Canada
13-digit ISBN: 978-1-891867-88-0
10-digit ISBN: 1-891867-88-1

Also by Joel Orff from Alternative Comics:

Waterwise
Strum and Drang: Great Moments in Rock 'n' Roll

BC # 34683

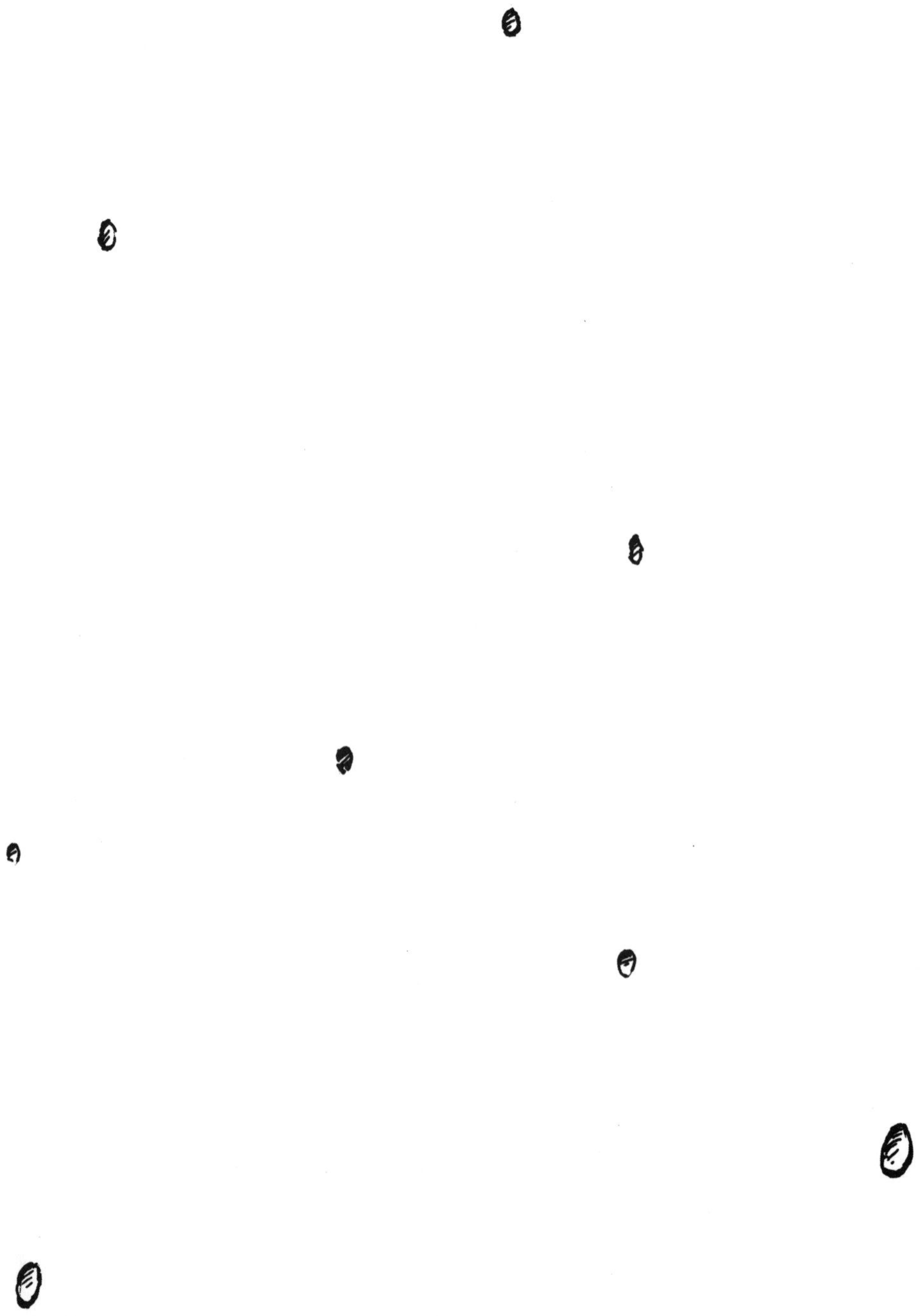

SCREEEE

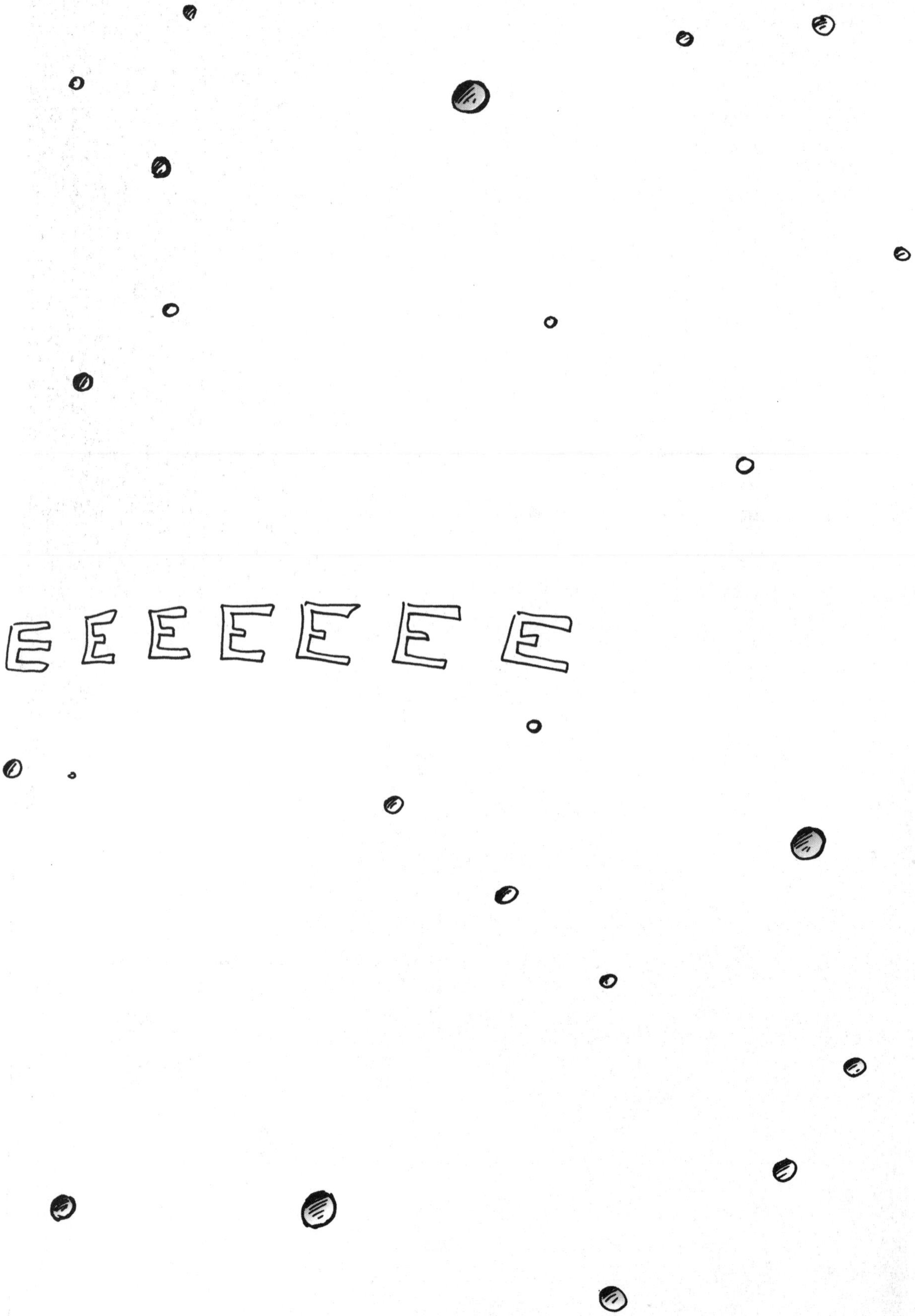
EEEEEEE

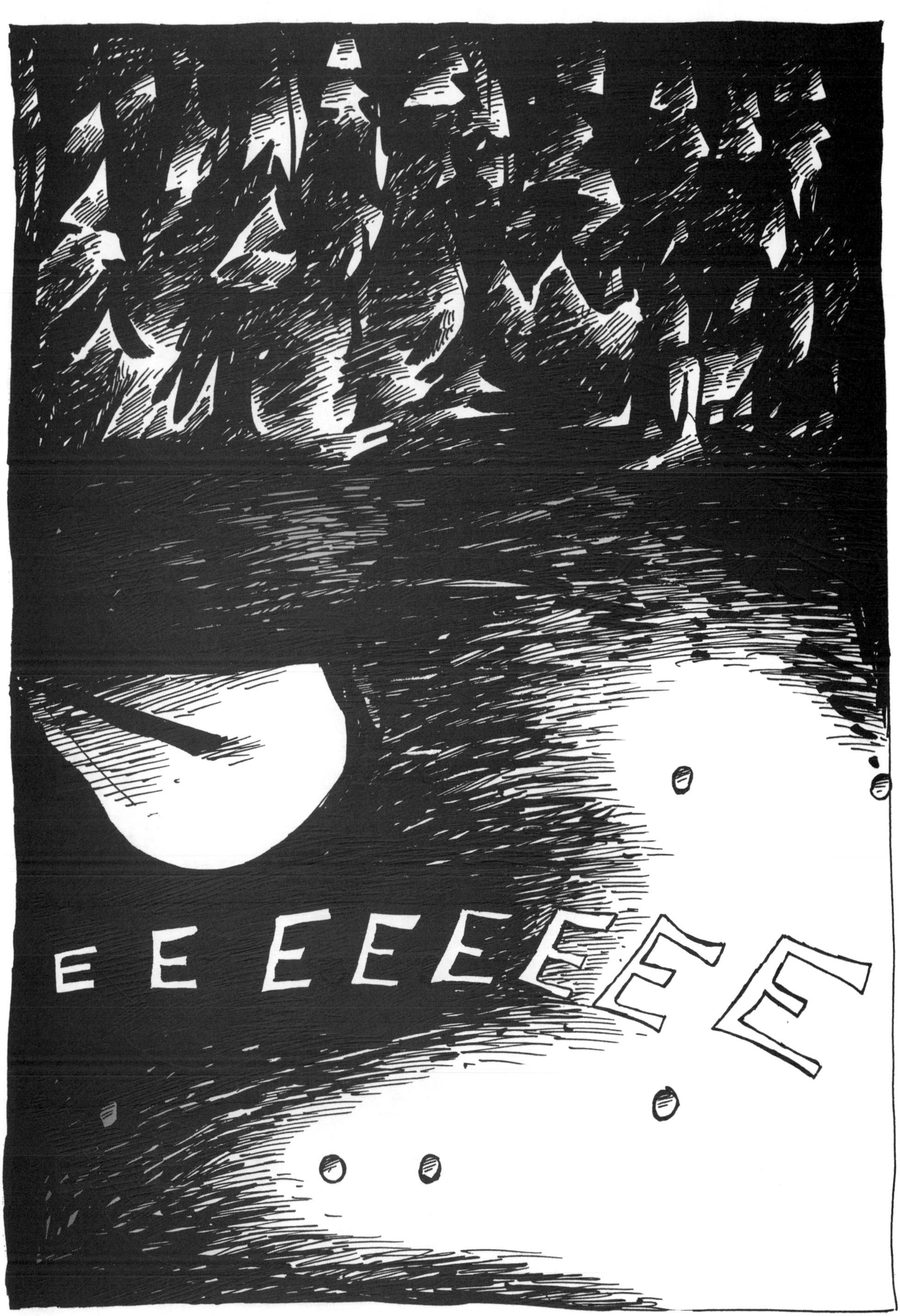
EEEEEEEE

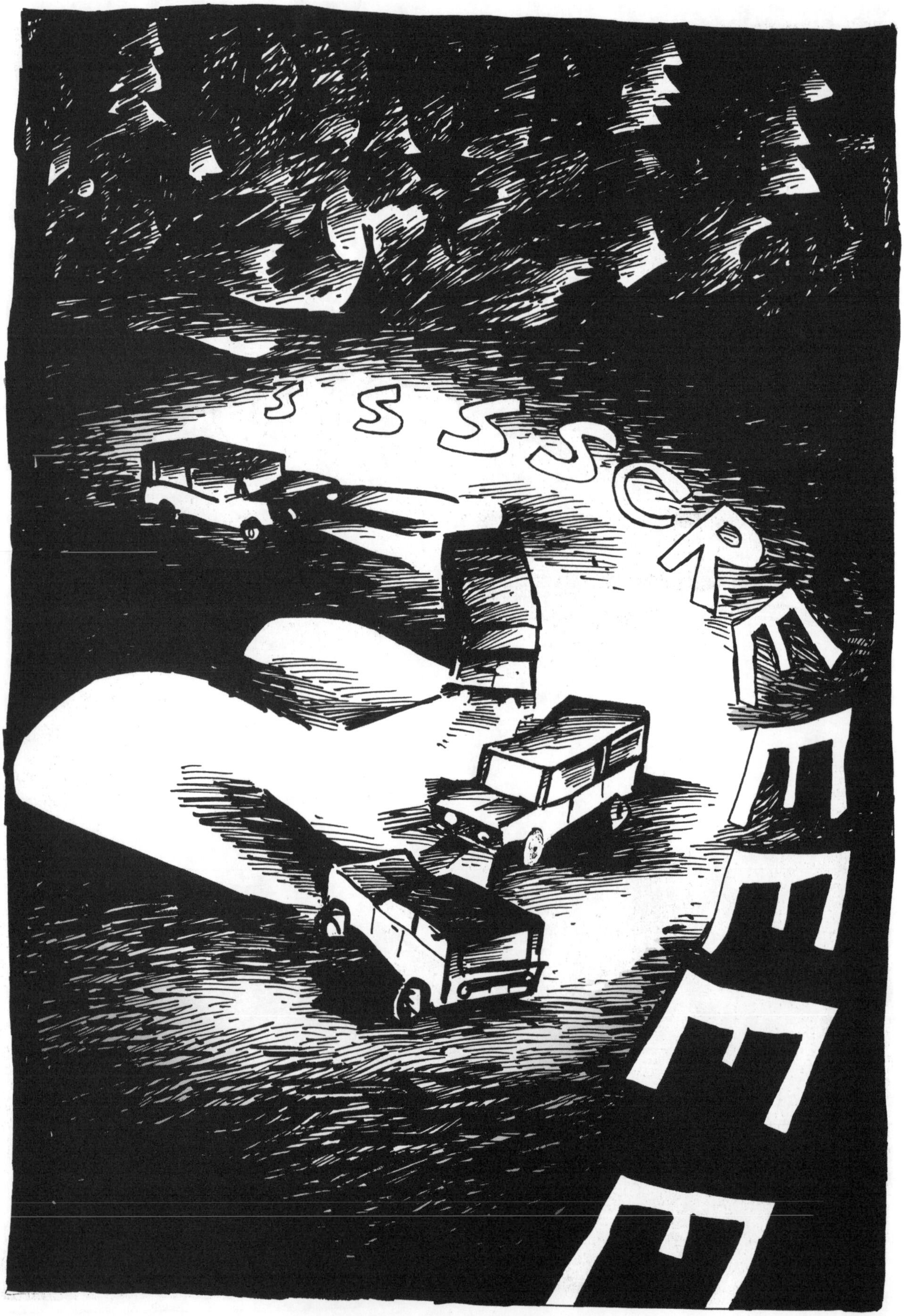
SSSSCREEEEE

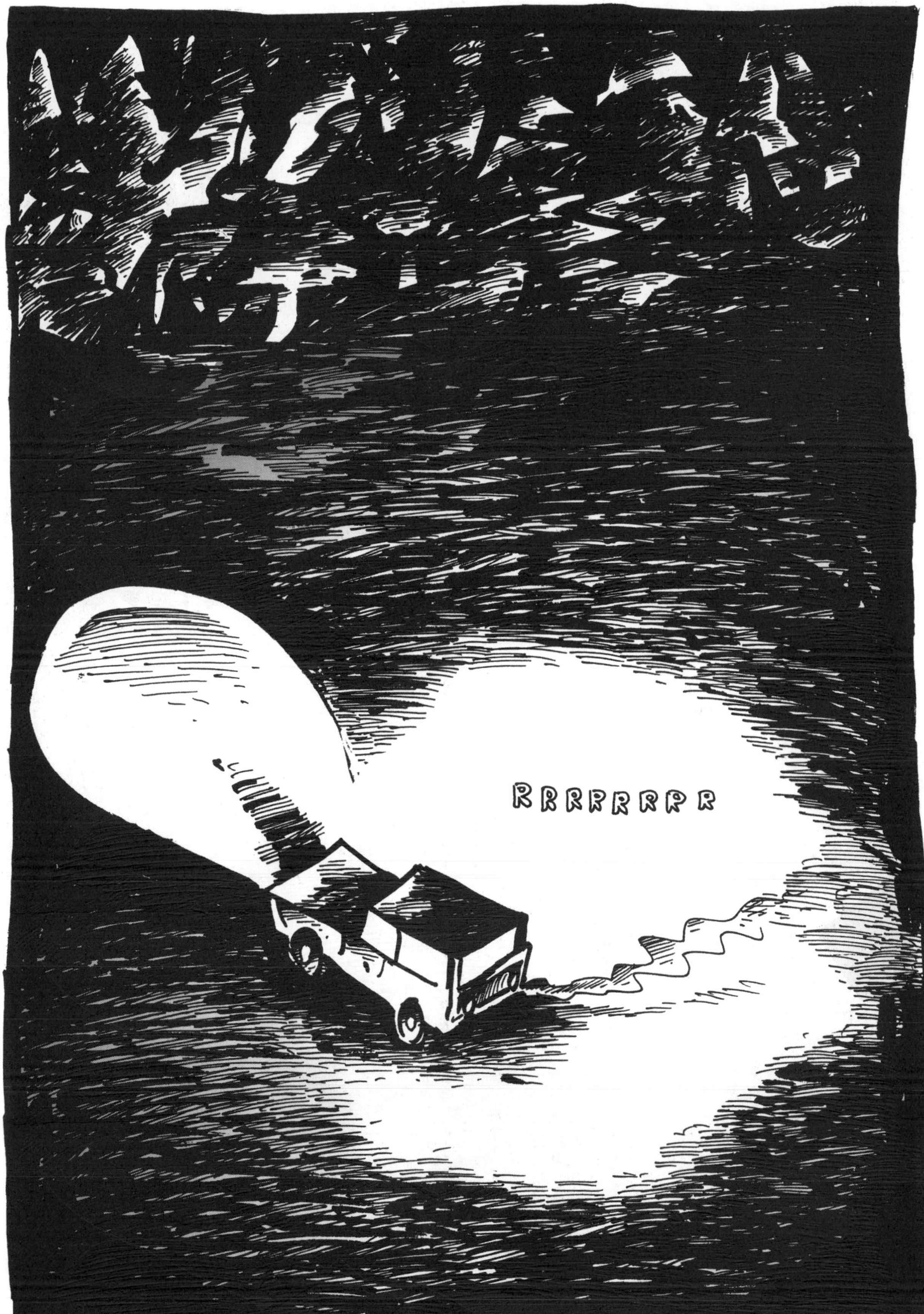
RRRRRRRR

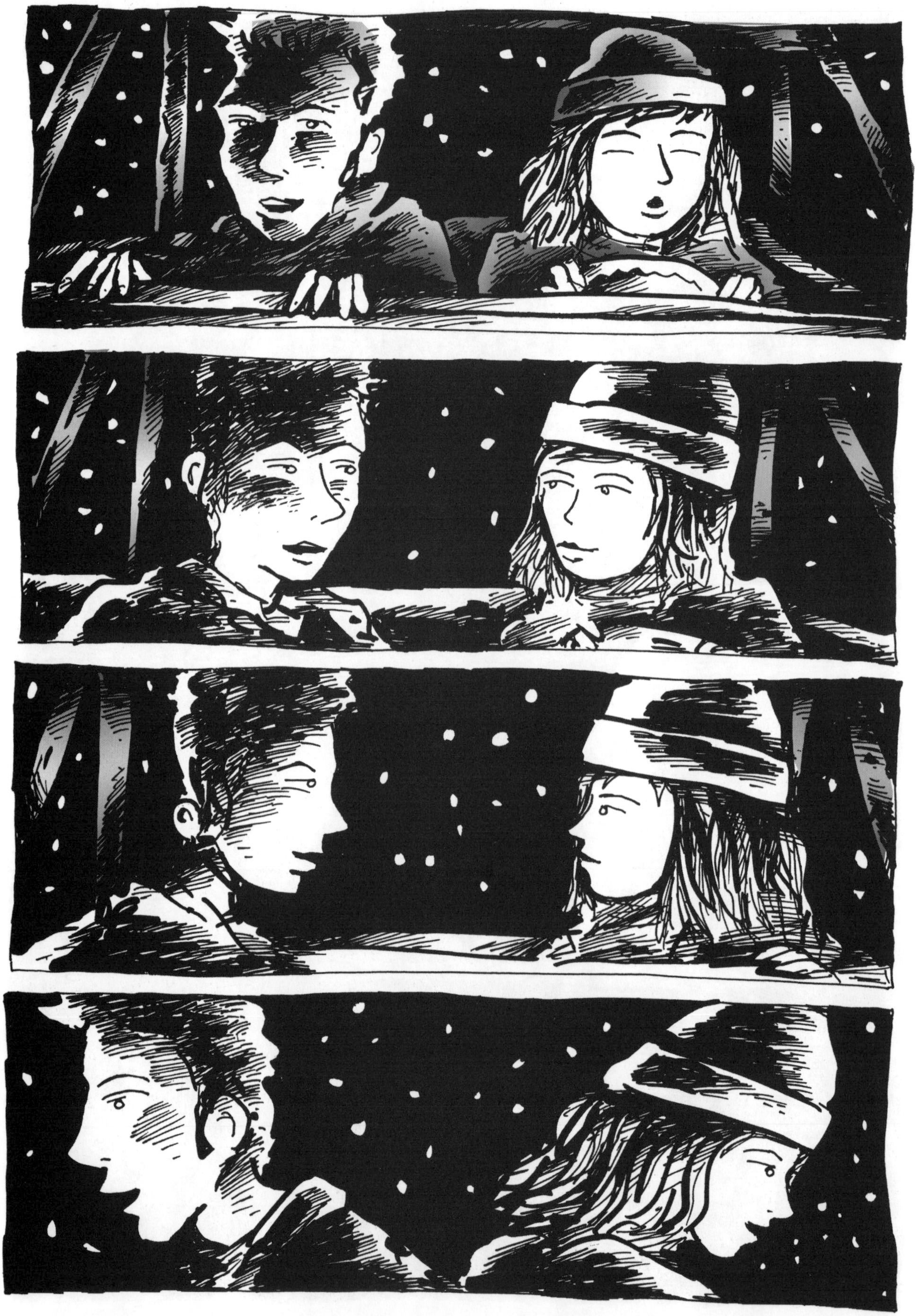

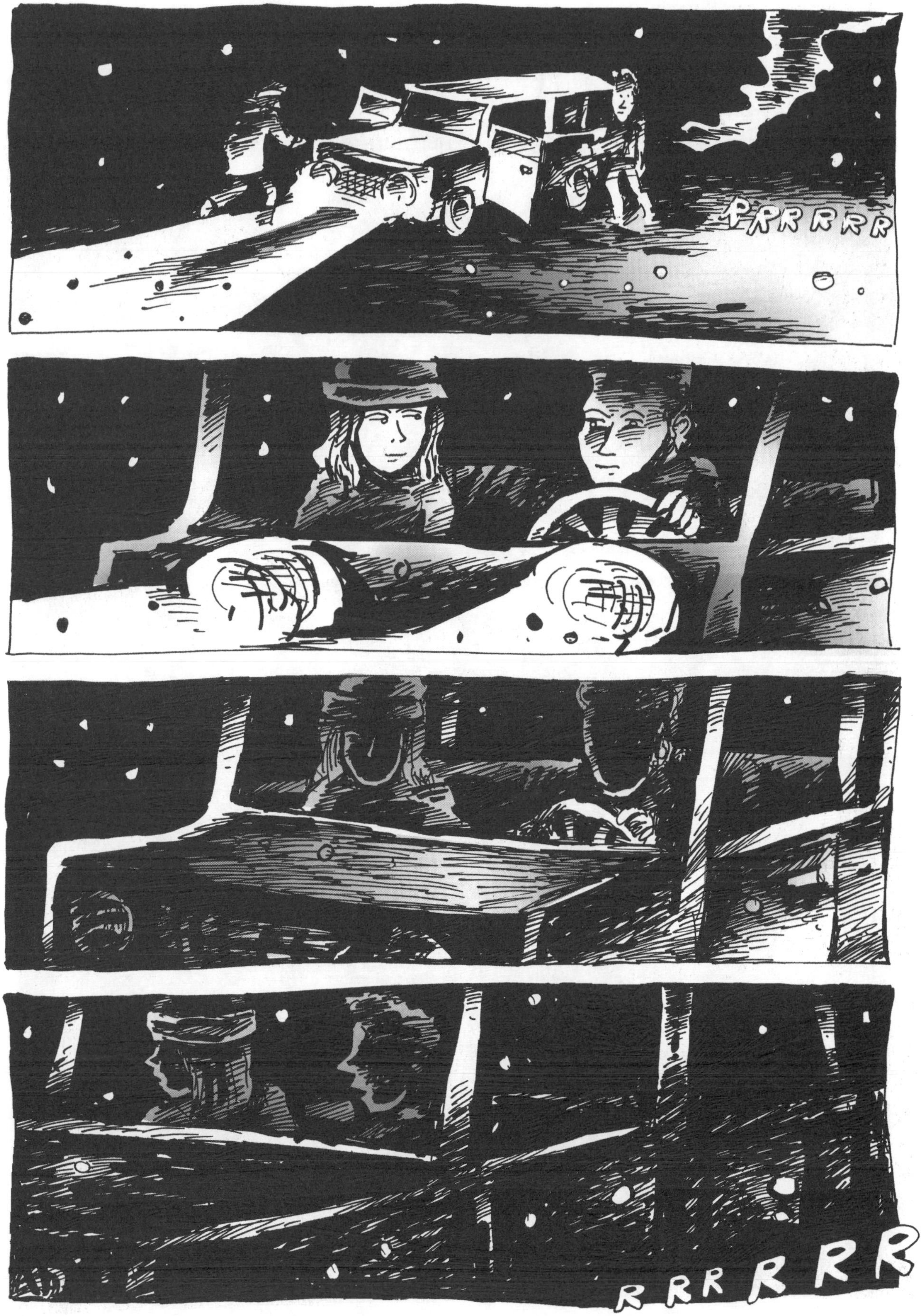
PRRRRRR
RRRRRR

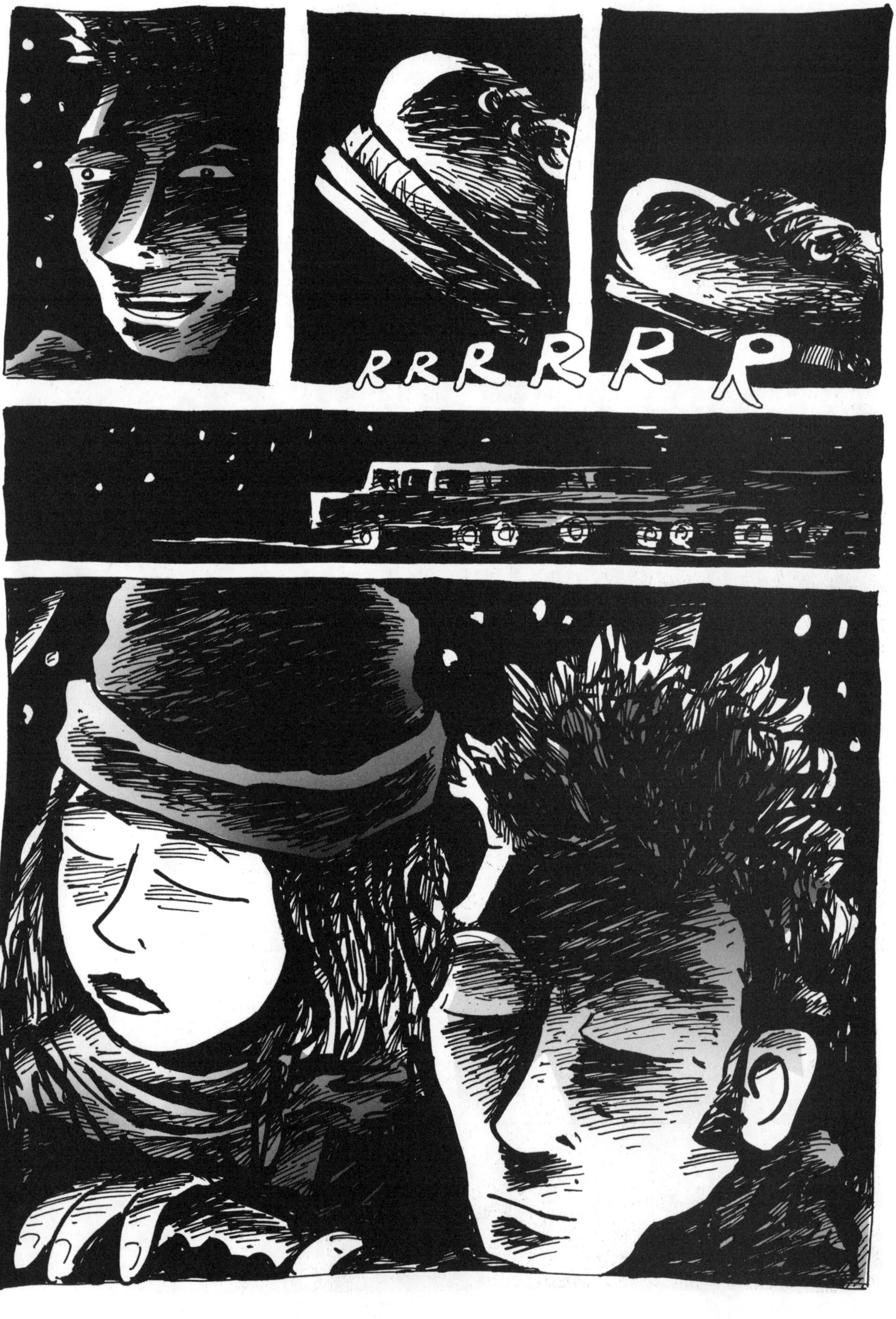
RRRRRR

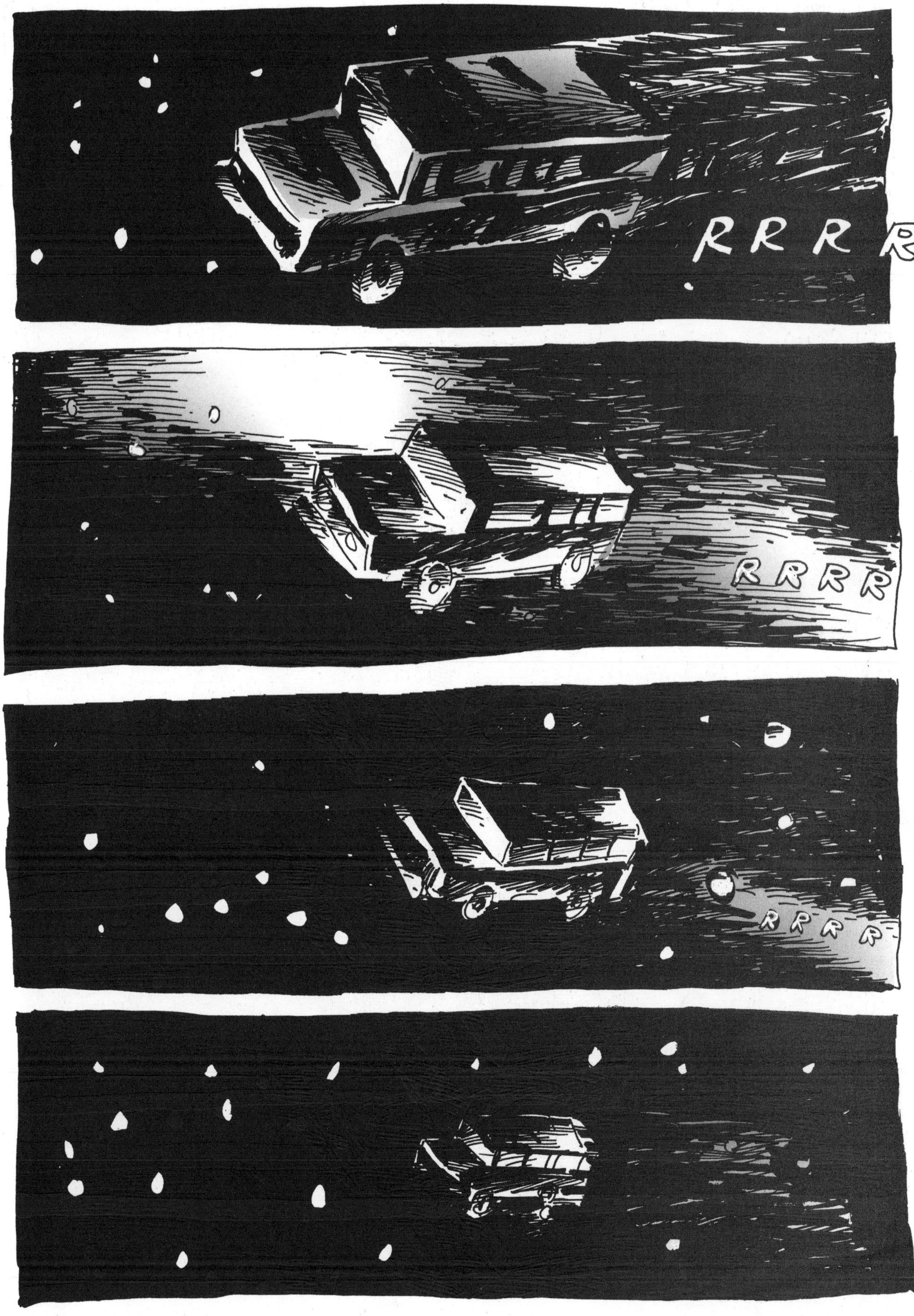
RRRR
RRRR
RRRRR

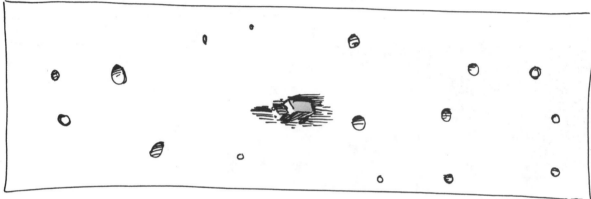

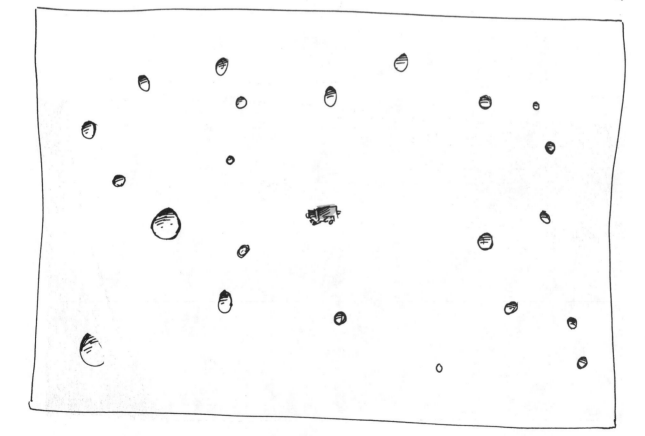

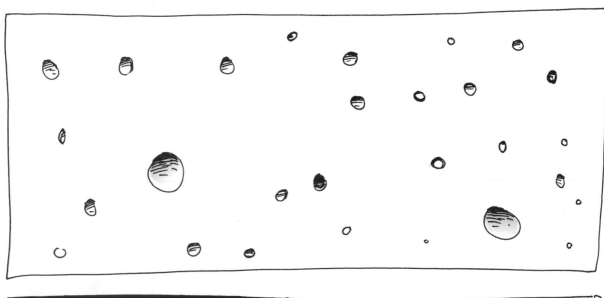

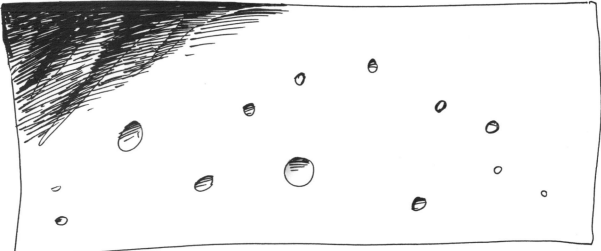

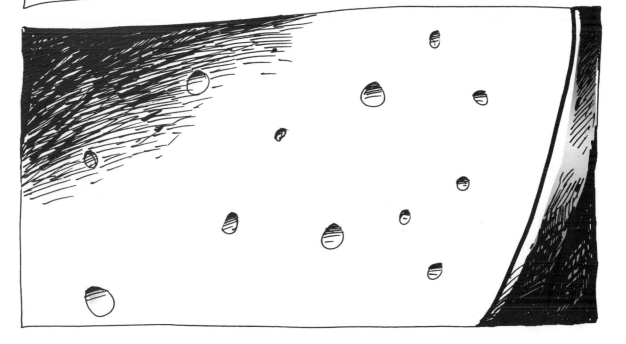

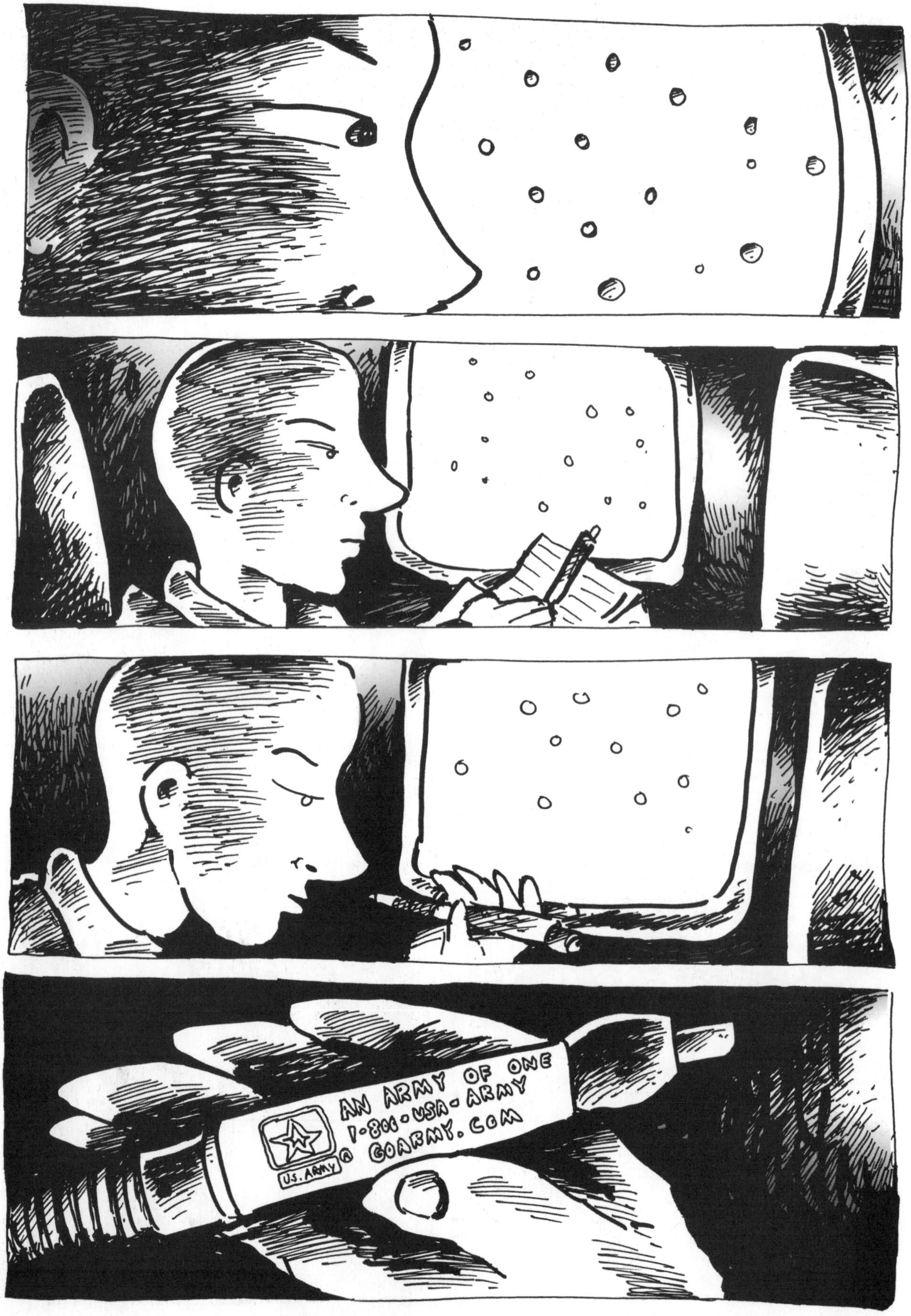

AN ARMY OF ONE
1-800-USA-ARMY
GOARMY.COM
U.S. ARMY

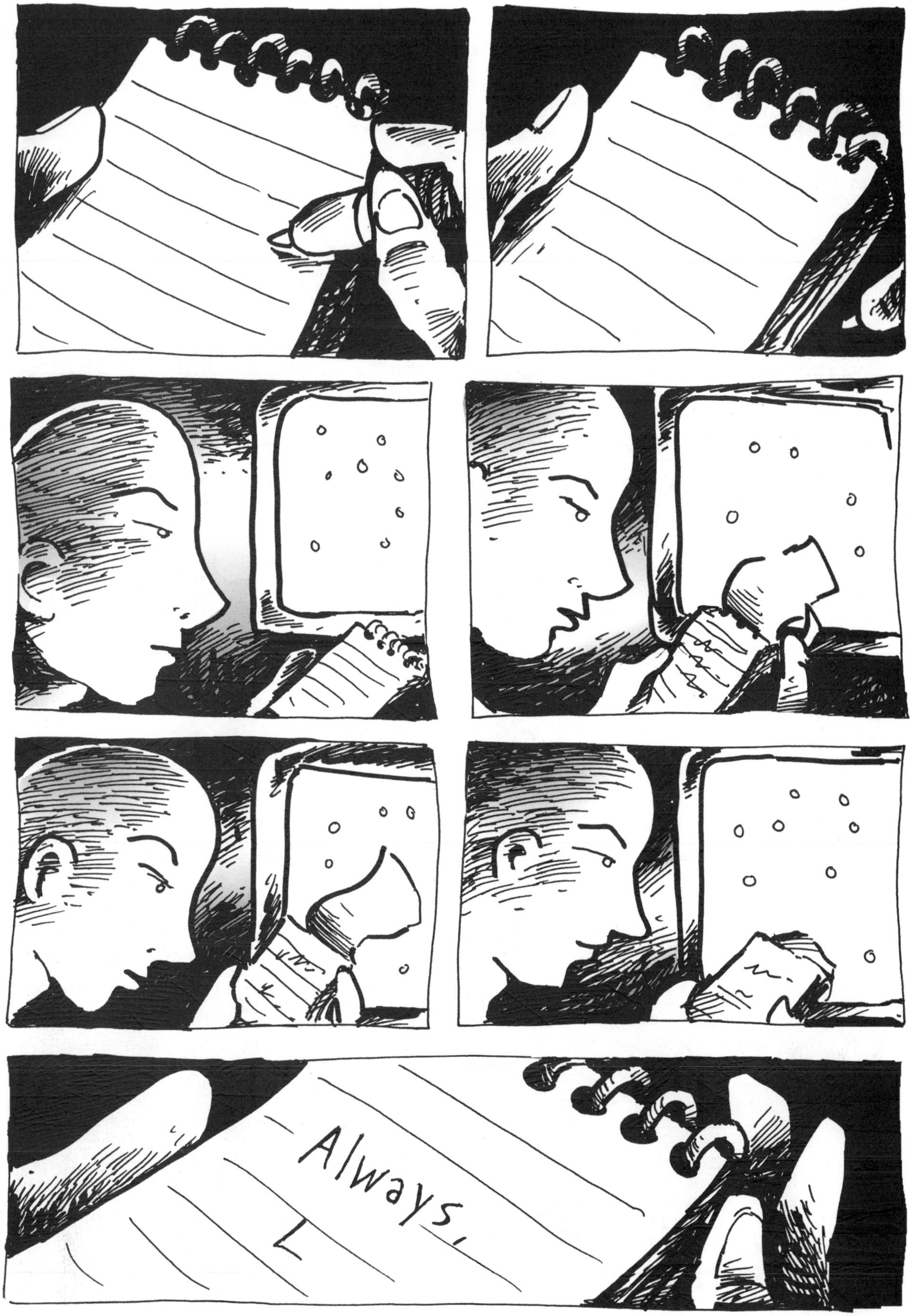
Always,
L

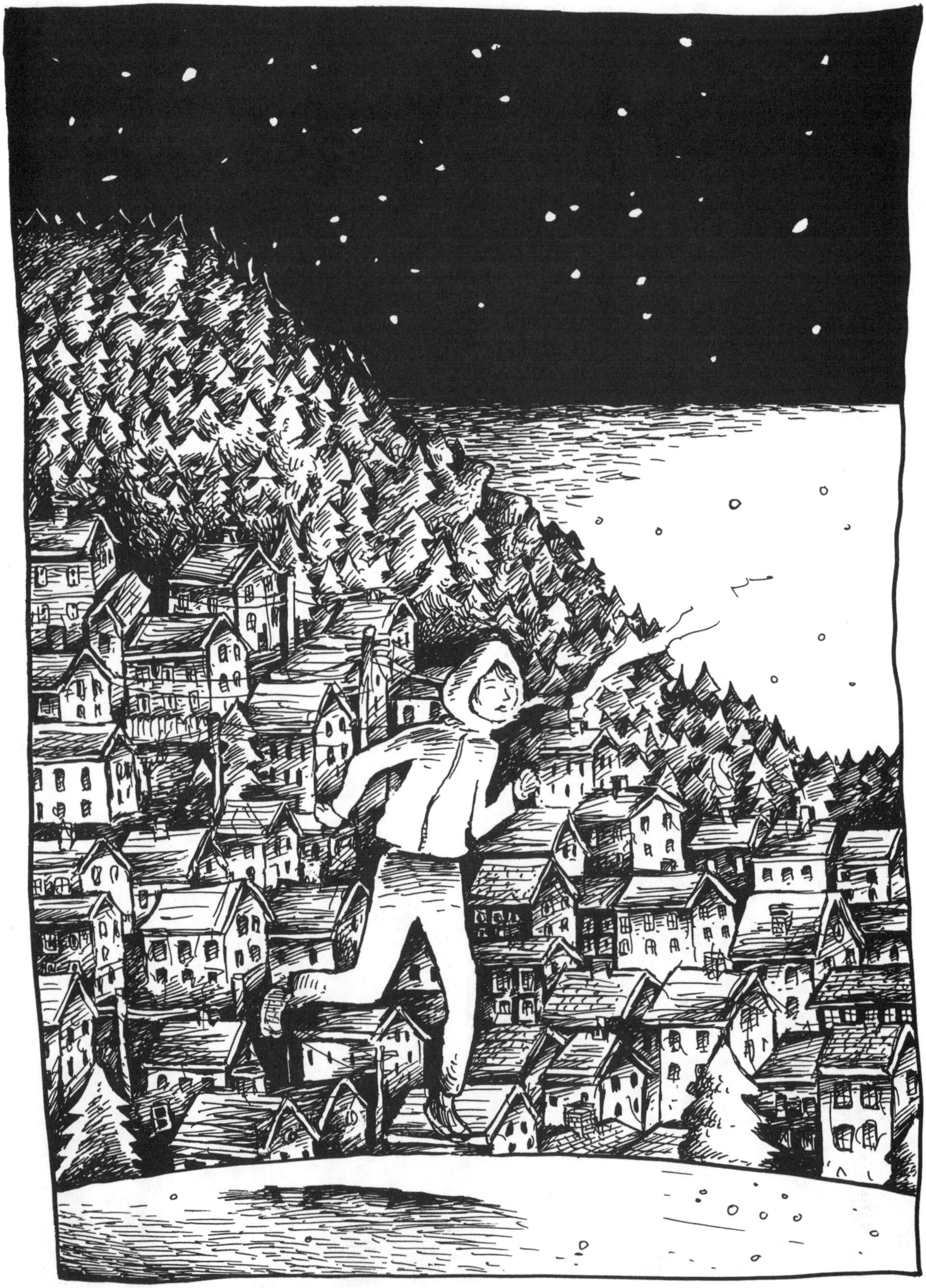

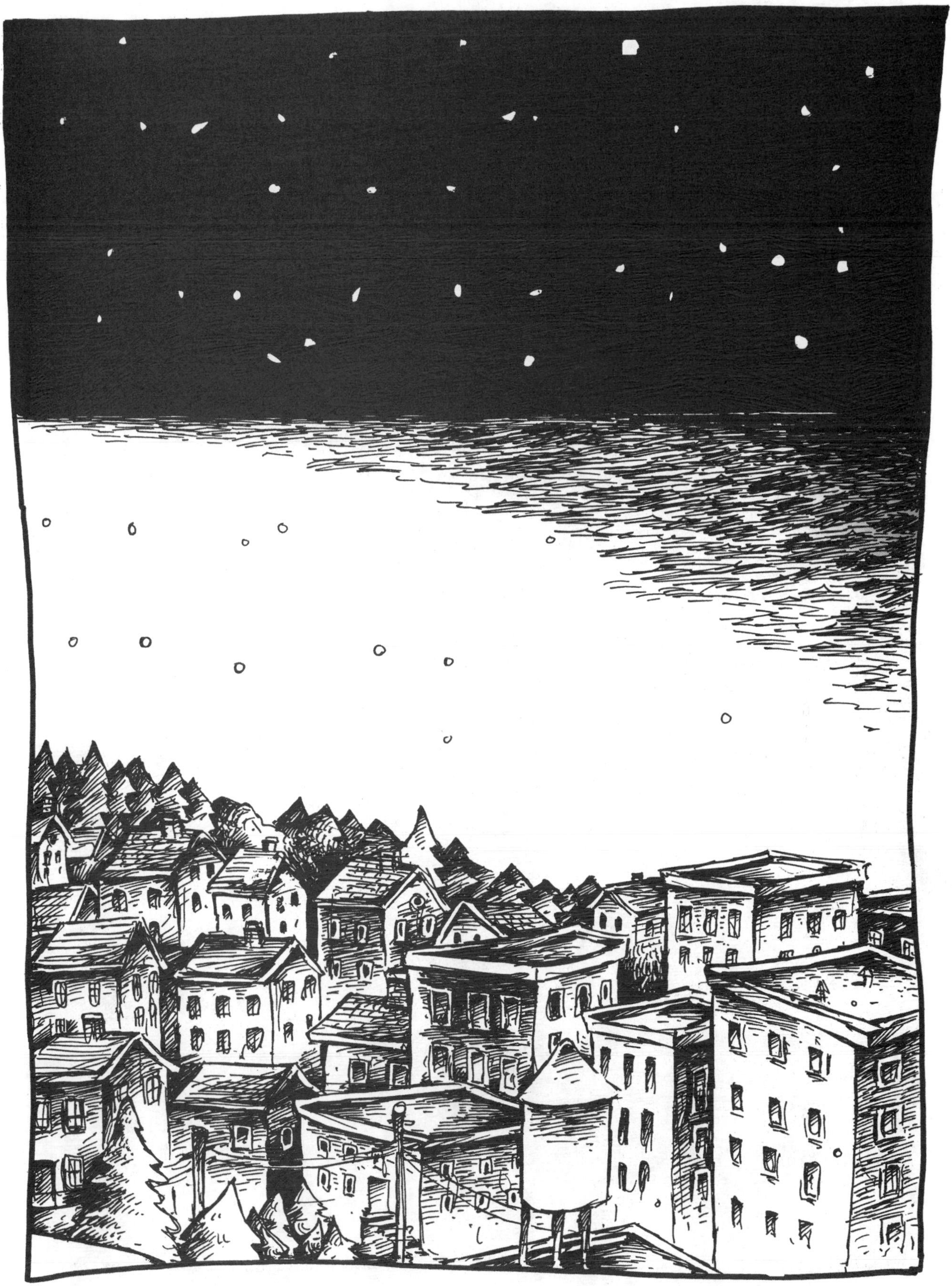

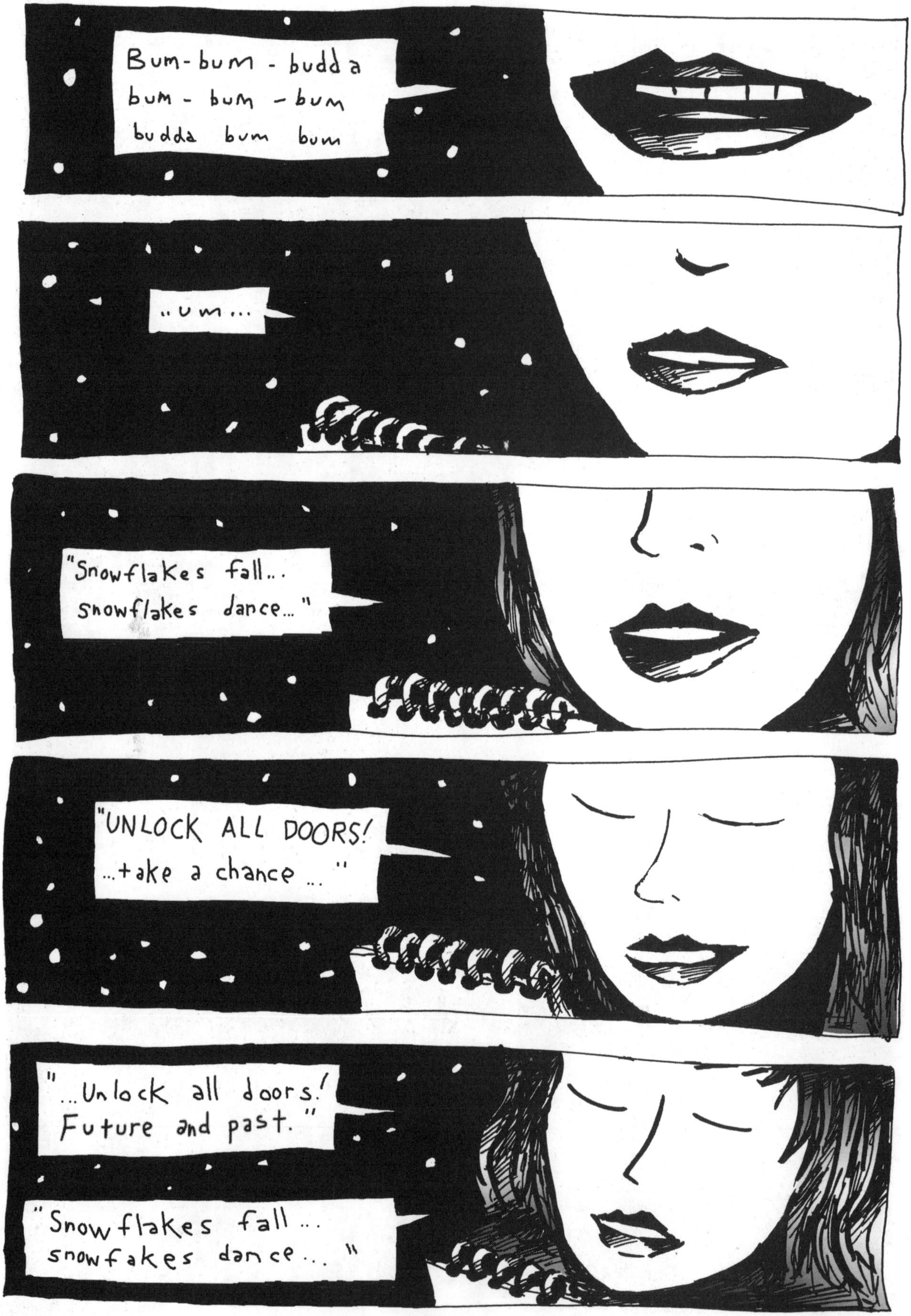
Bum-bum-budda bum-bum-bum budda bum bum
..um...
"Snowflakes fall... snowflakes dance..."
"UNLOCK ALL DOORS! ...take a chance..."
"...Unlock all doors! Future and past."
"Snowflakes fall... snowfakes dance..."

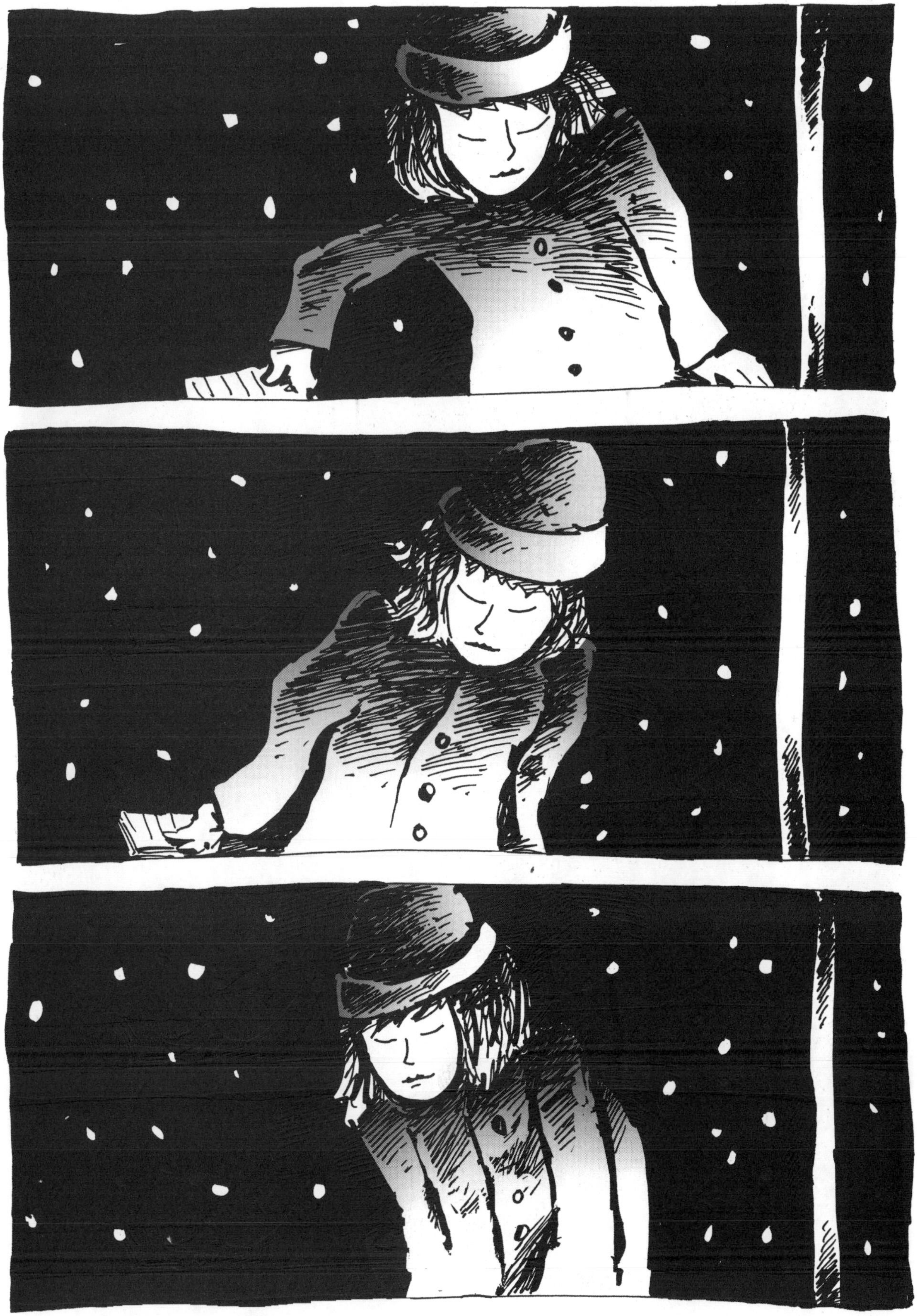

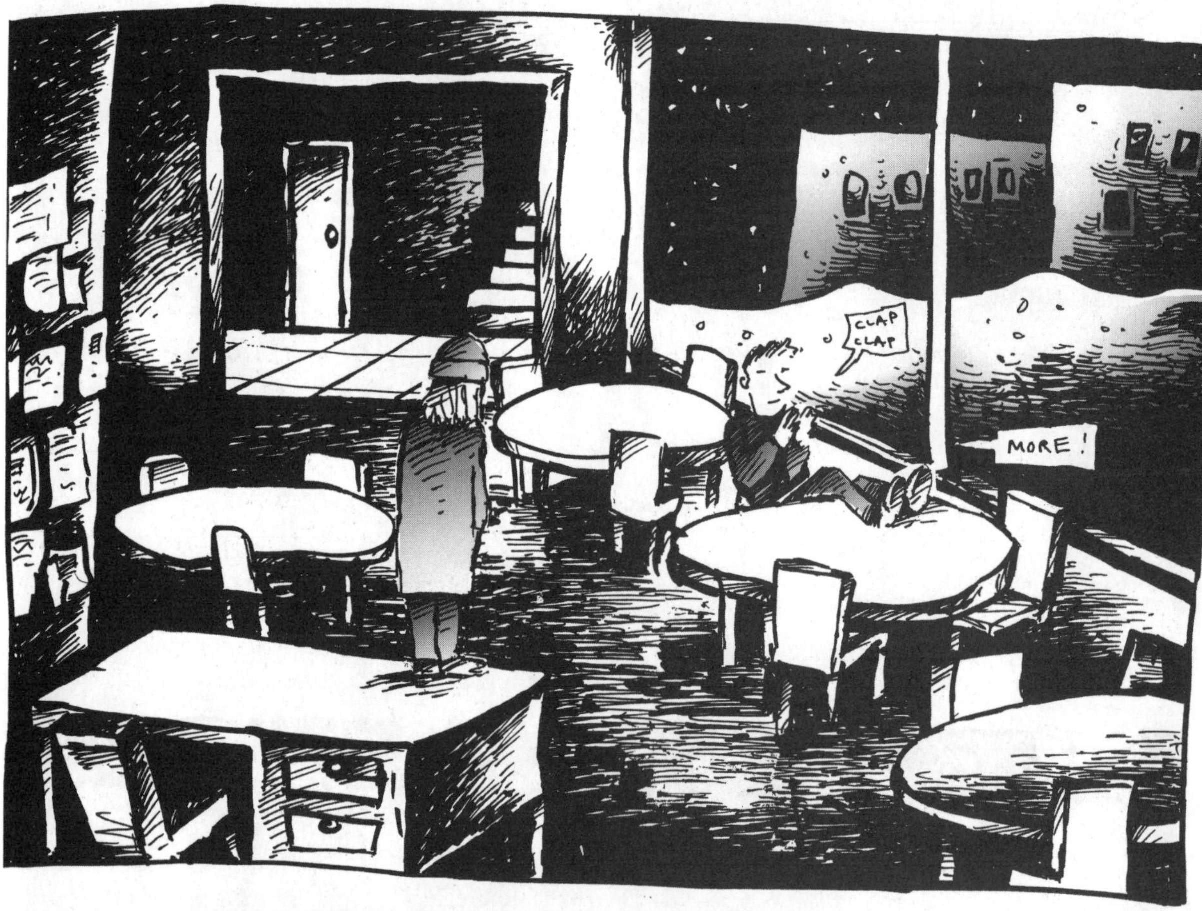
CLAP CLAP
MORE!

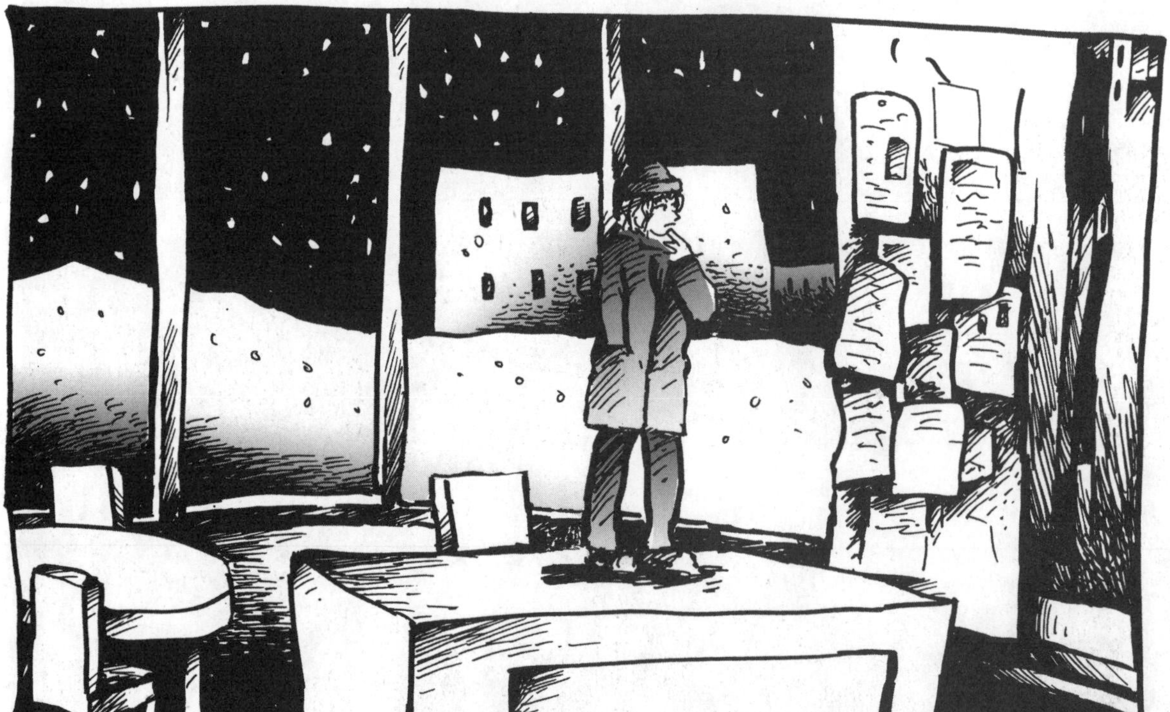

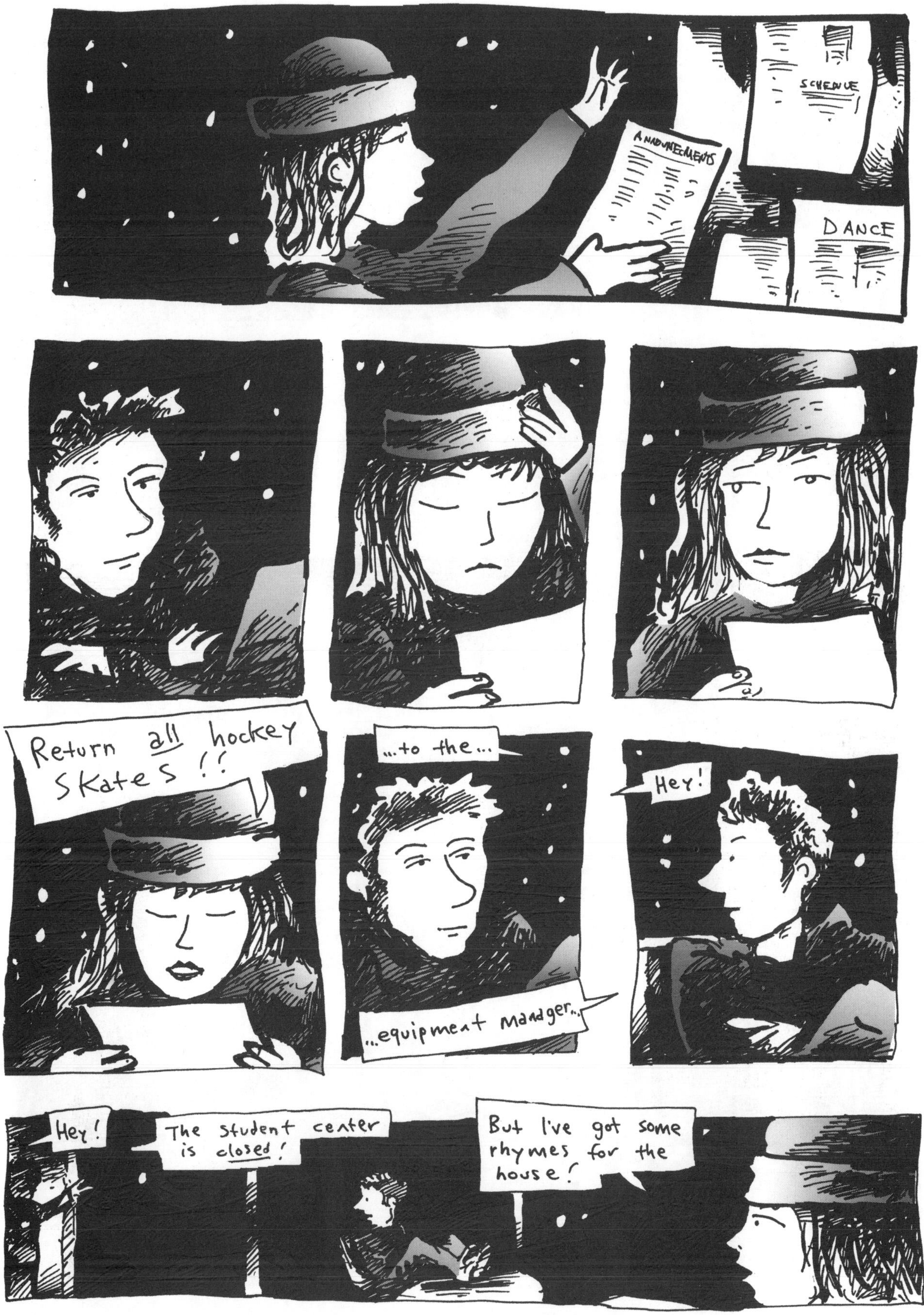
ANNOUNCEMENTS
SCHEDULE
DANCE
Return all hockey skates!?
...to the...
...equipment manager...
Hey!
Hey!
The student center is closed!
But I've got some rhymes for the house!

STUDENT
CENTER
S
C

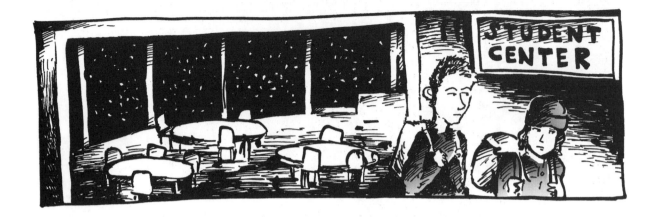

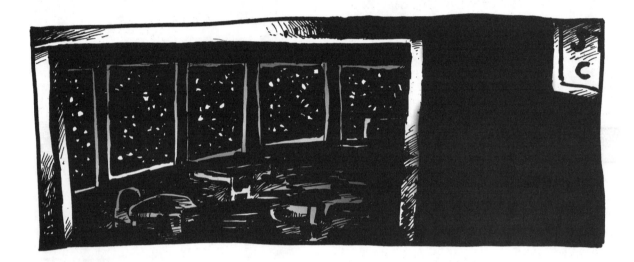

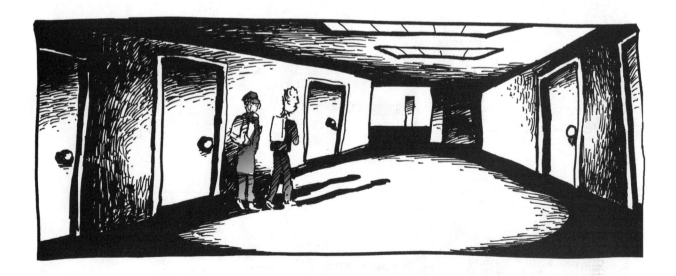

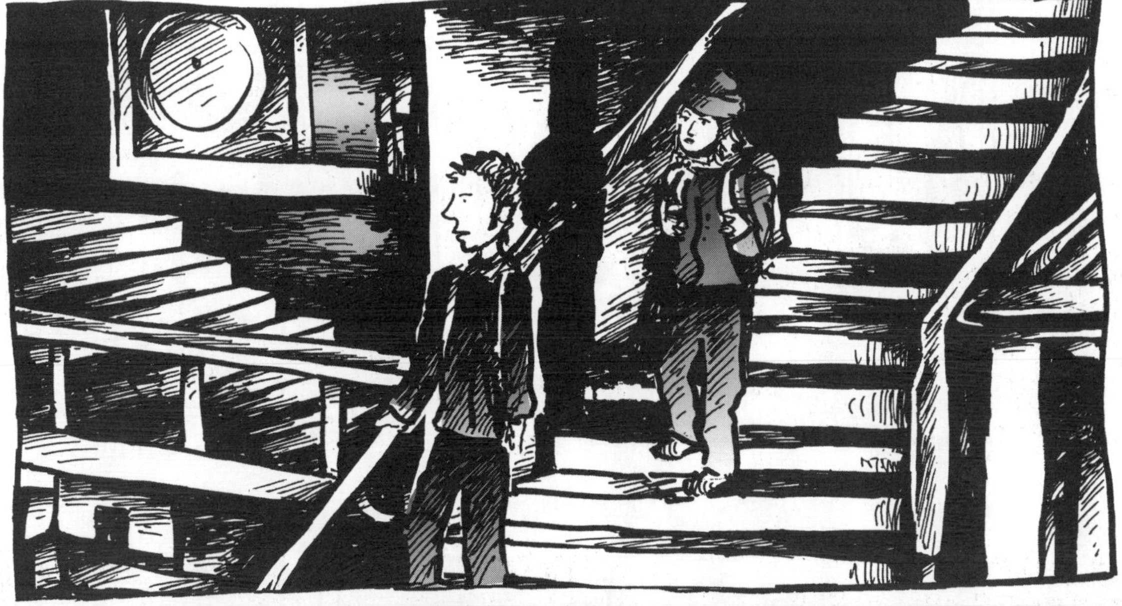
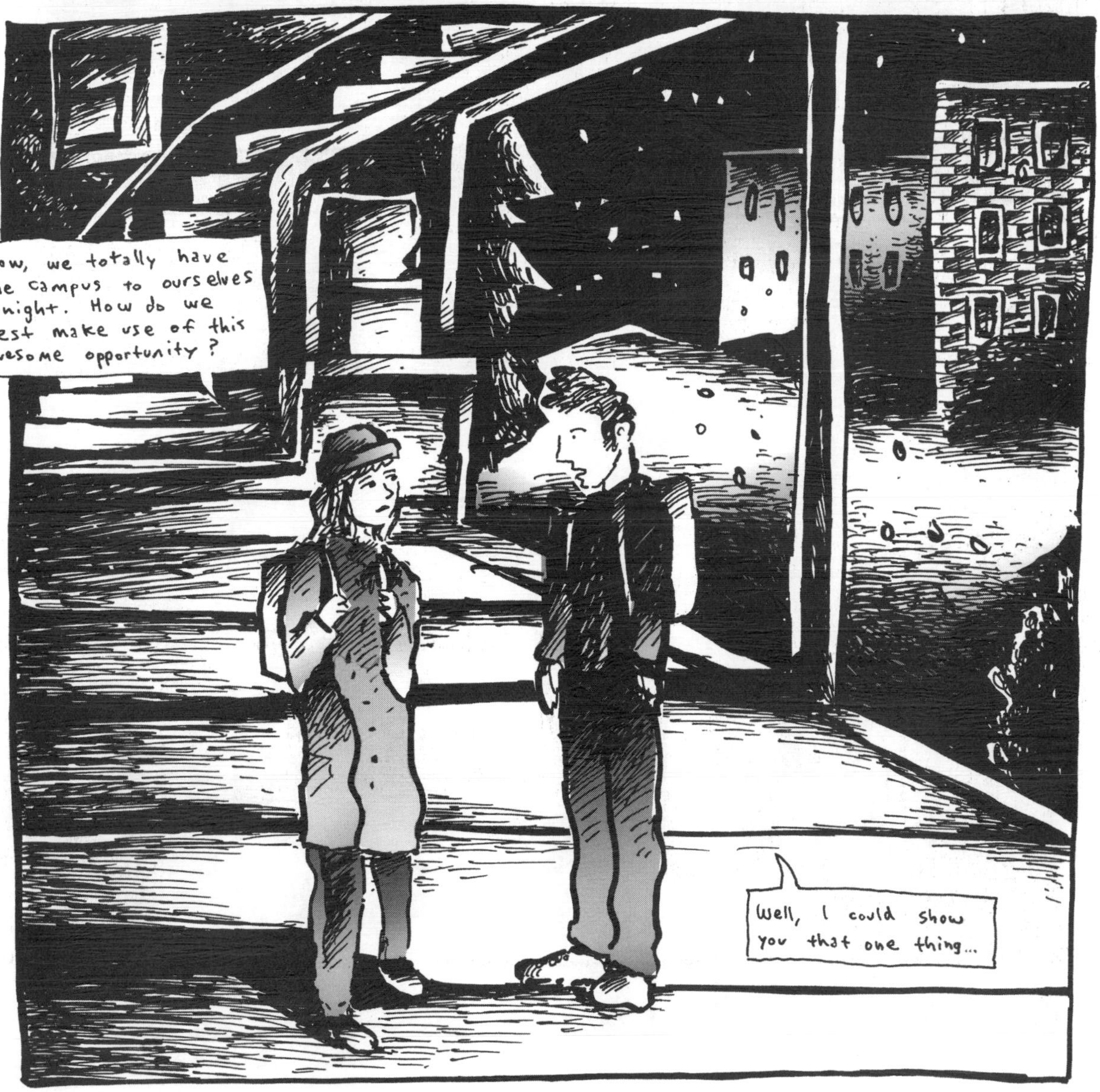
Wow, we totally have the campus to ourselves tonight. How do we best make use of this awesome opportunity?
Well, I could show you that one thing...

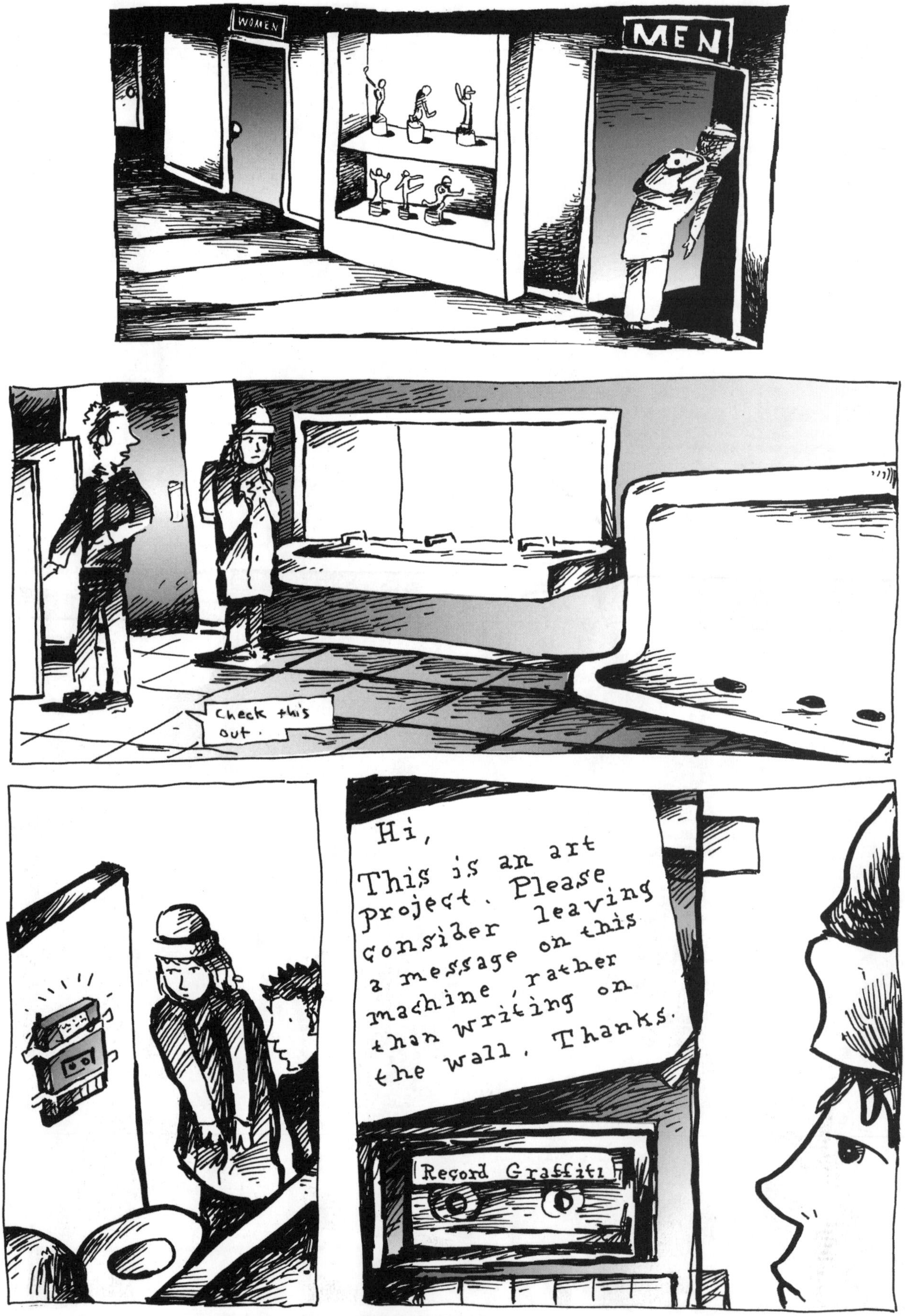
WOMEN
MEN
Check this out.
Hi,
This is an art project. Please consider leaving a message on this machine, rather than writing on the wall. Thanks.
Record Graffiti

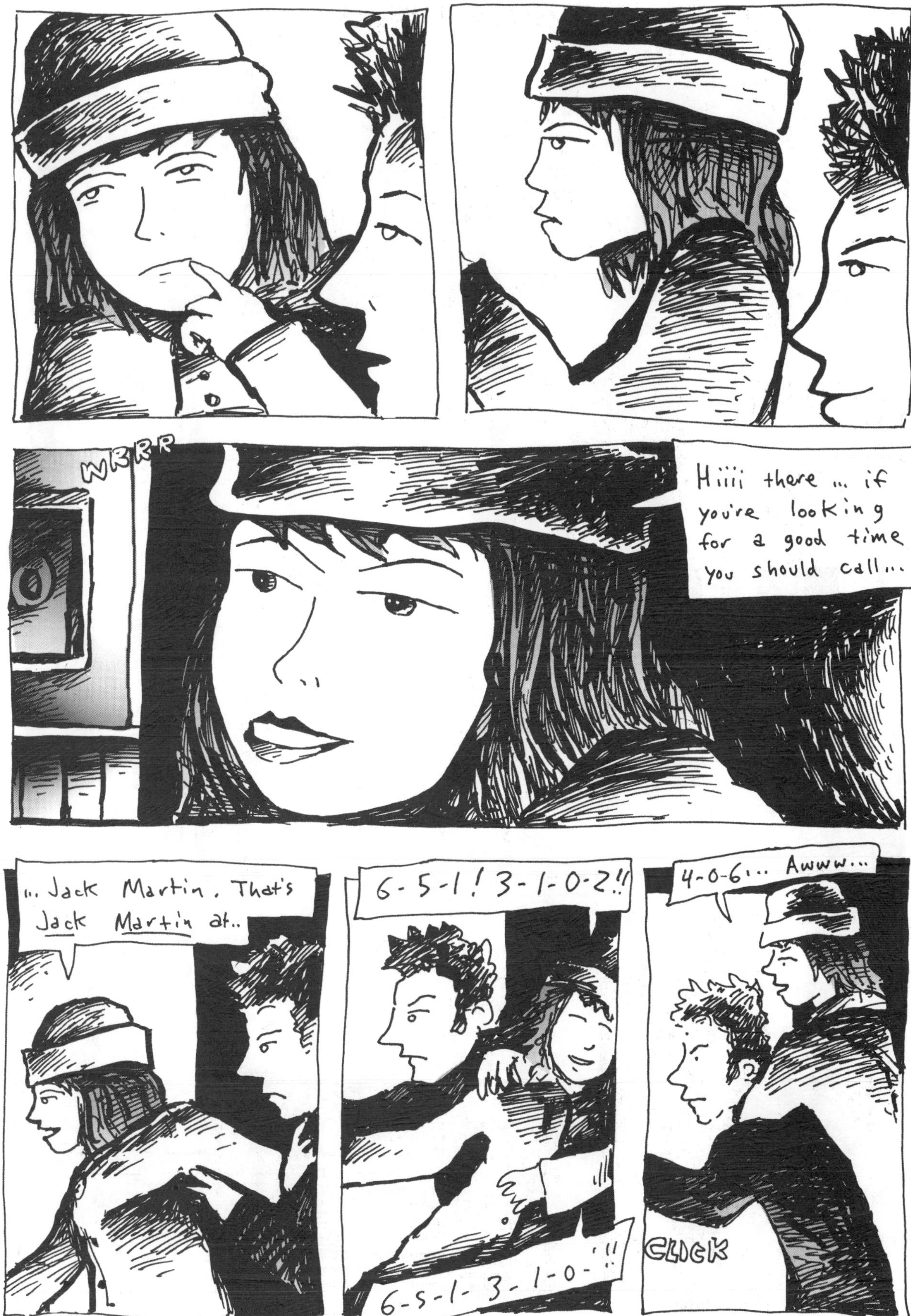
WRRR
Hiiii there ... if you're looking for a good time you should call...
... Jack Martin. That's Jack Martin at...
6-5-1! 3-1-0-2!!
6-5-1- 3-1-0-!!
4-0-6... Awww...
CLICK

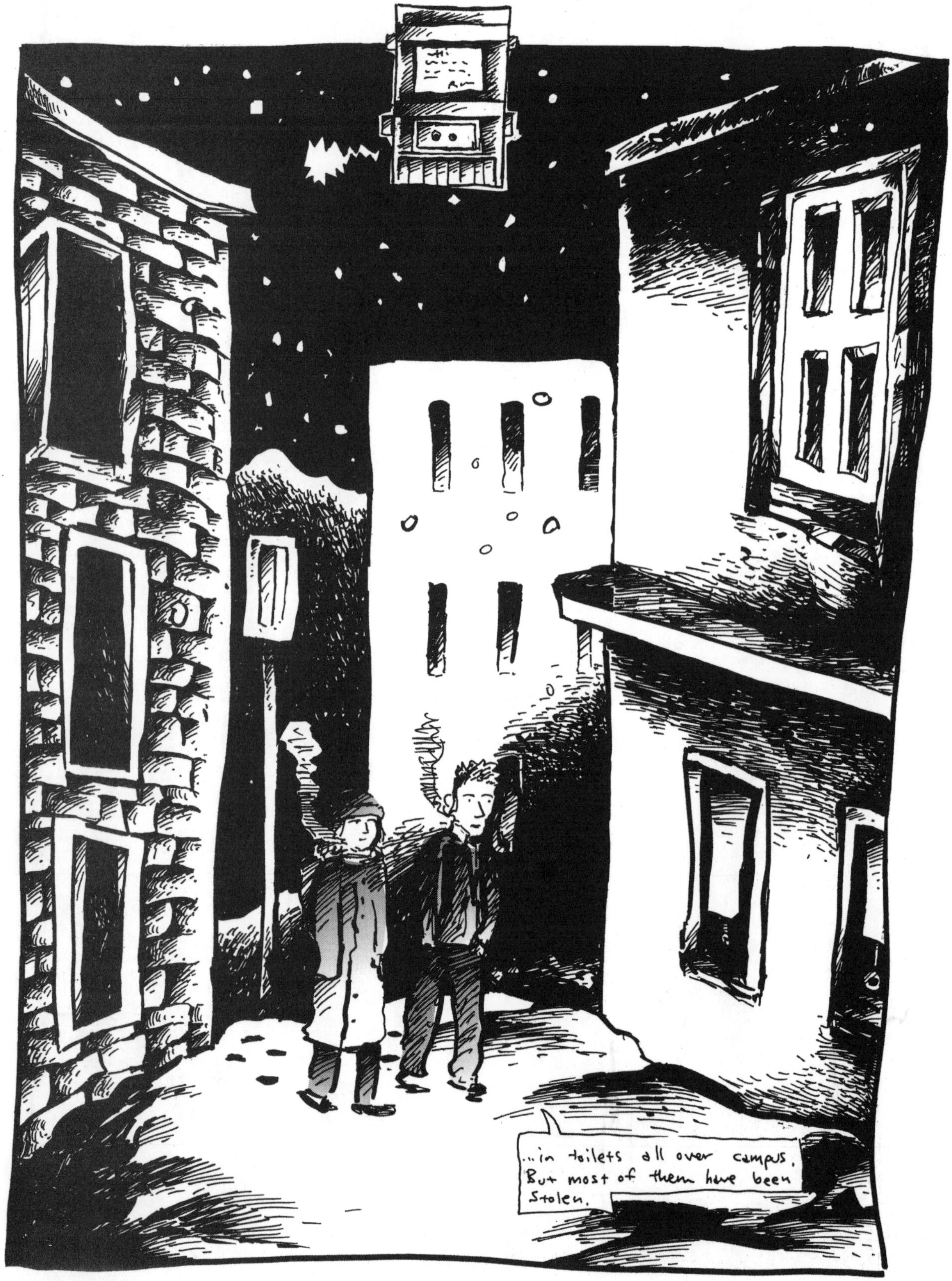
...in toilets all over campus. But most of them have been stolen.

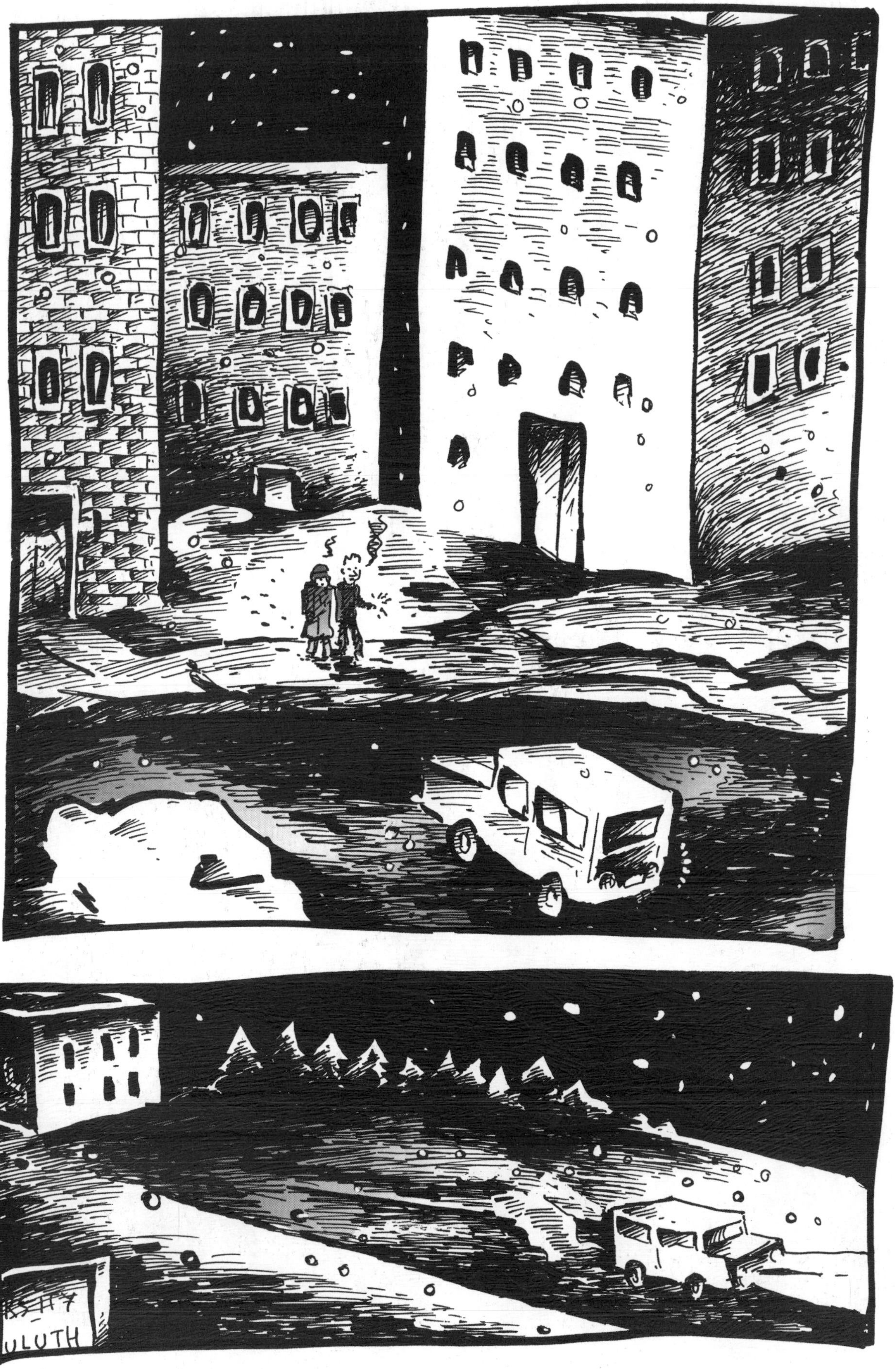

ULUTH

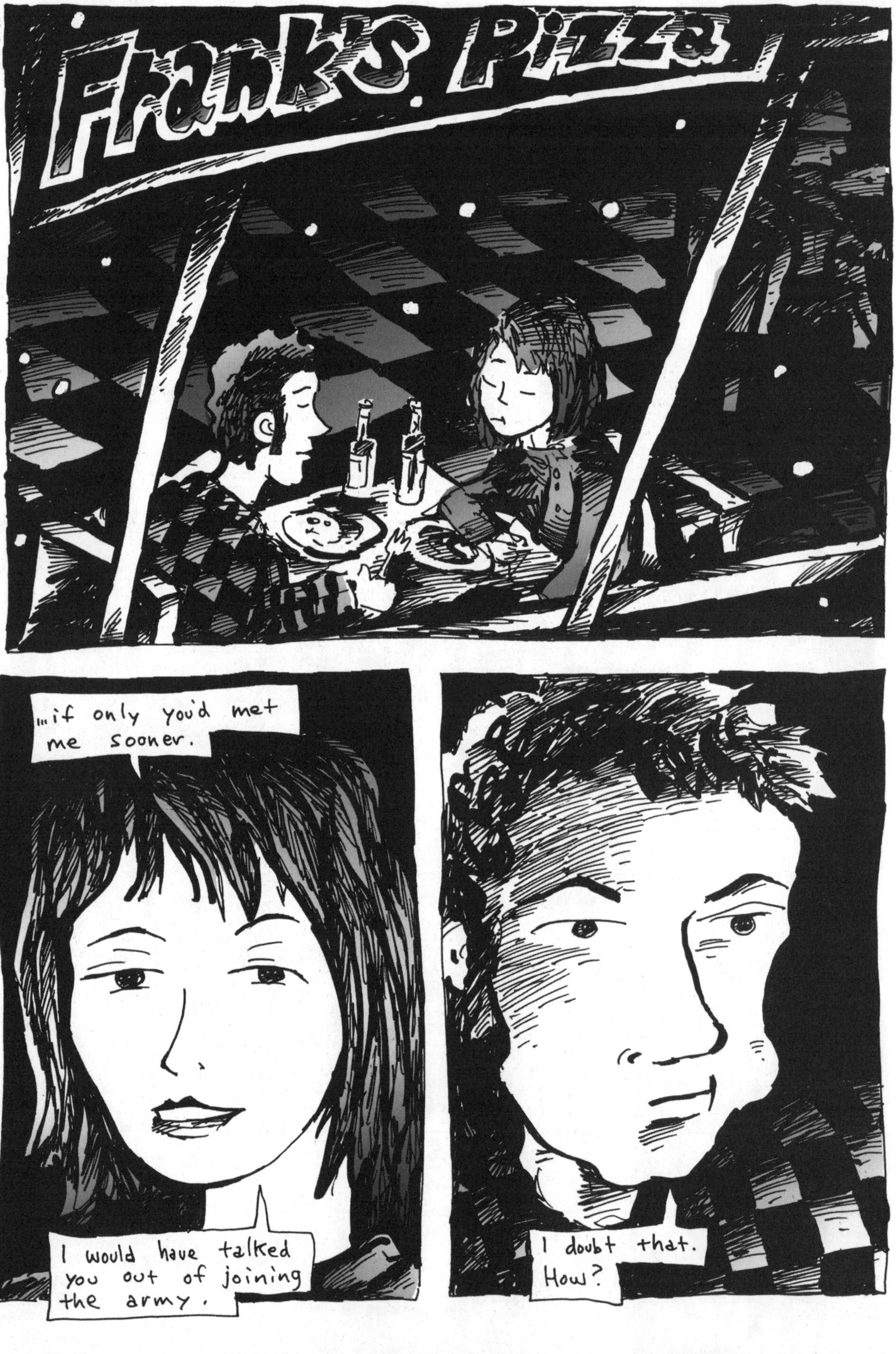
Frank's Pizza
...if only you'd met me sooner.
I would have talked you out of joining the army.
I doubt that. How?

I can be very persuasive.

That's true.

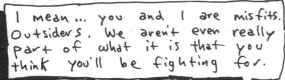

I mean... you and I are misfits. Outsiders. We aren't even really part of what it is that you think you'll be fighting for.

You know?

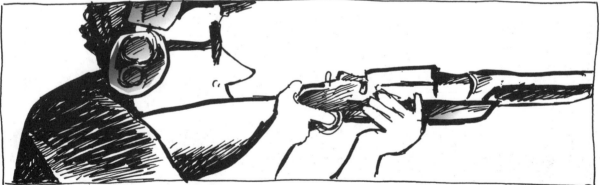

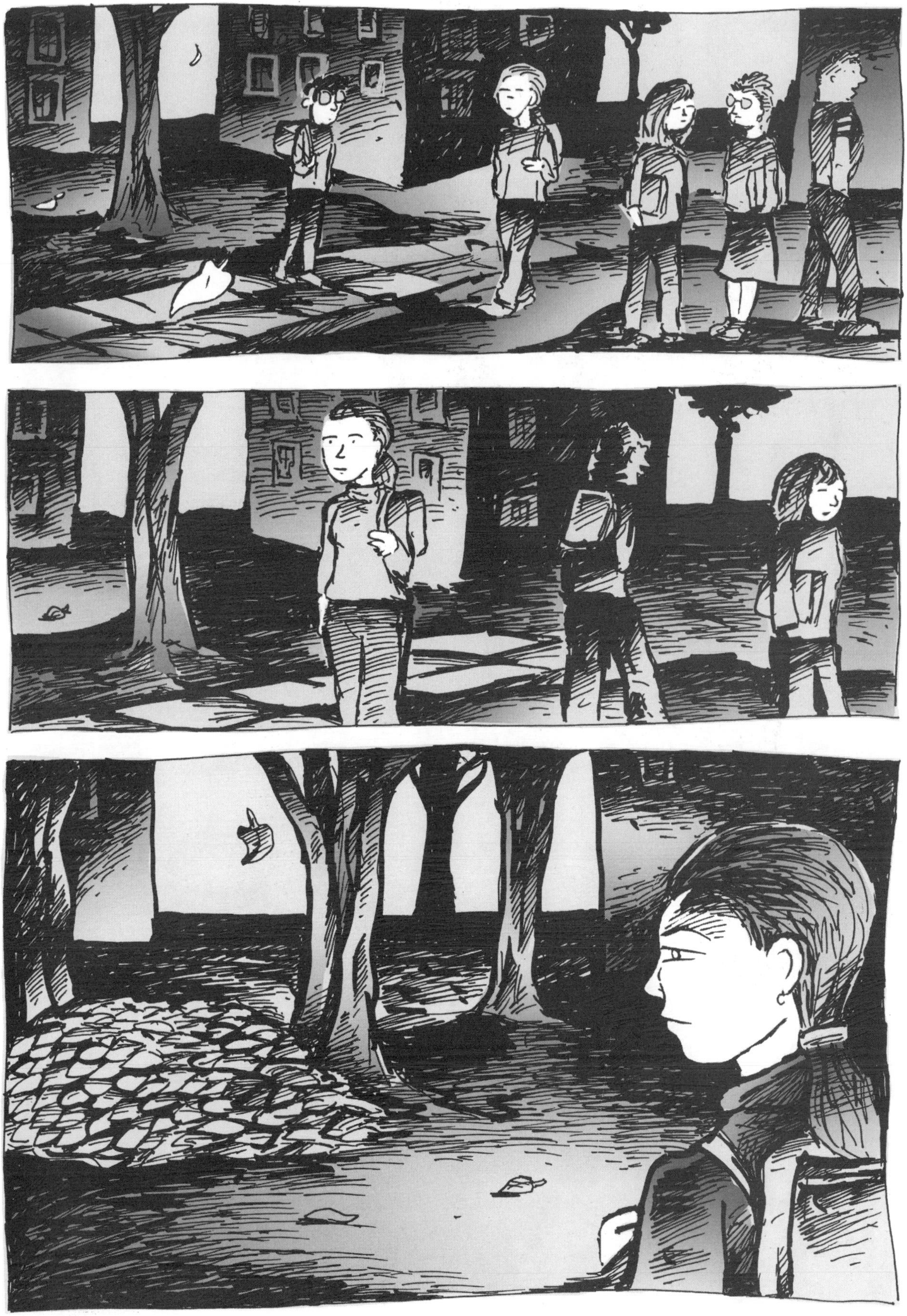

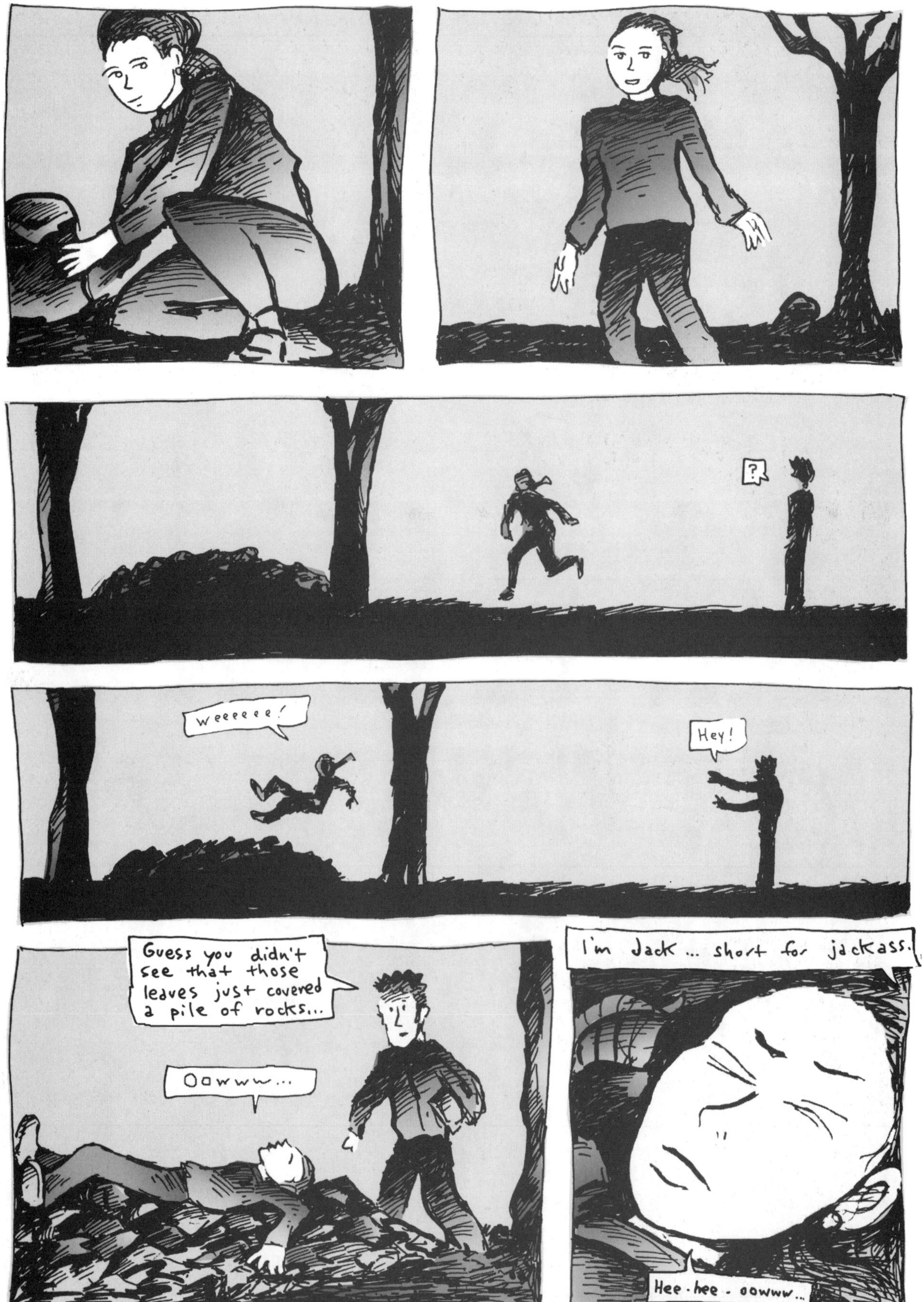
?
weeeeee!
Hey!
Guess you didn't see that those leaves just covered a pile of rocks...
Oowww...
I'm Jack... short for jackass.
Hee-hee-oowww...

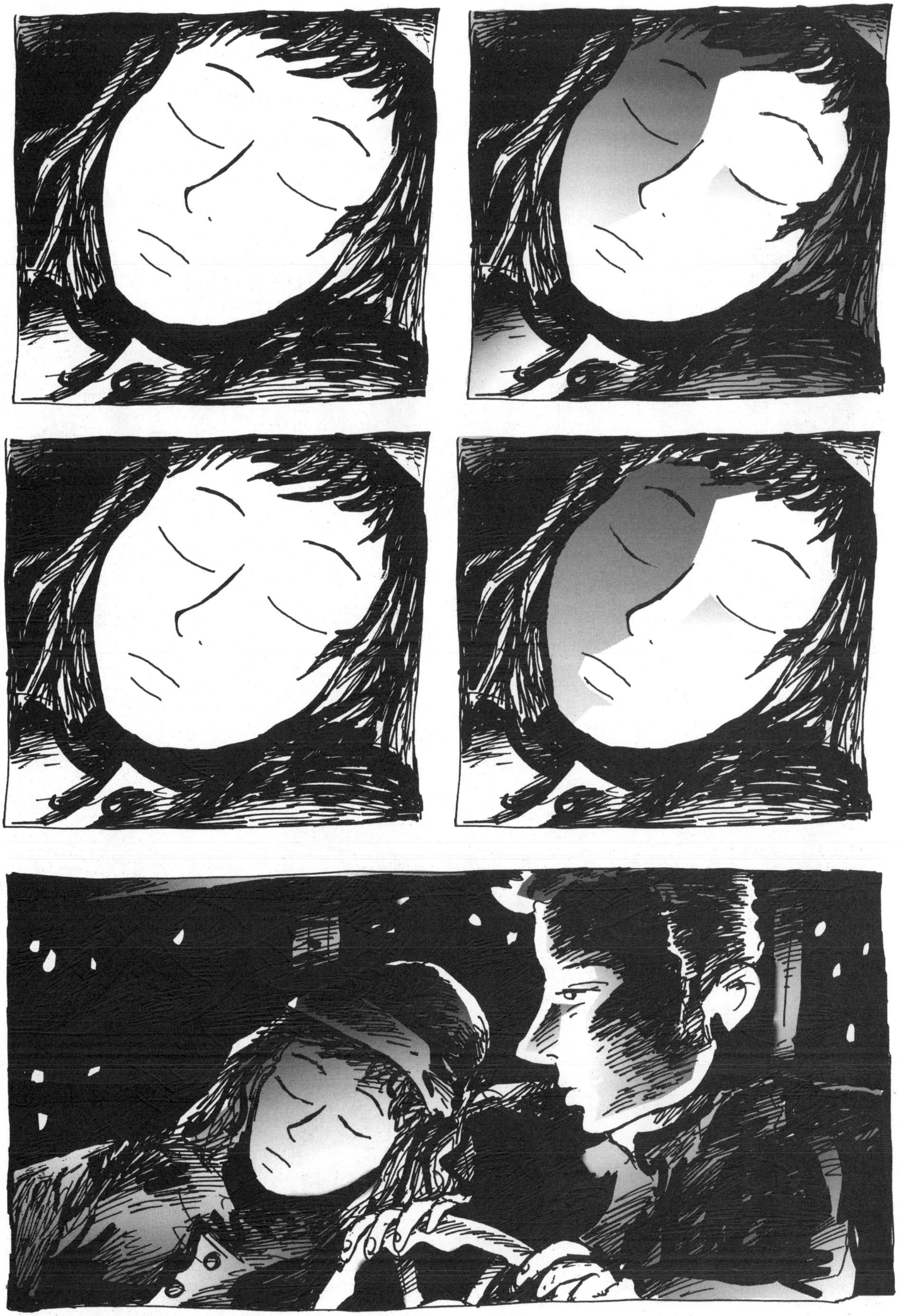

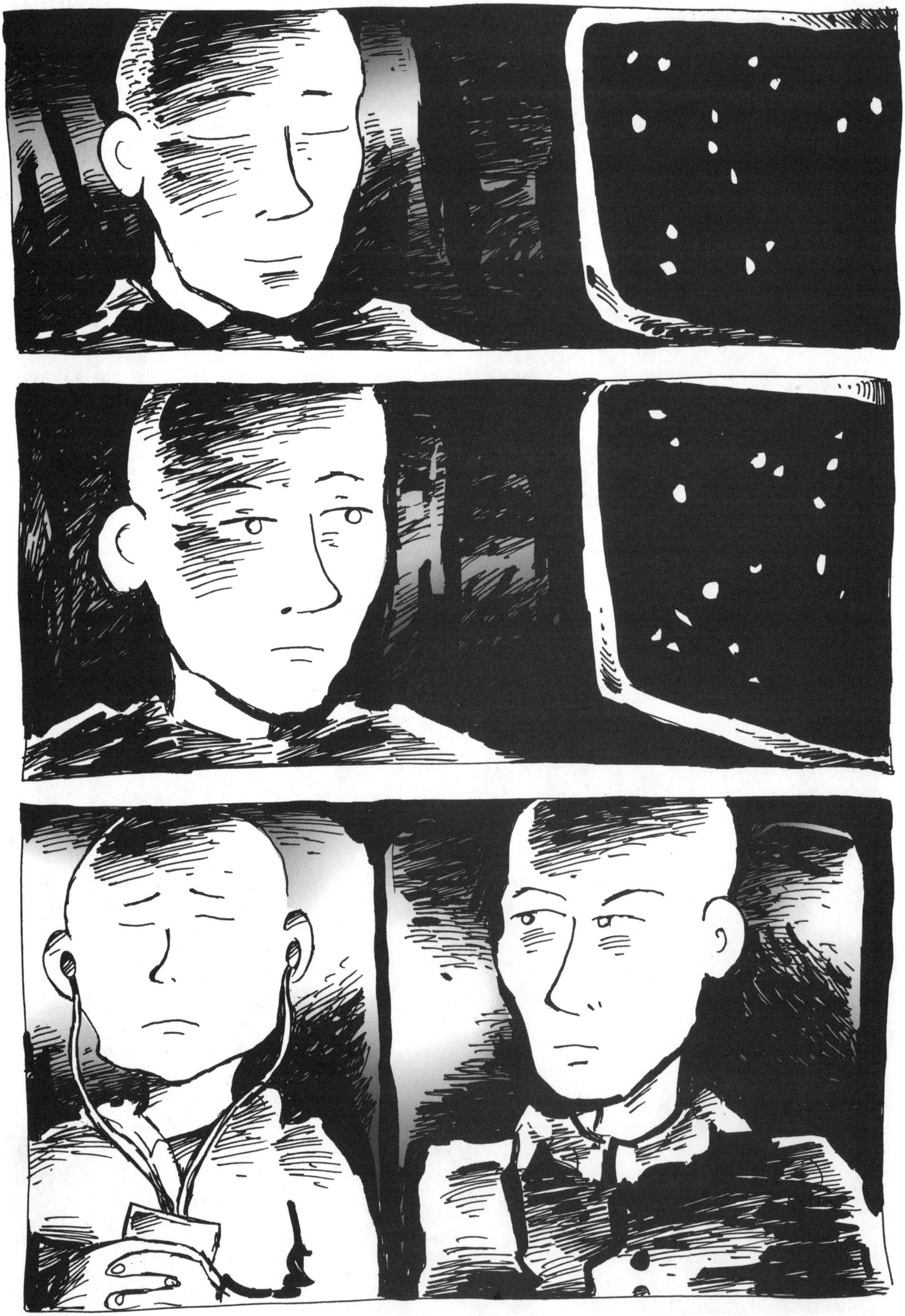

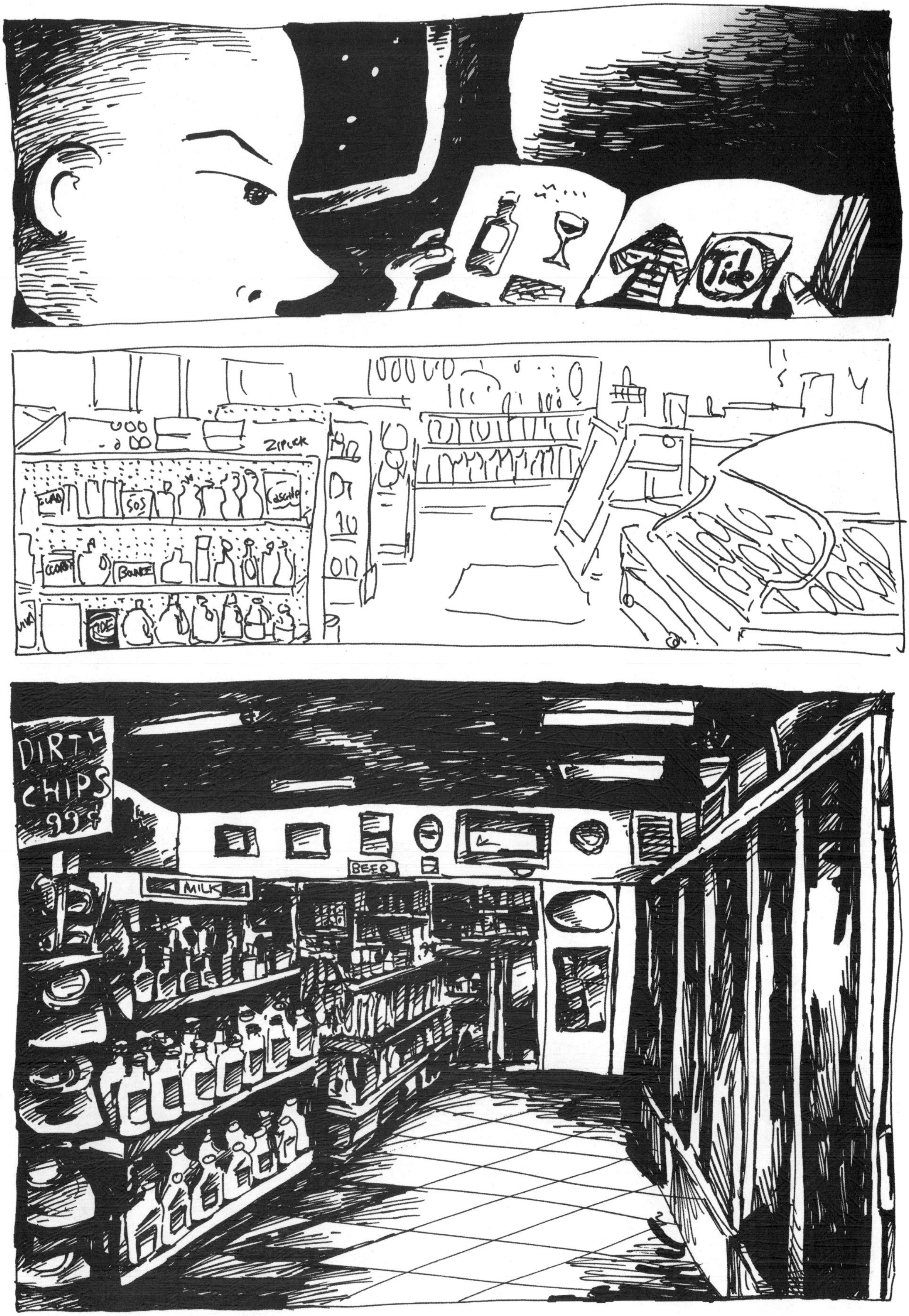
Tide
ZIPLOCK
SOS
BOUNCE
TIDE
DIRTY CHIPS 99¢
BEER
MILK

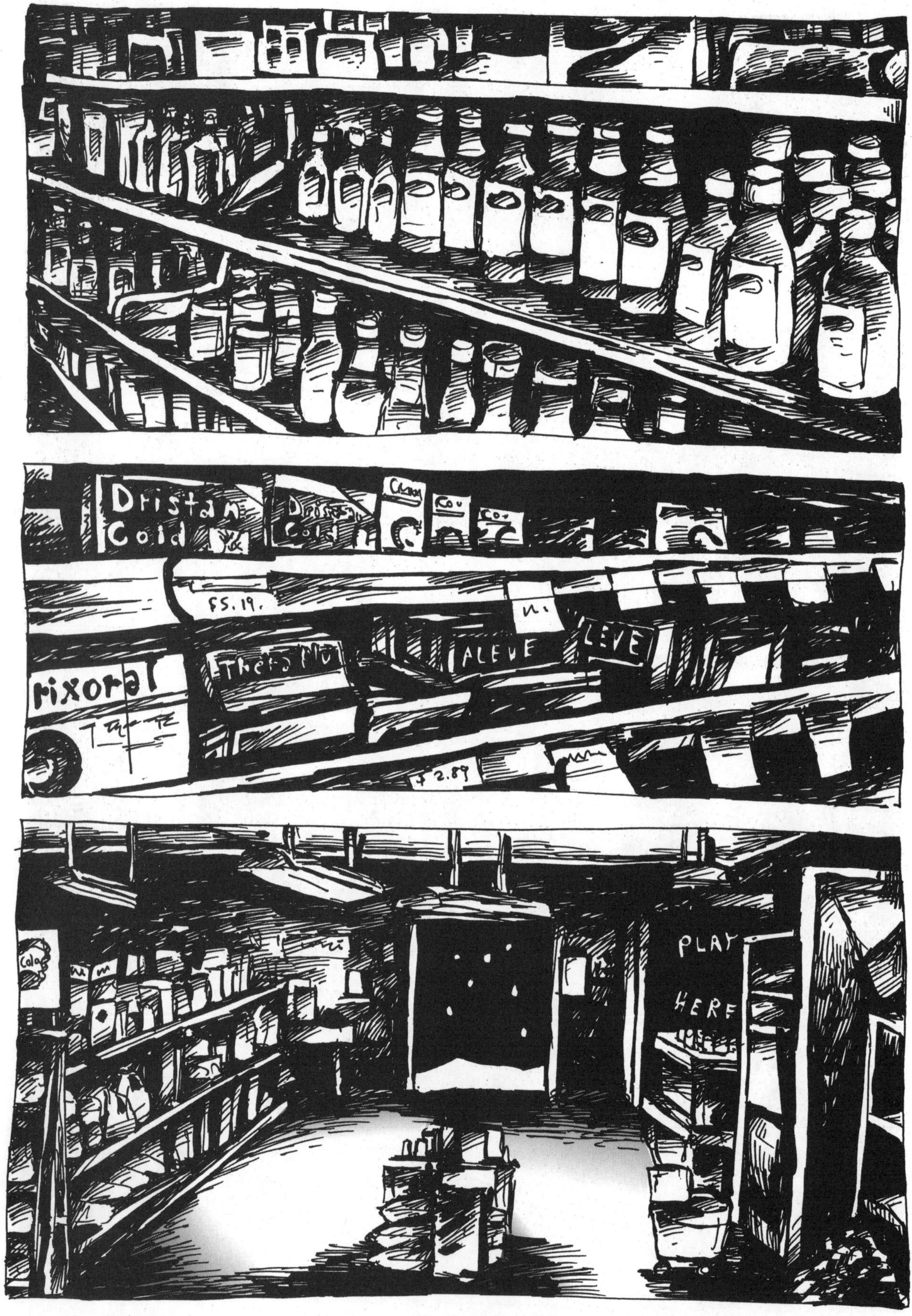
Dristan
Cold
ALEVE
LEVE
rixoral
$2.89
PLAY
HERE

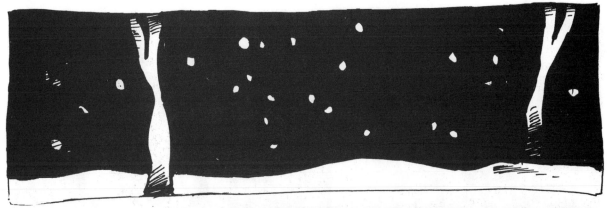

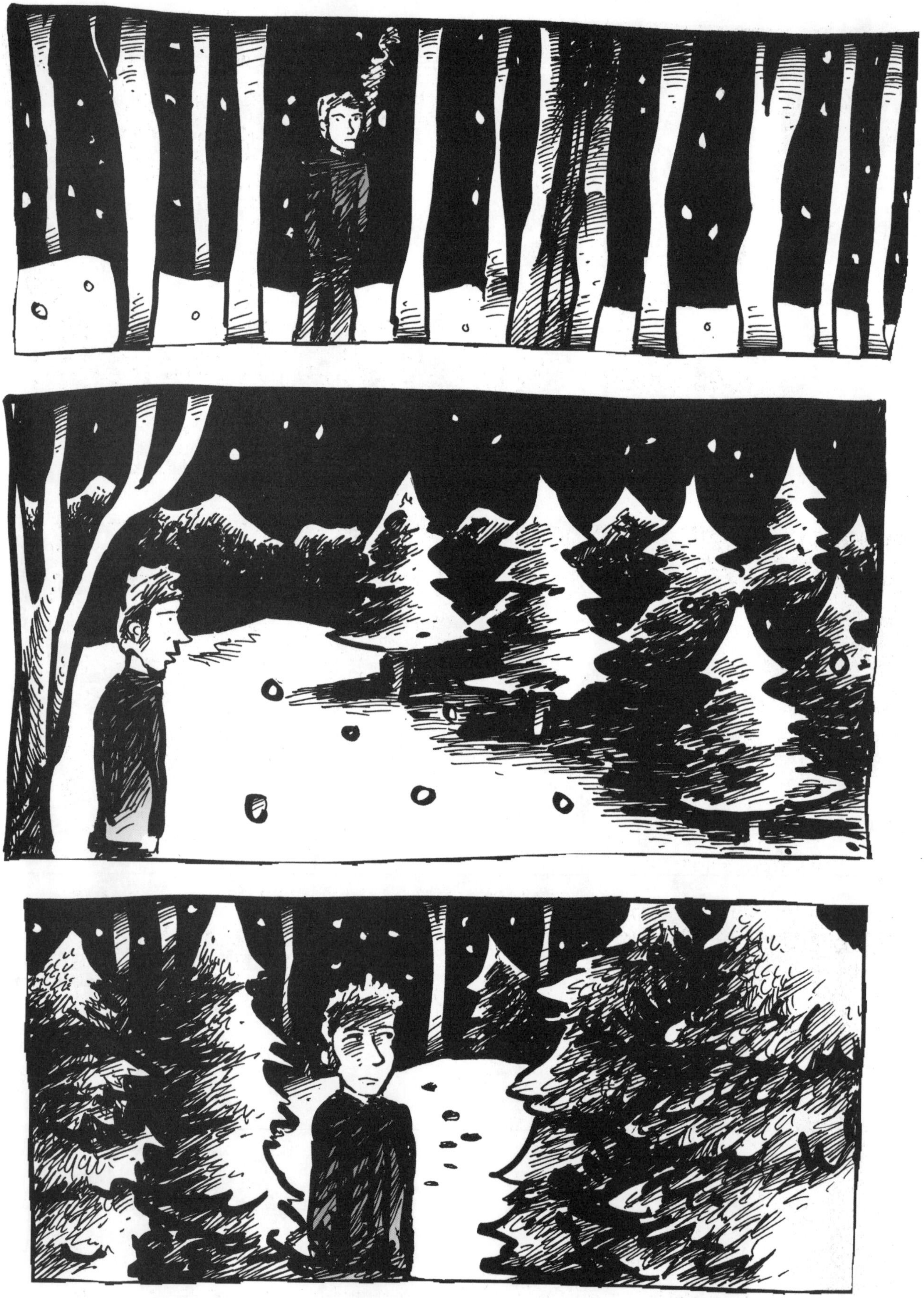

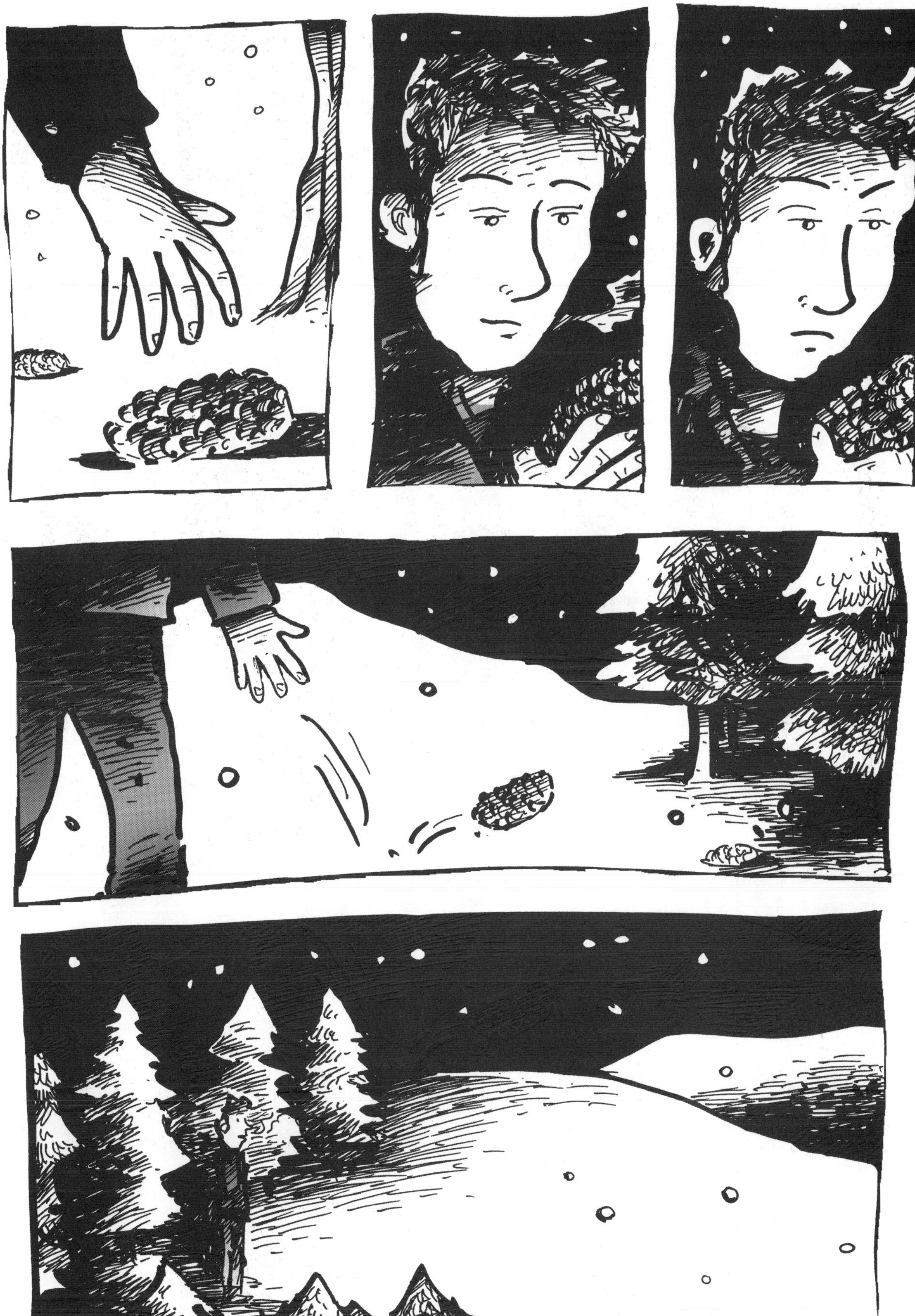

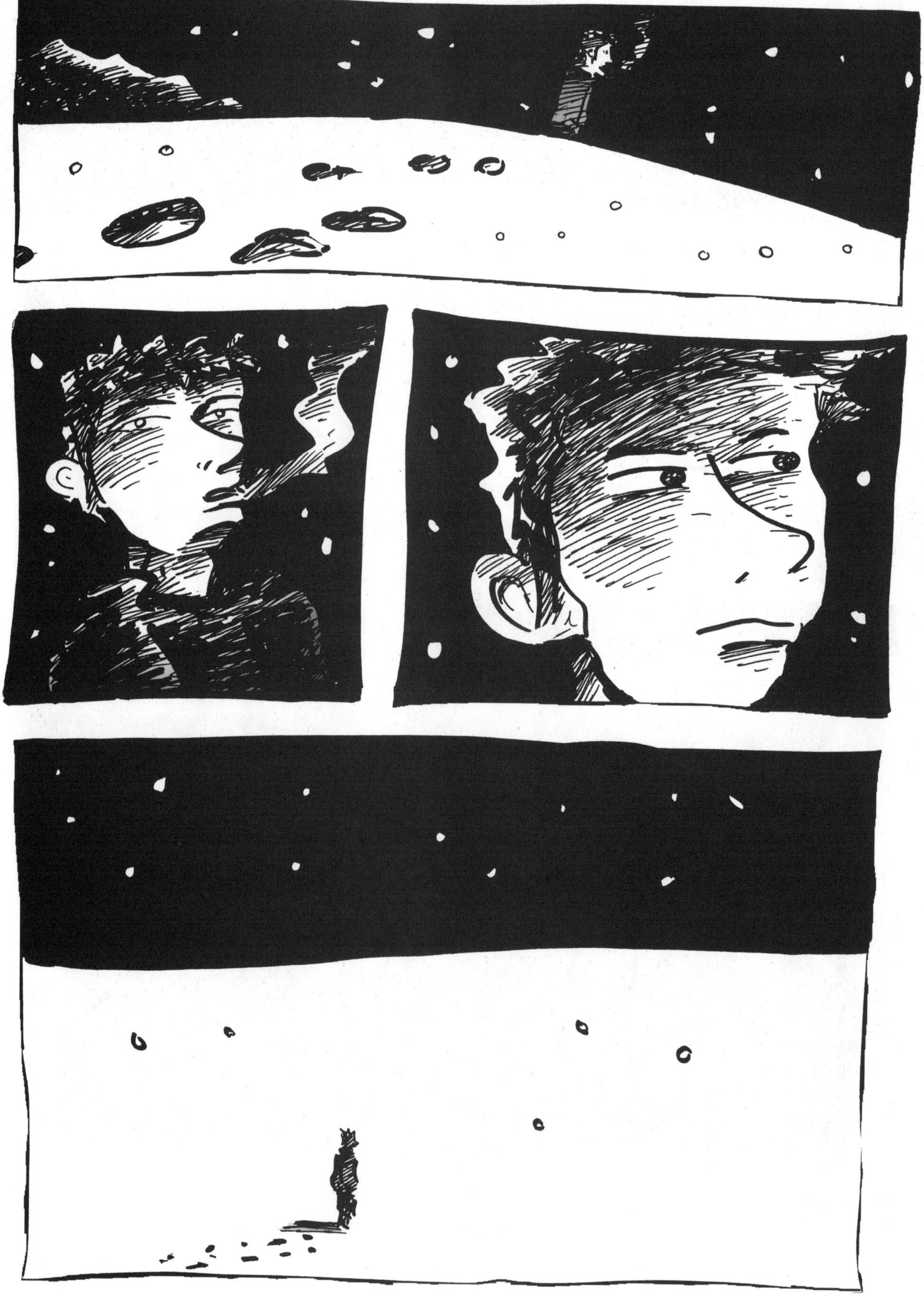

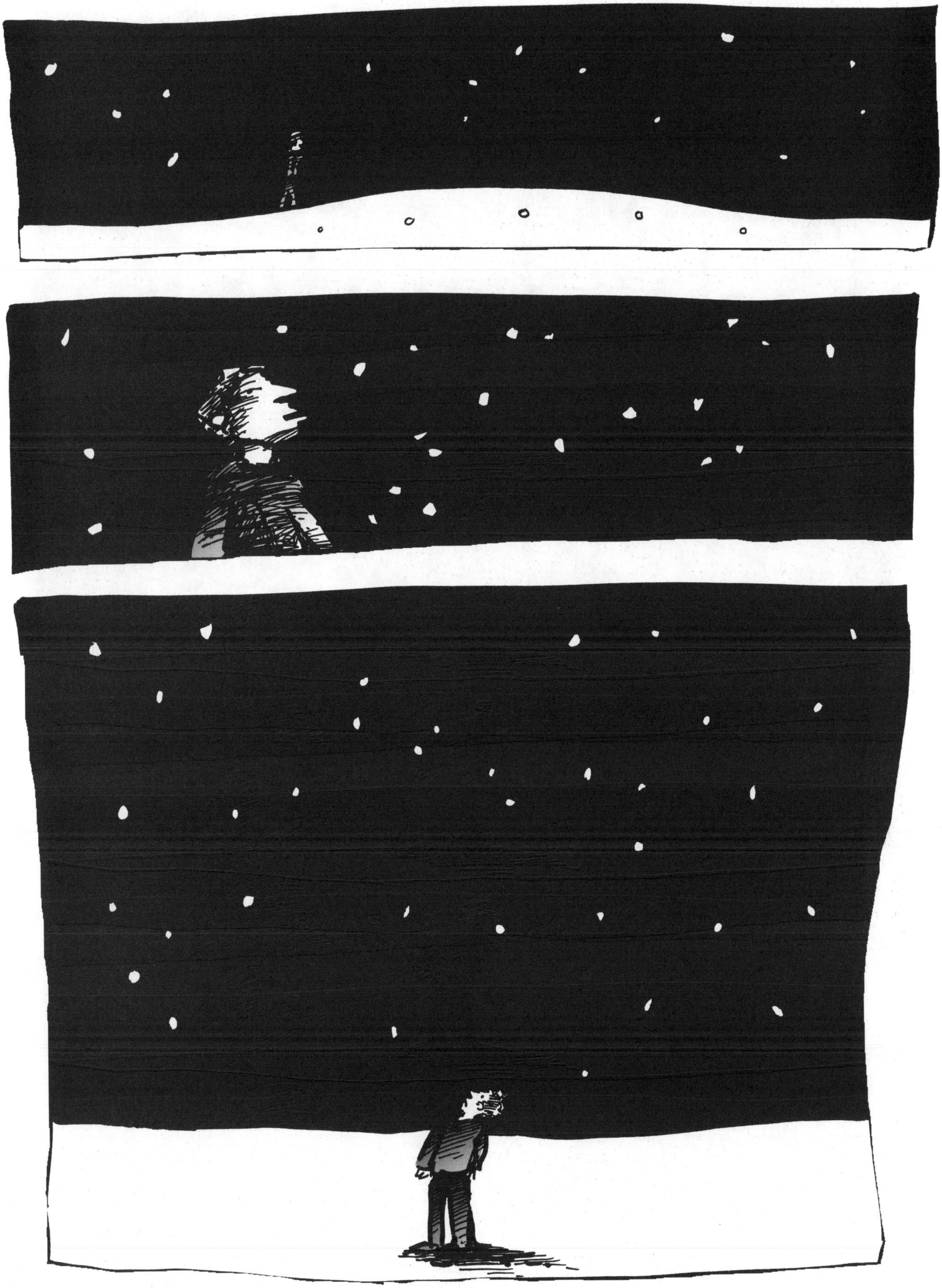

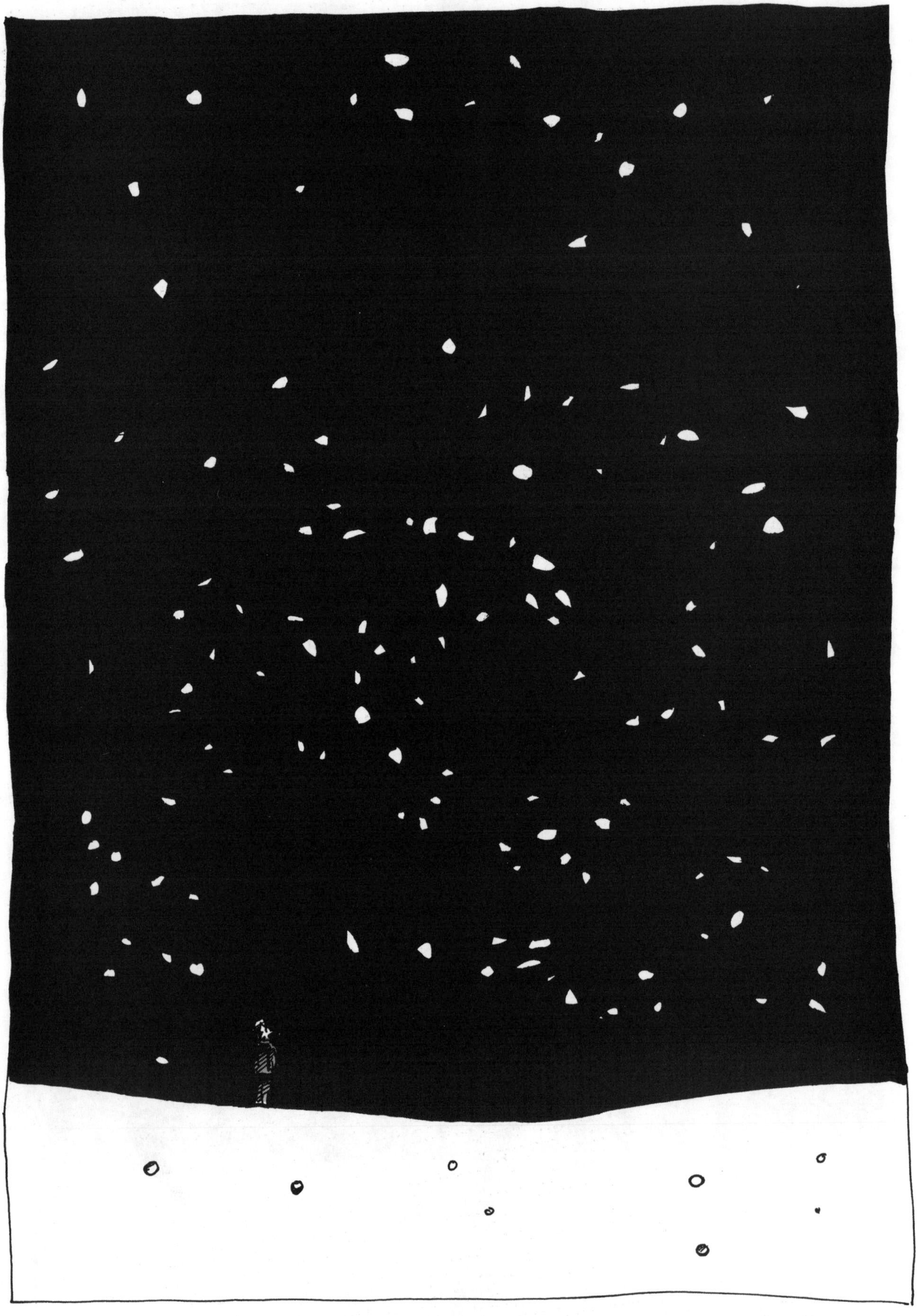

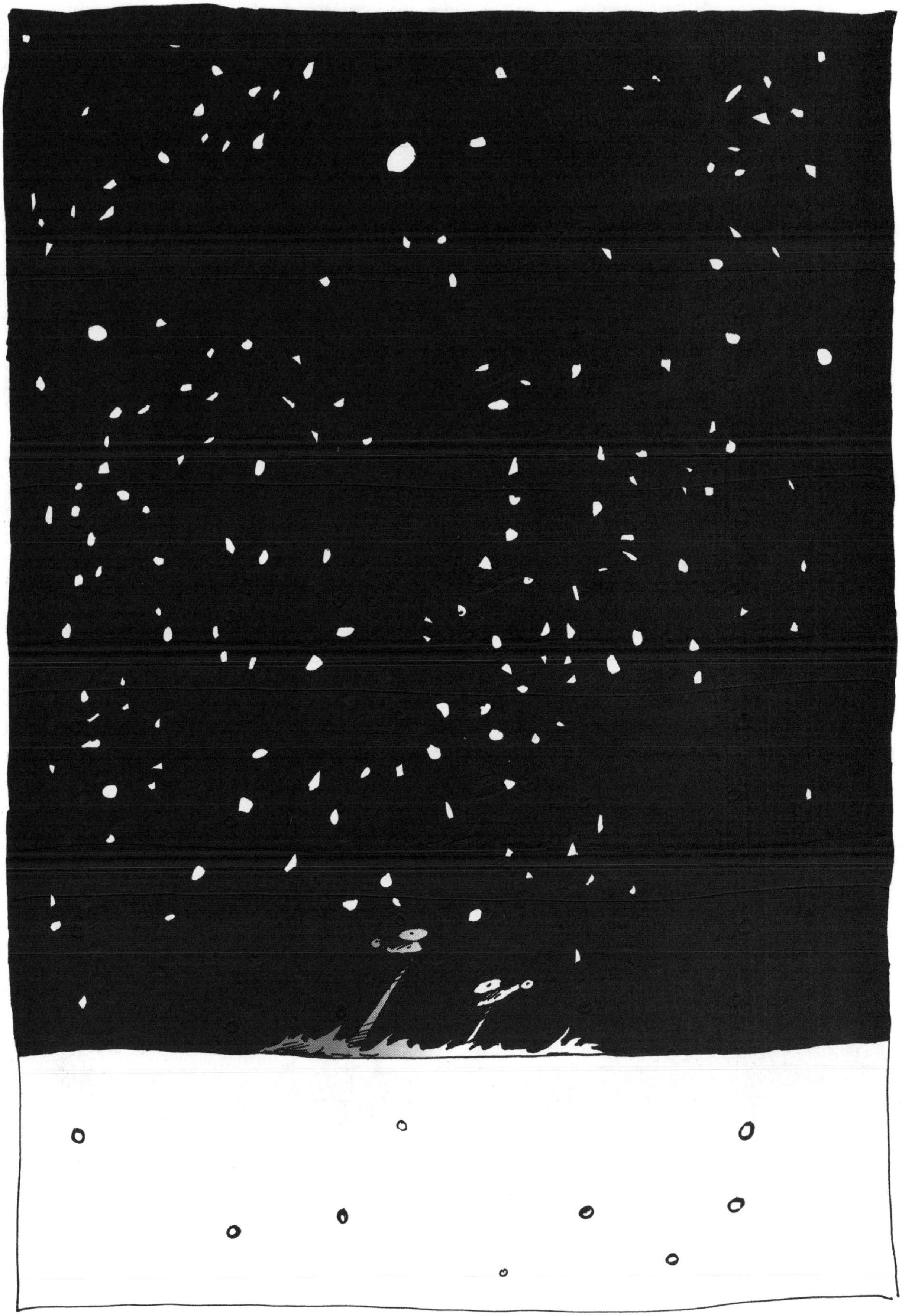

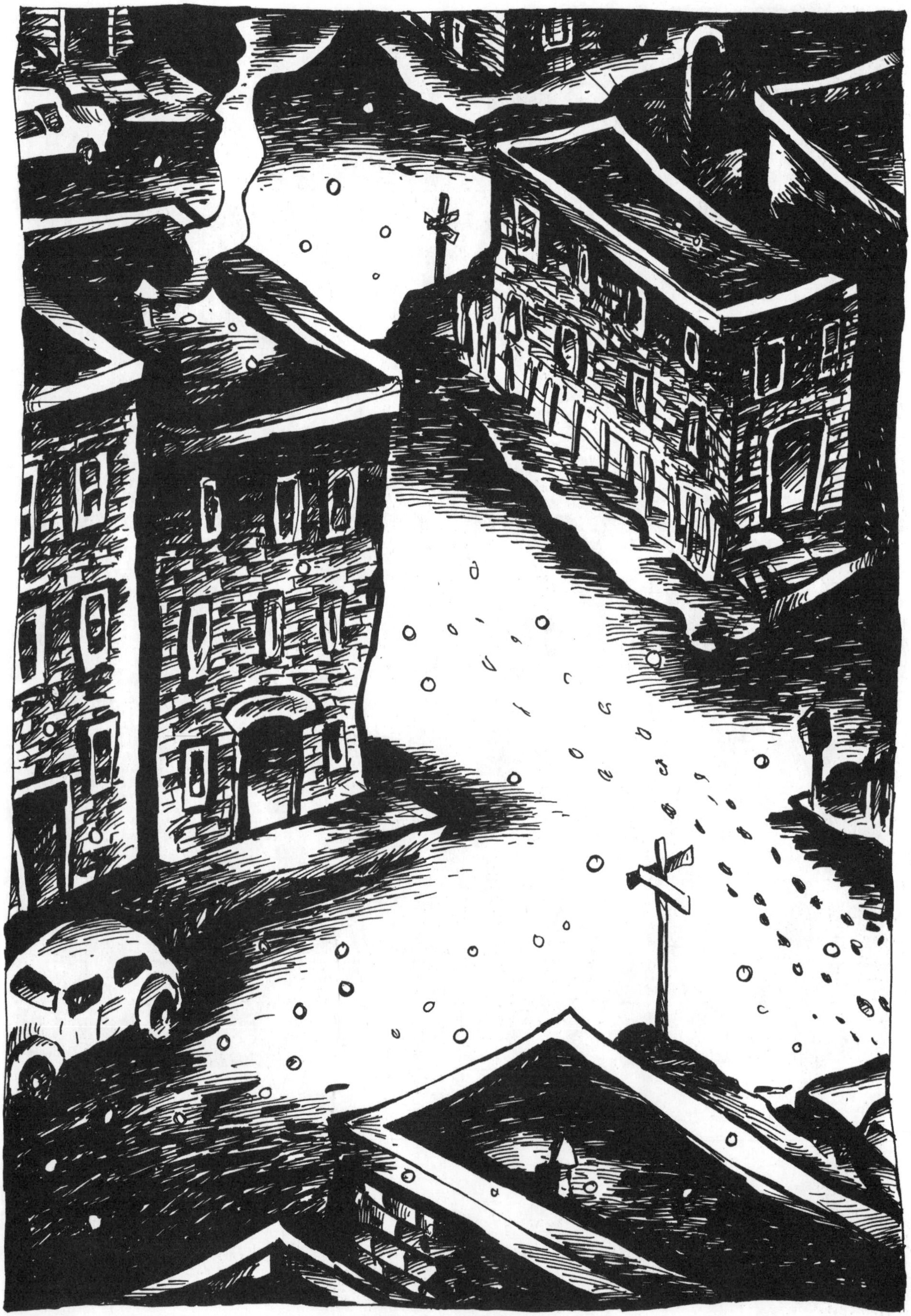

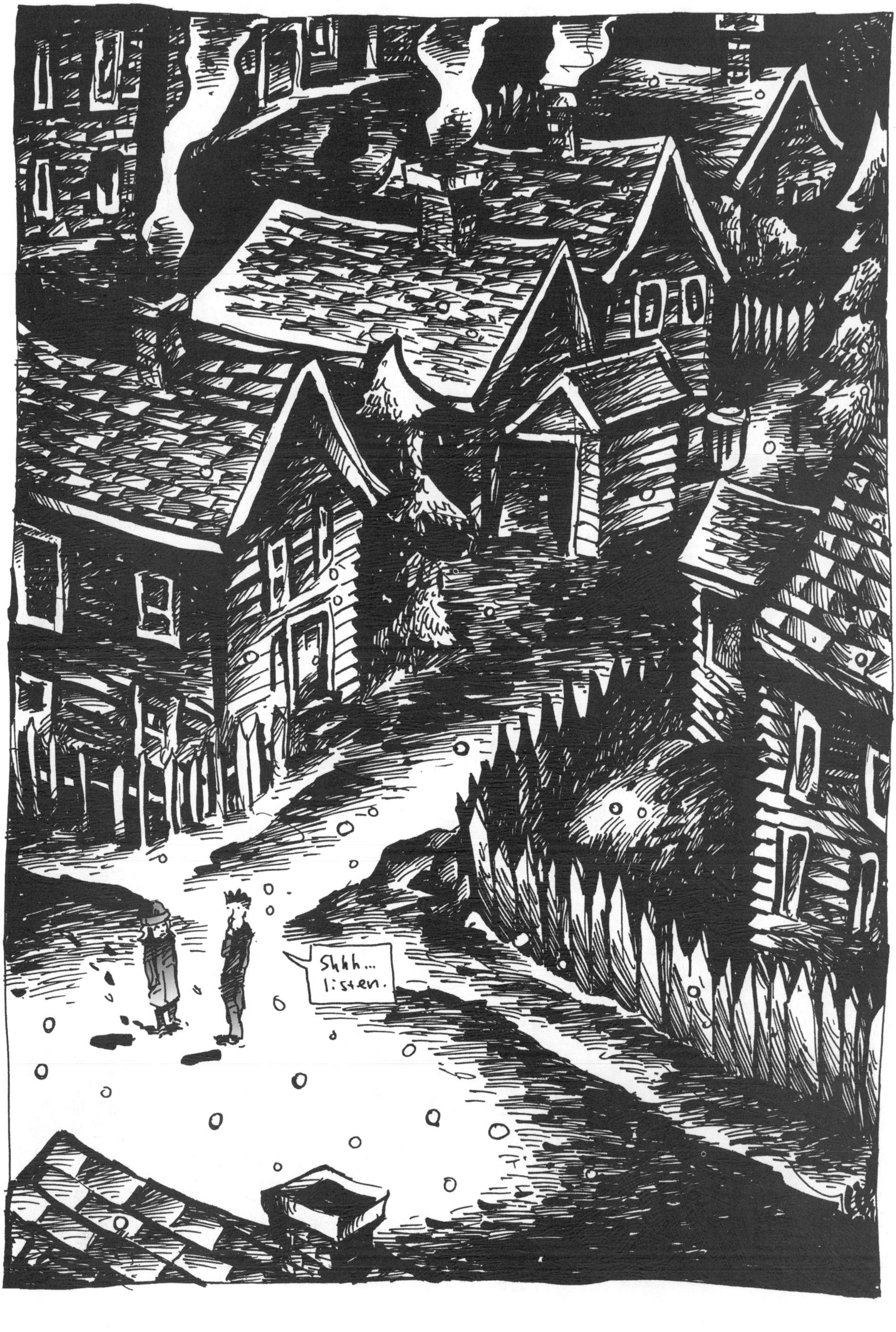
Shhh... listen.

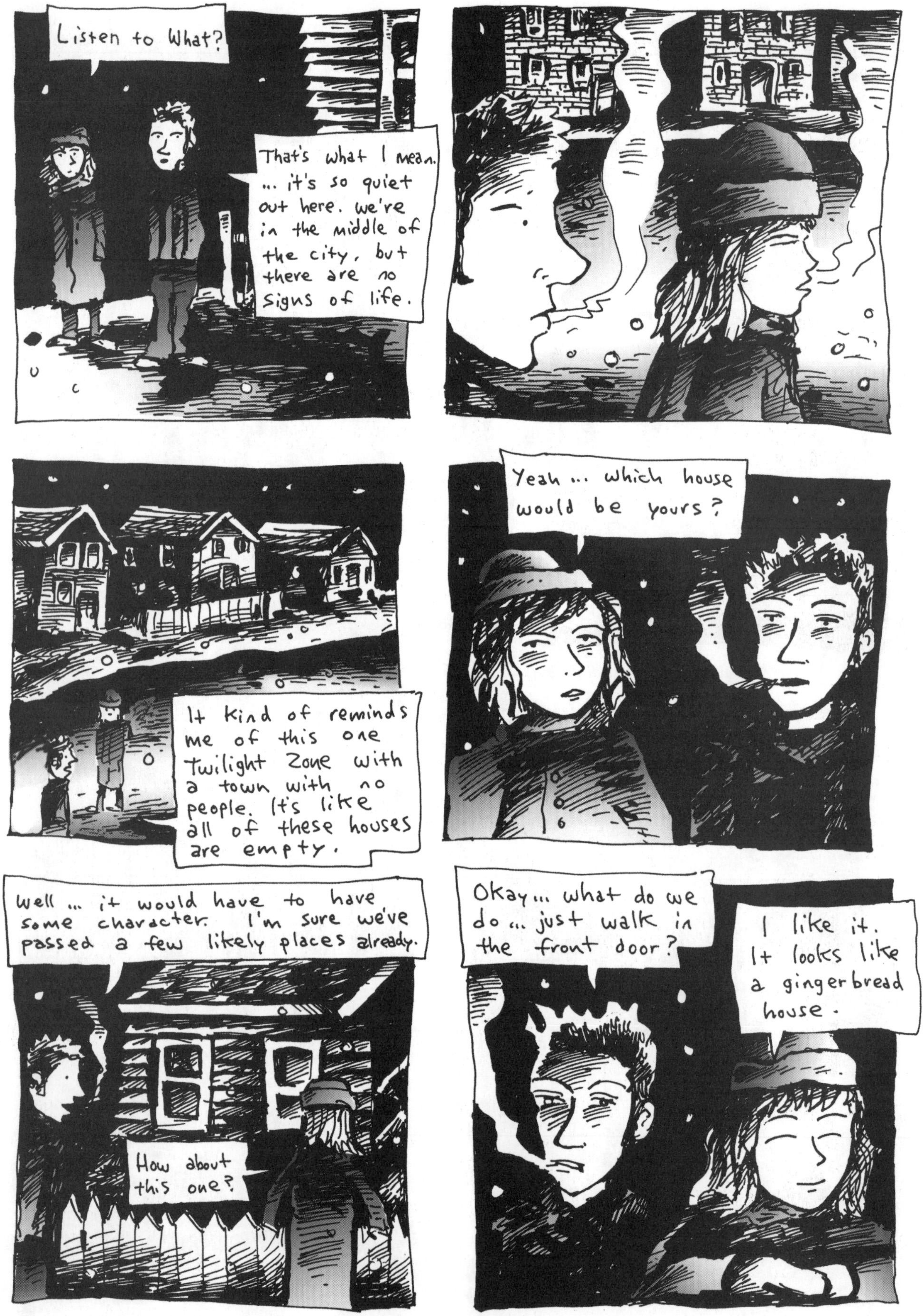
Listen to What?
That's what I mean. ... it's so quiet out here. we're in the middle of the city, but there are no signs of life.
It kind of reminds me of this one Twilight Zone with a town with no people. It's like all of these houses are empty.
Yeah ... which house would be yours?
well ... it would have to have some character. I'm sure we've passed a few likely places already.
How about this one?
Okay ... what do we do ... just walk in the front door?
I like it. It looks like a gingerbread house.

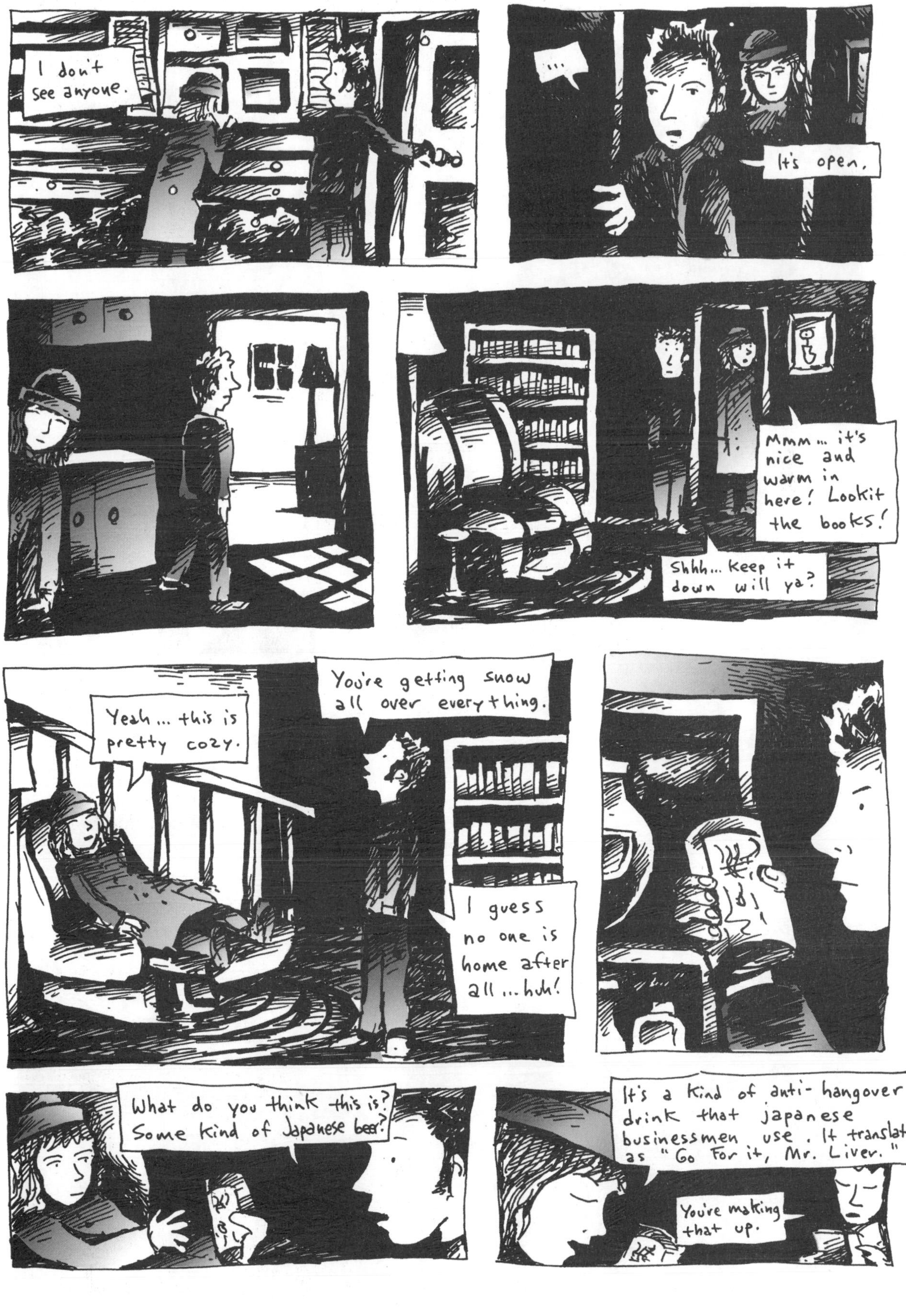
I don't see anyone.
...
It's open.
Mmm... it's nice and warm in here! Lookit the books!
Shhh... keep it down will ya?
Yeah... this is pretty cozy.
You're getting snow all over everything.
I guess no one is home after all... huh!
What do you think this is? Some kind of Japanese beer?
It's a kind of anti-hangover drink that japanese businessmen use. It translates as "Go For it, Mr. Liver."
You're making that up.

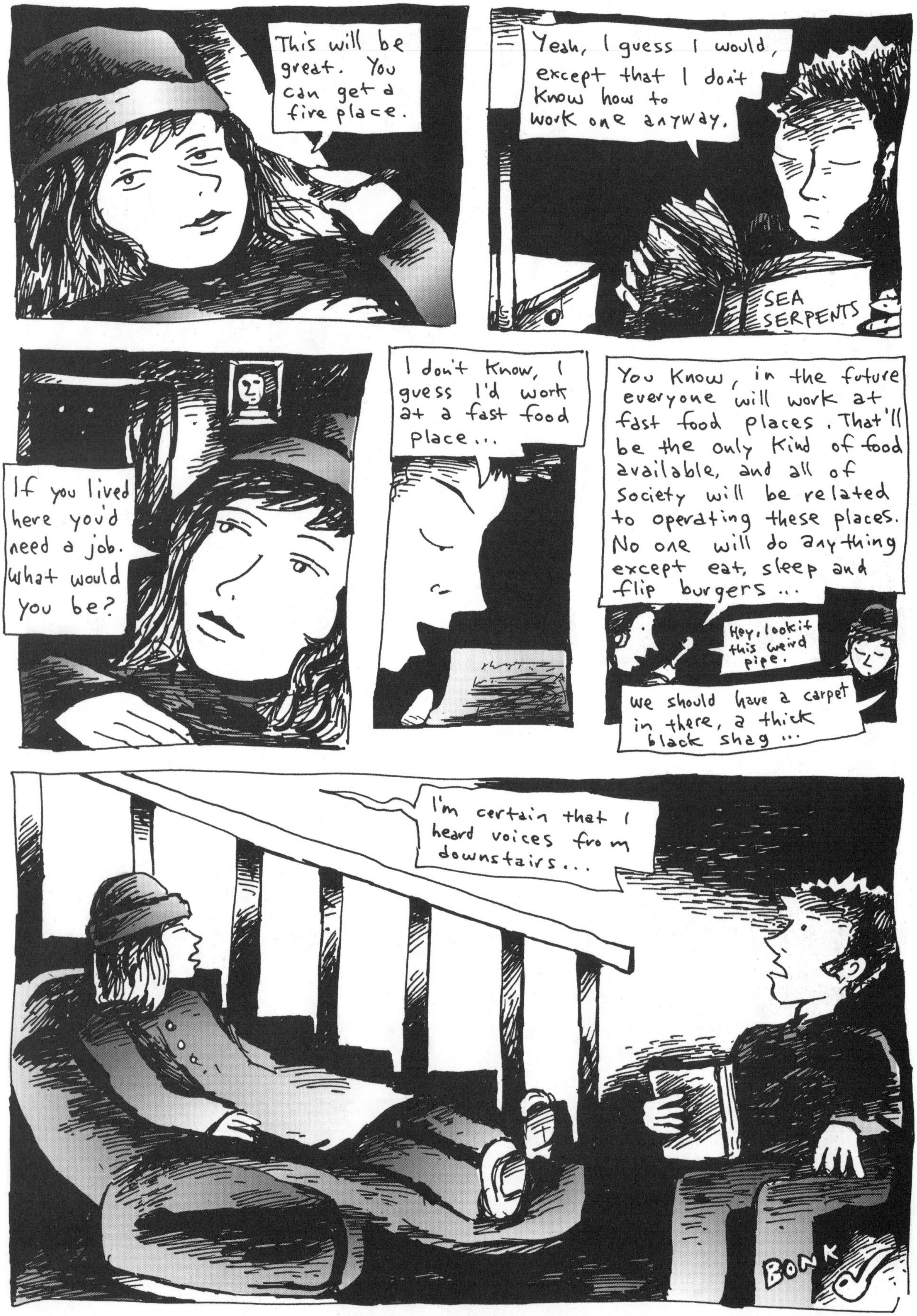
This will be great. You can get a fire place.
Yeah, I guess I would, except that I don't know how to work one anyway.
SEA SERPENTS
If you lived here you'd need a job. What would you be?
I don't know, I guess I'd work at a fast food place...
You know, in the future everyone will work at fast food places. That'll be the only kind of food available, and all of society will be related to operating these places. No one will do anything except eat, sleep and flip burgers...
Hey, lookit this weird pipe.
We should have a carpet in there, a thick black shag...
I'm certain that I heard voices from downstairs...
BONK

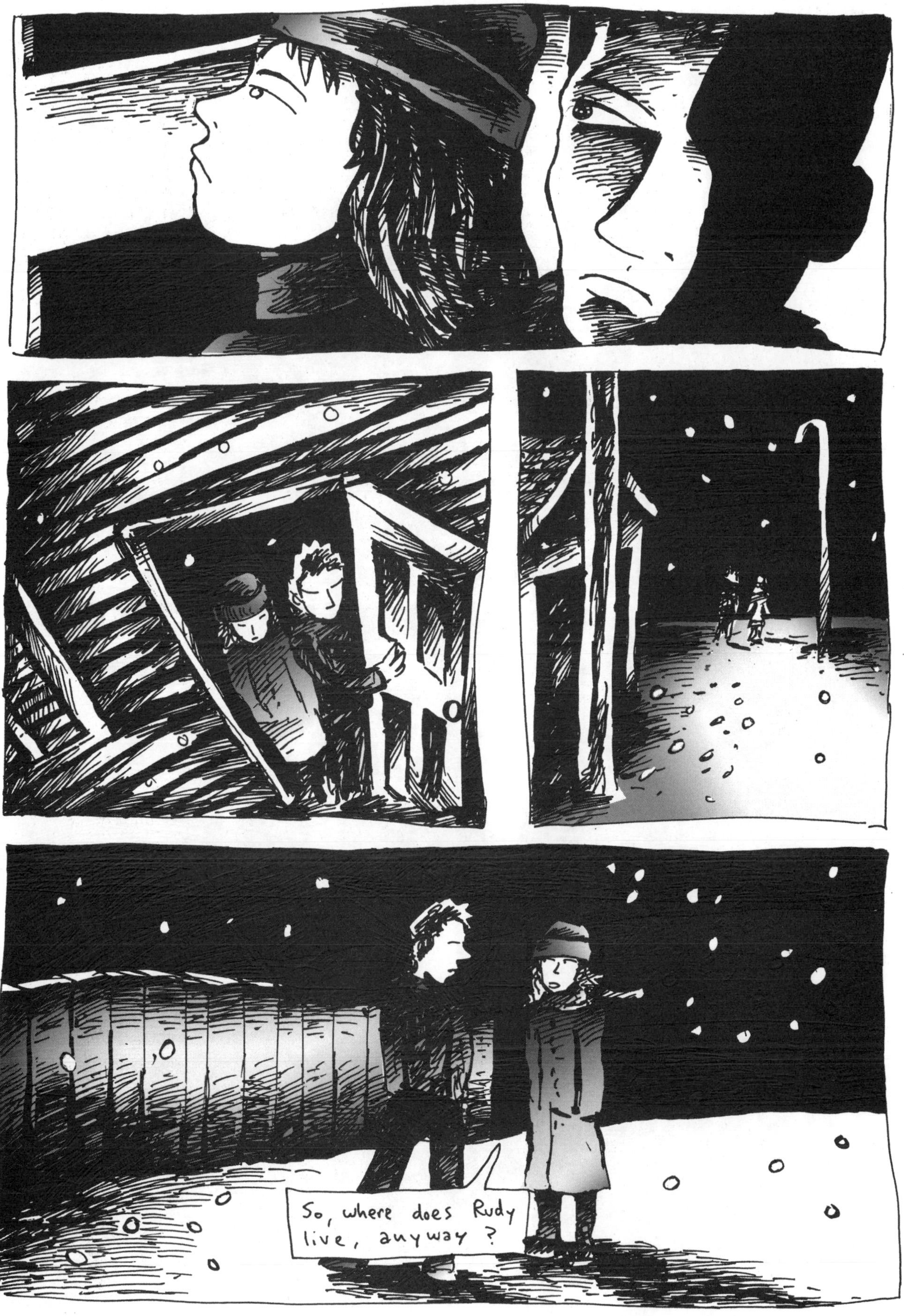
So, where does Rudy live, anyway ?

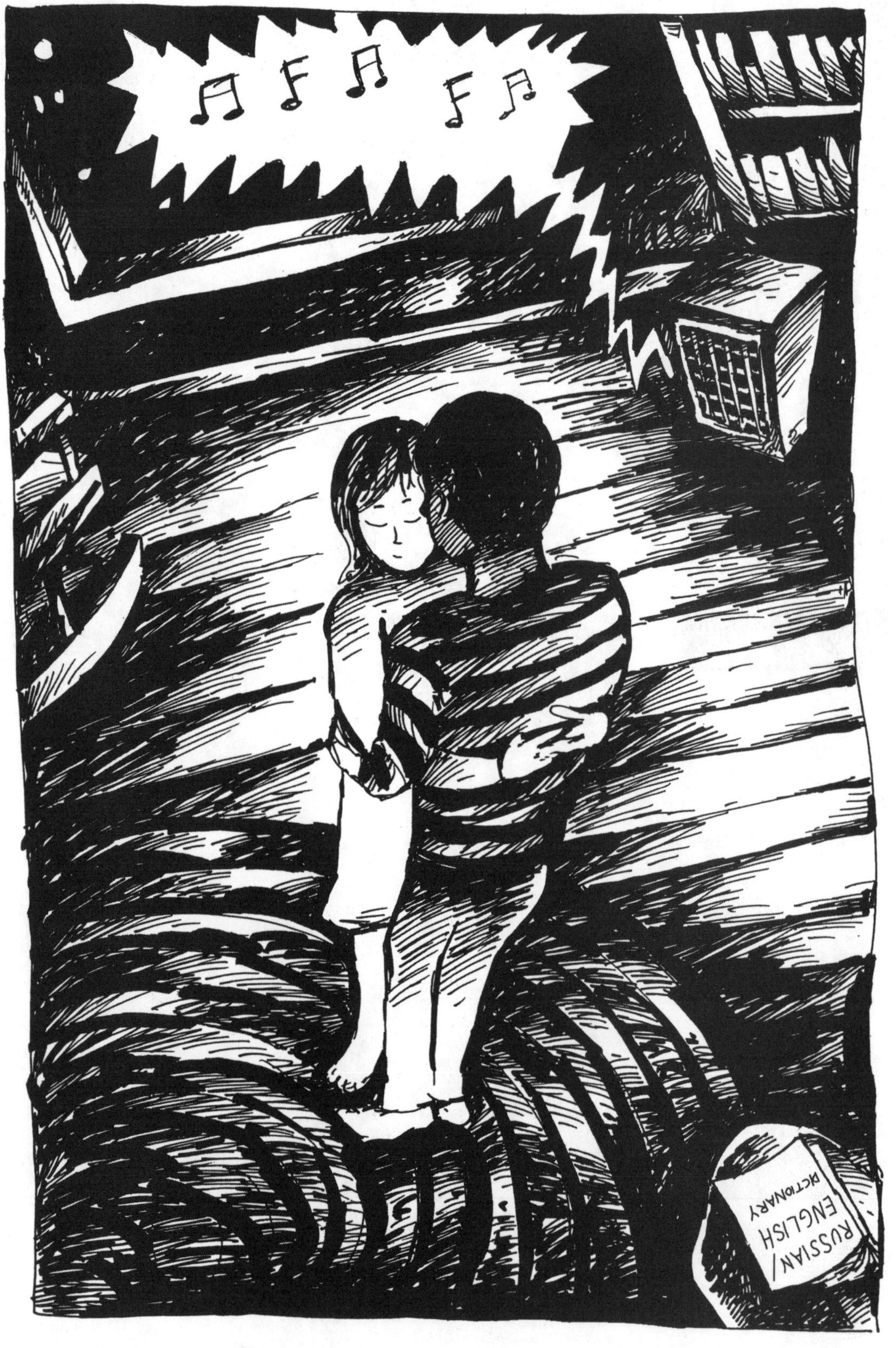
RUSSIAN/
ENGLISH
DICTIONARY

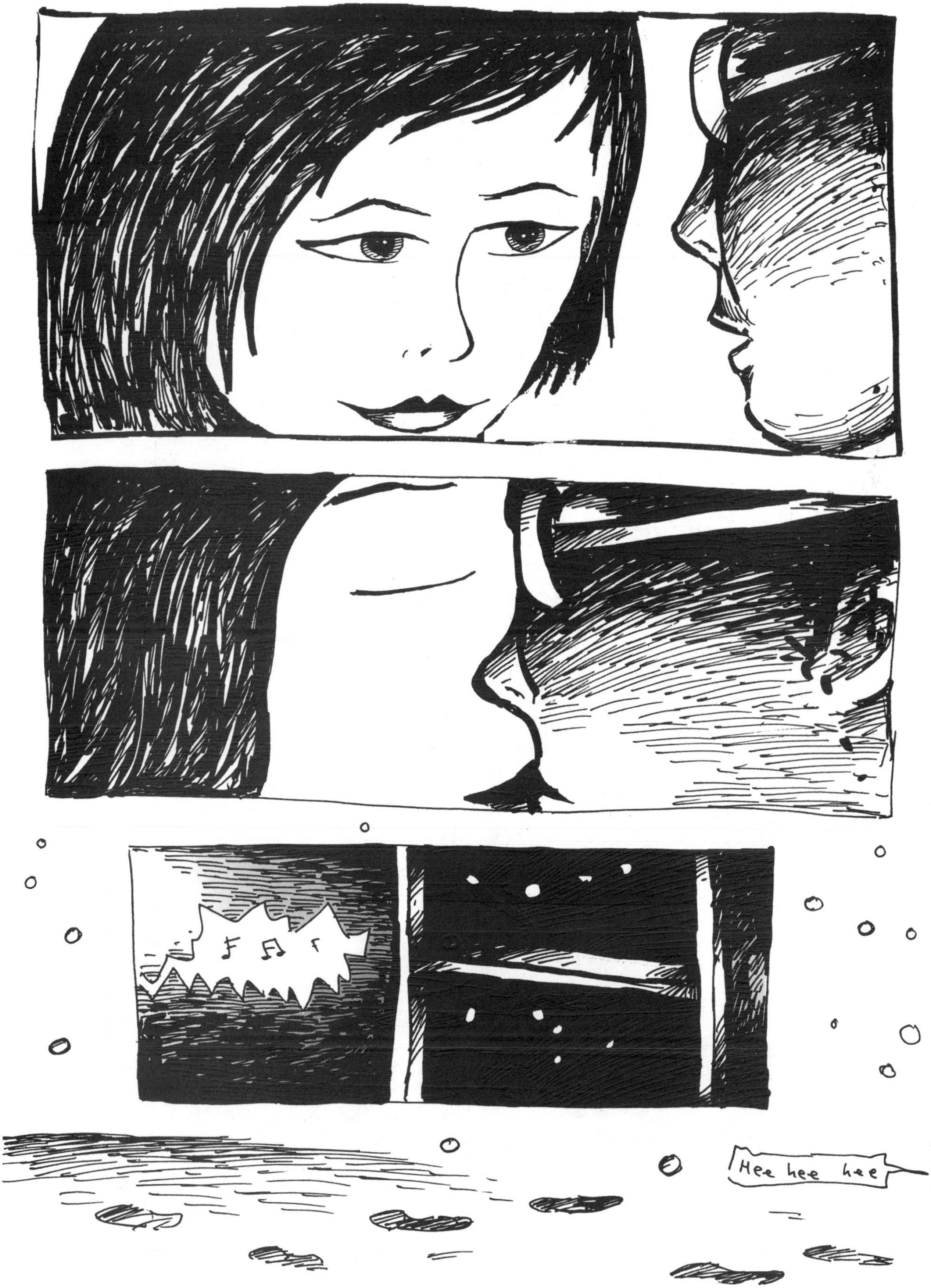
Hee hee hee

HEEEY ROOOODY!!!!
Hey Rudy, up yours!
WOO OOO hoo!
Wooooo!
Yeah!
Yeah!
RUUUUDY!!
Screw you, Rudy!

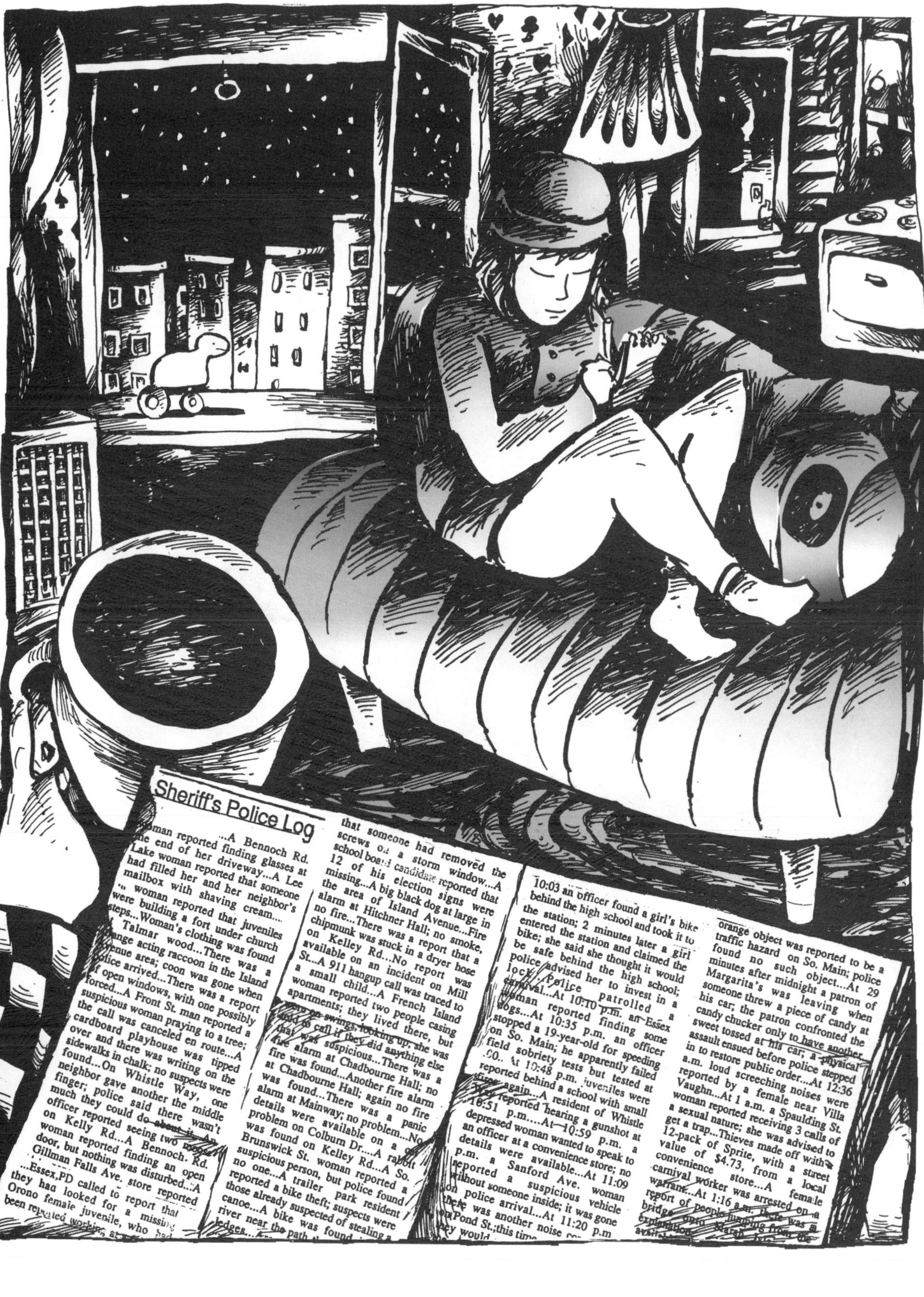
Sheriff's Police Log
...A Bennoch Rd.
end of her driveway...A Lee
Lake woman reported that someone
had filled her and her neighbor's
mailbox with shaving cream....
woman reported that juveniles
were building a fort under church
steps...Woman's clothing was found
Talmar wood...There was a
acting raccoon in the Island
area; coon was gone when
arrived...There was a report
open windows, with one possibly
forced...A Front St. man reported a
suspicious woman praying to a tree;
the call was canceled en route...A
cardboard playhouse was tipped
over and there was writing on the
sidewalks in chalk; no suspects were
found...On Whistle Way, one
neighbor gave another the middle
finger; police said there wasn't
much they could do
officer reported seeing two
on Kelly Rd...A Bennoch. Rd.
woman reported finding an open
door, but nothing was disturbed...A
Gillman Falls Ave. store reported
...Essex PD called to report that
they had looked for a missing
Orono female juvenile, who had
that someone had removed the
screws on a storm window...A
school board candidate reported that
12 of his election signs were
missing...A big black dog at large in
the area of Island Avenue...Fire
alarm at Hitchner Hall; no smoke,
no fire...There was a report that a
chipmunk was stuck in a dryer hose
on Kelley Rd...No report was
available on an incident on Mill
St...A 911 hangup call was traced to
a small child...A French Island
woman reported two people casing
apartments; they lived there, but
that was suspicious...There was a
fire alarm at Chadbourne Hall; no
fire was found...Another fire alarm
at Chadbourne Hall; again no fire
was found...There was a panic
alarm at Mainway; no problem...No
details were available on a
problem on Colburn Dr....A rabbit
was found on Kelley Rd...A So.
Brunswick St. woman reported a
suspicious person, but police found
no one...A trailer park resident
reported a bike theft; suspects were
those already suspected of stealing a
canoe...A bike was found
river near the path
10:03 an officer found a girl's bike
behind the high school and took it to
the station; 2 minutes later a girl
entered the station and claimed the
bike; she said she thought it would
be safe behind the high school;
police advised her to invest in a
lock...Police patrolled a
carnival...At 10:10 p.m. an Essex
woman reported finding some
dogs...At 10:35 p.m. an officer
stopped a 19-year-old for speeding
on So. Main; he apparently failed
field sobriety tests but tested at
.00...At 10:48 p.m. juveniles were
reported behind a school with small
fires again...A resident of Whistle
Way reported hearing a gunshot at
10:51 p.m....At 10:59 p.m. a
depressed woman wanted to speak to
an officer at a convenience store; no
details were available...At 11:09
p.m. a Sanford Ave. woman
reported a suspicious vehicle
without someone inside; it was gone
on police arrival...At 11:20 p.m
there was another noise
on Pond St.;this time
they would
orange object was reported to be a
traffic hazard on So. Main; police
found no such object...At 29
minutes after midnight a patron of
Margarita's was leaving when
someone threw a piece of candy at
his car; the patron confronted the
candy chucker only to have another
sweet tossed at his car; a physical
assault ensued before police stepped
in to restore public order...At 12:36
a.m. loud screeching noises were
reported by a female near Villa
Vaughn...At 1 a.m. a Spaulding St.
woman reported receiving 3 calls of
a sexual nature; she was advised to
get a trap...Thieves made off with a
12-pack of Sprite, with a street
value of $4.73, from a local
convenience store...A female
carnival worker was arrested on a
warrant...At 1:16 a.m. there was a
report of people jumping from the
bridge

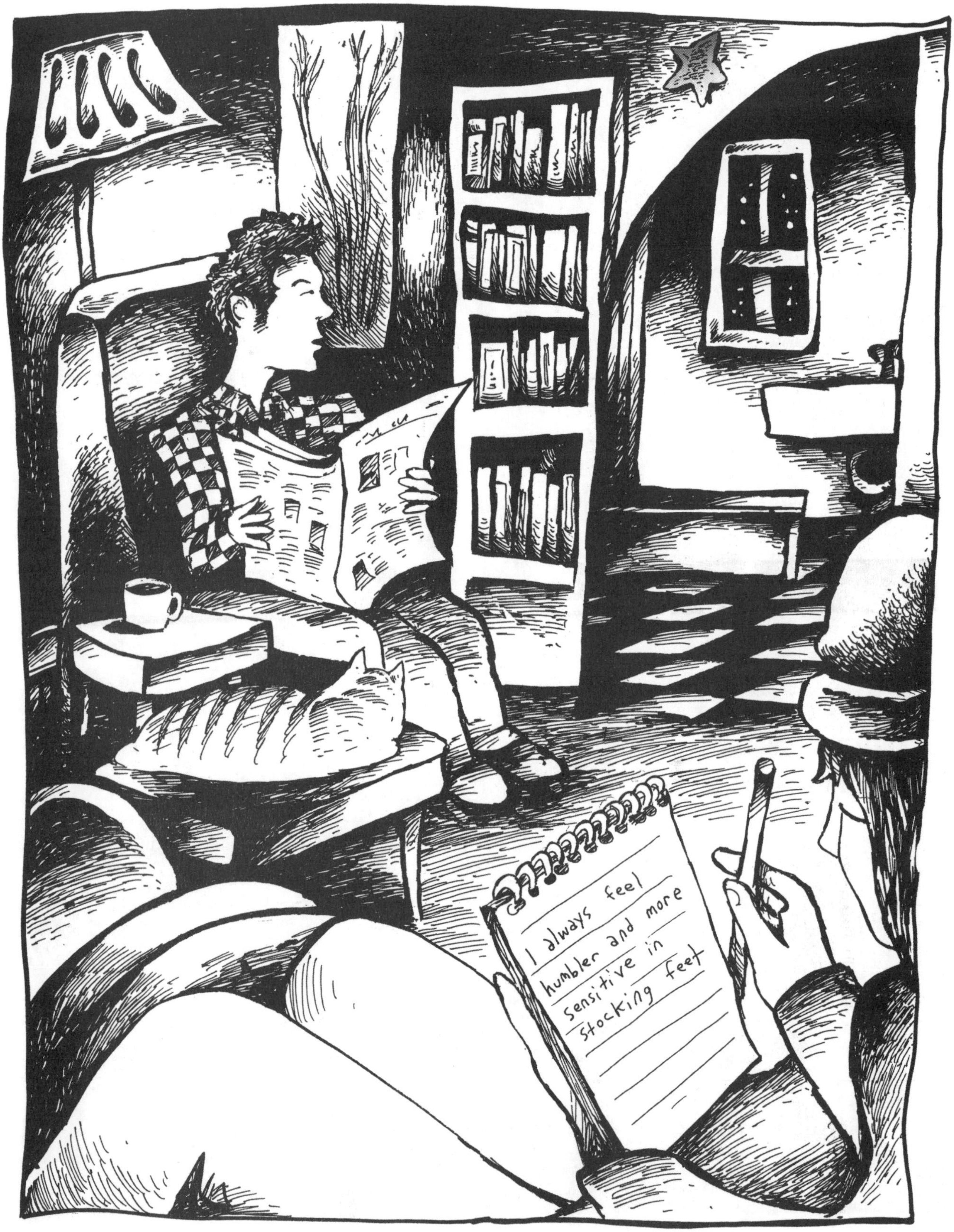
I always feel
humbler and more
sensitive in
stocking feet

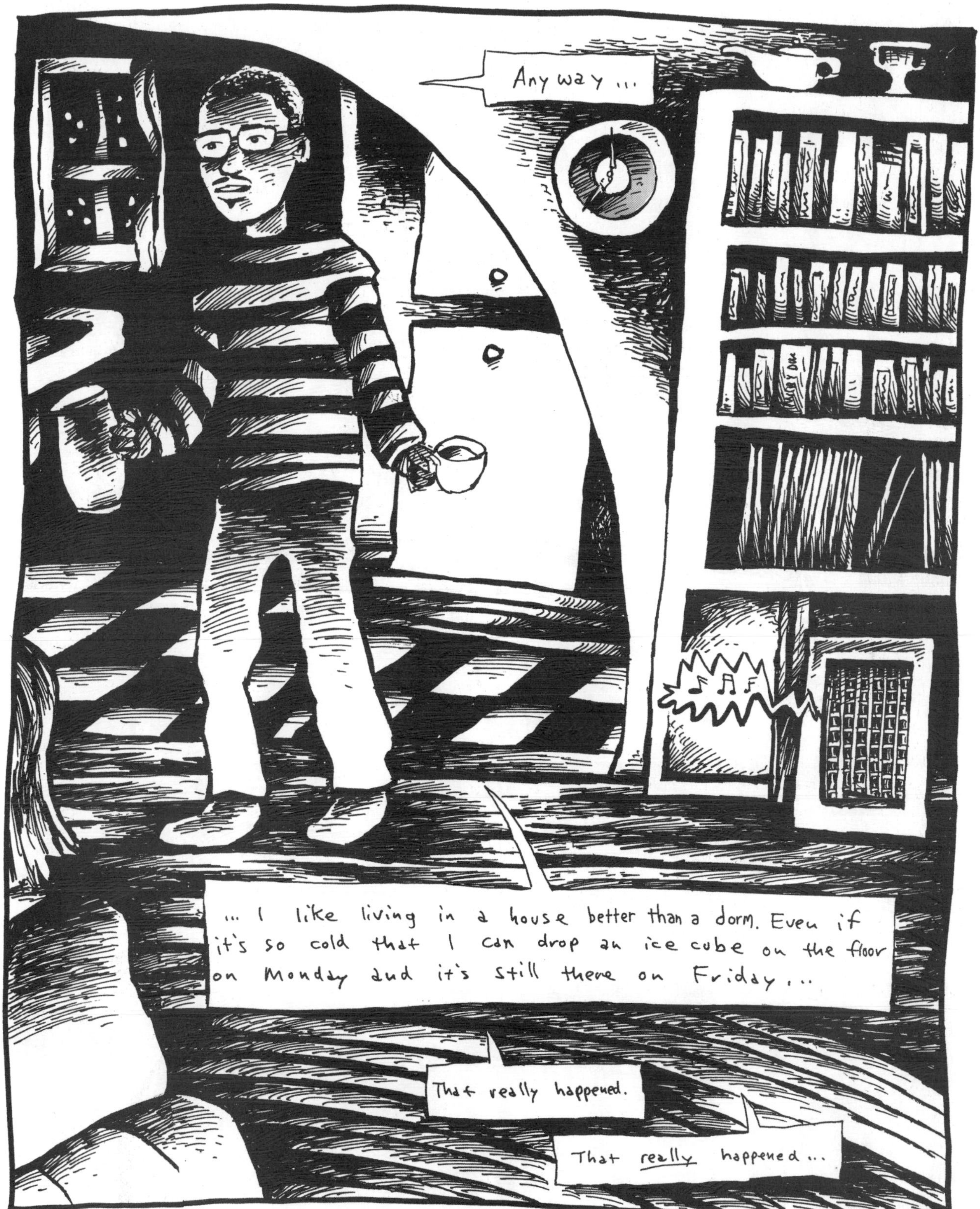
Anyway ...
... I like living in a house better than a dorm. Even if it's so cold that I can drop an ice cube on the floor on Monday and it's still there on Friday ...
That really happened.
That really happened ...

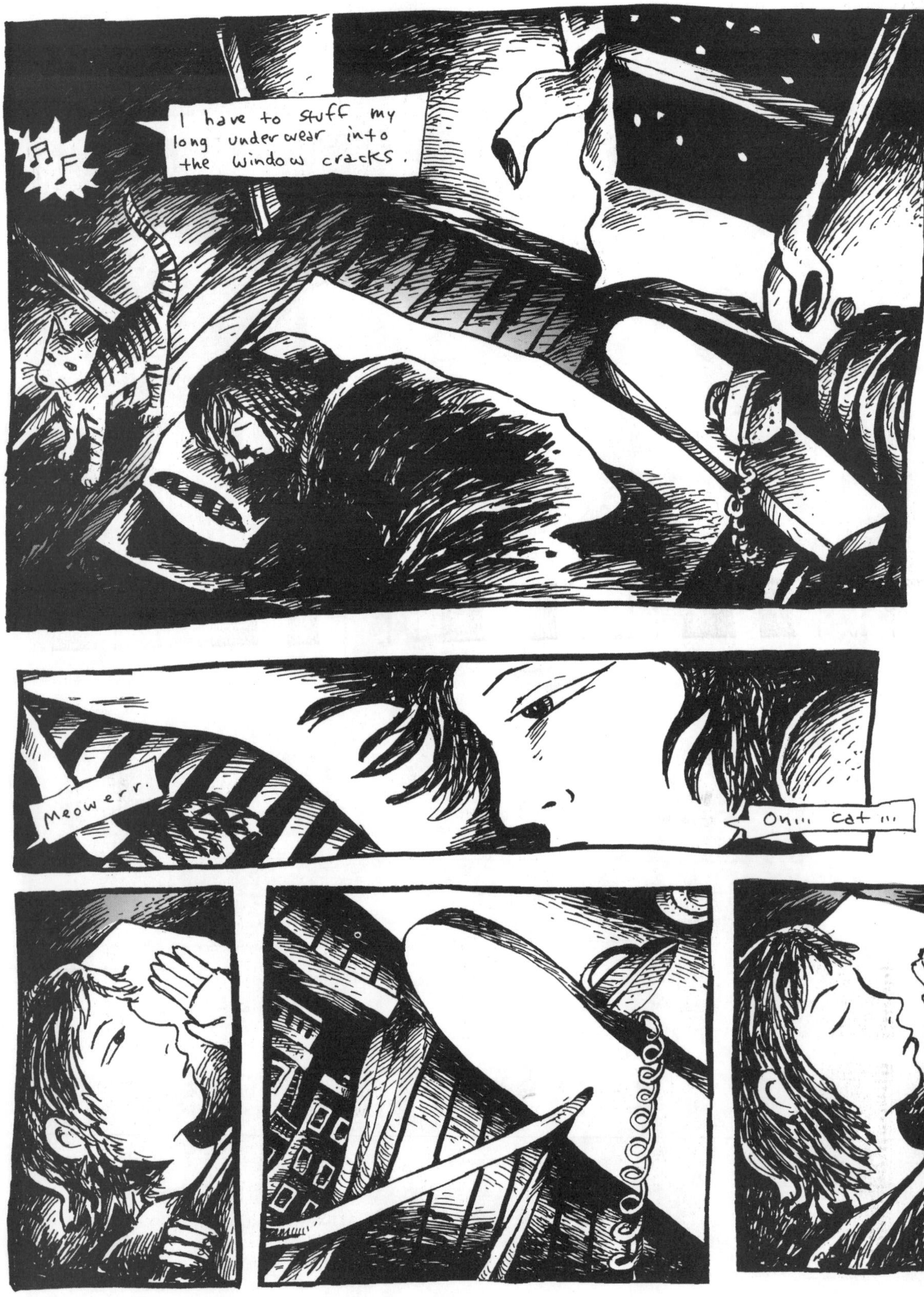

I have to stuff my long underwear into the window cracks.
Meowerr.
Oh... cat...

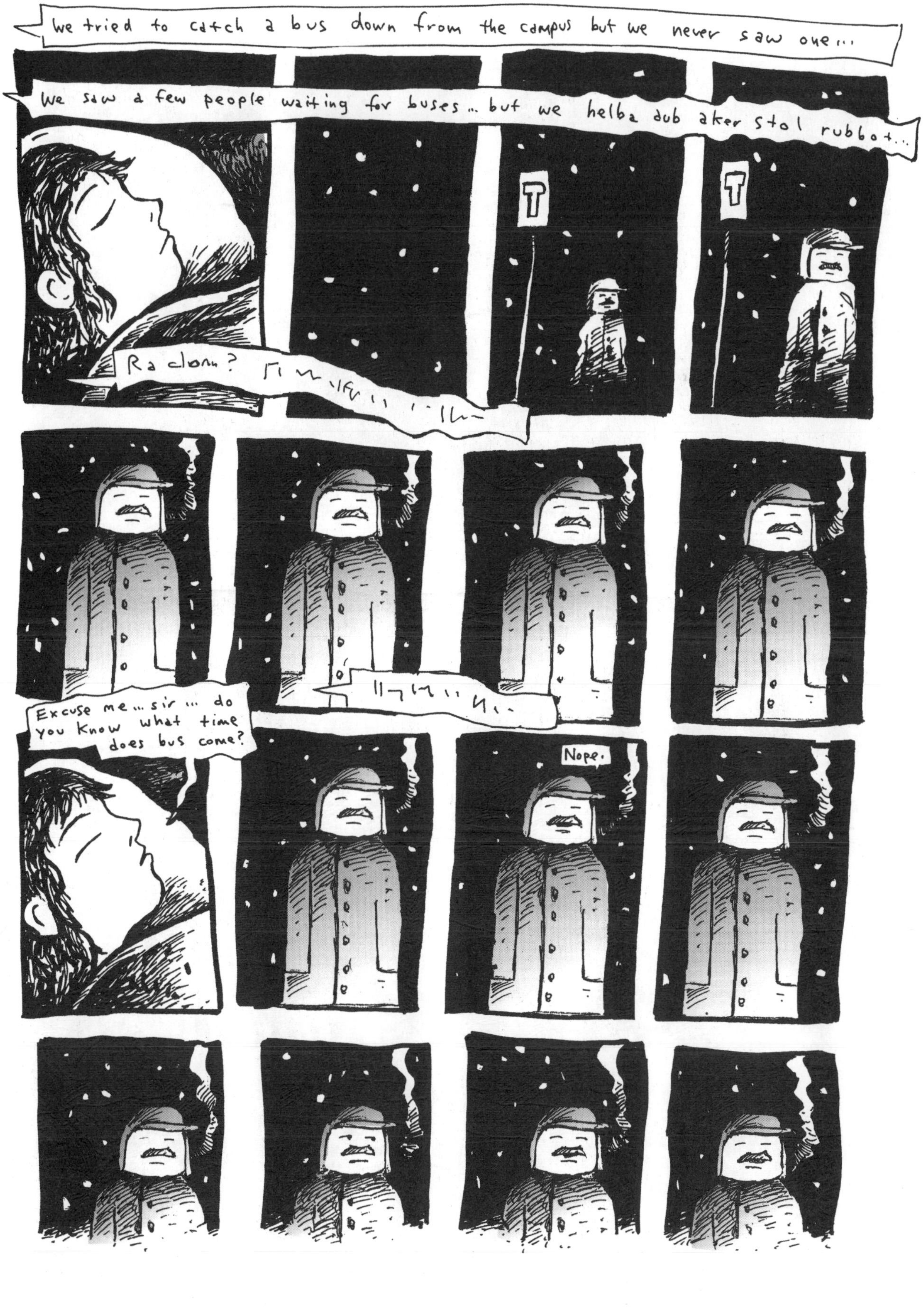
we tried to catch a bus down from the campus but we never saw one...
we saw a few people waiting for buses... but we helba dub aker stol rubbot...
Ra clonn?
Excuse me... sir... do you know what time does bus come?
Nope.

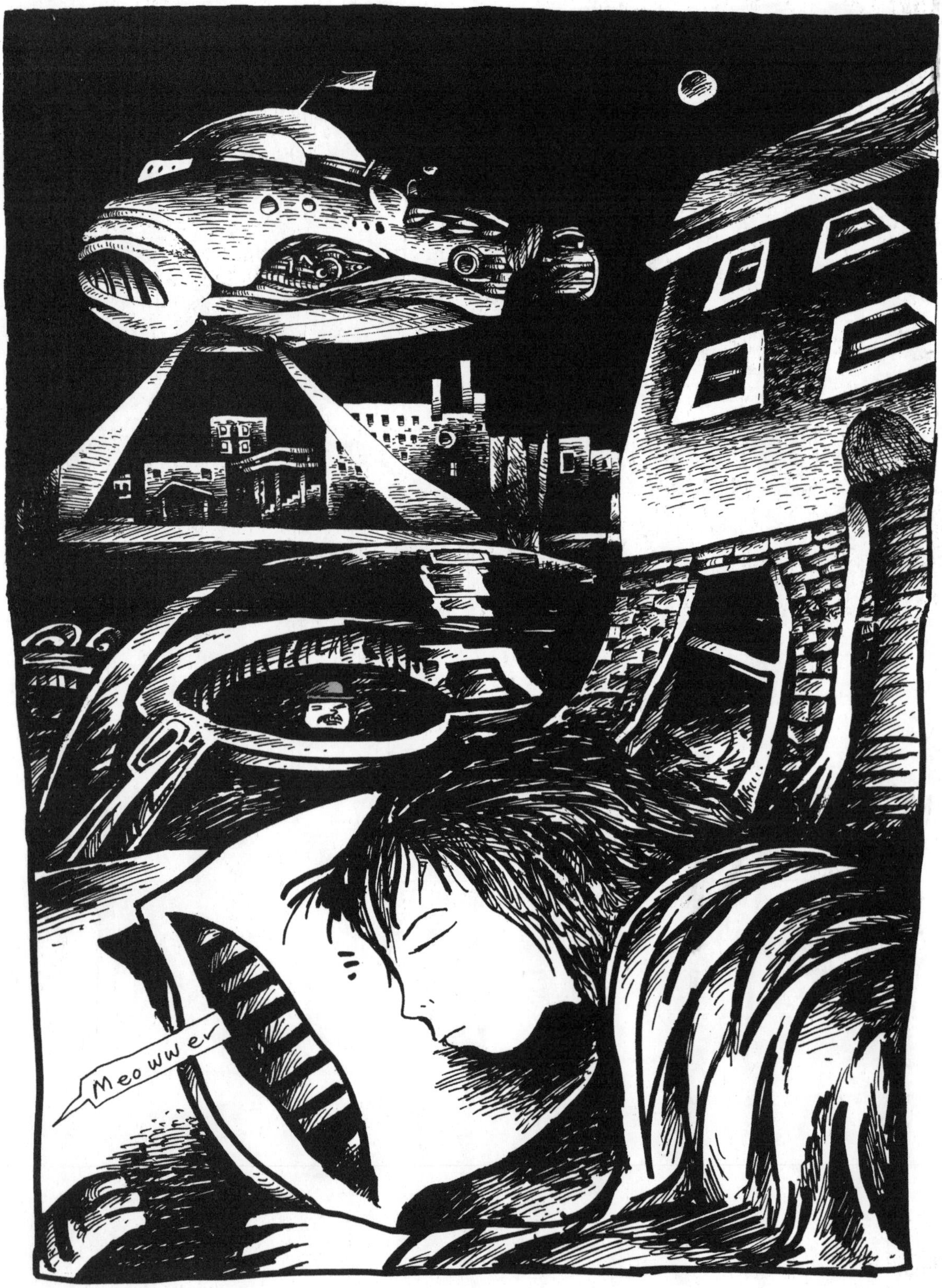
Meowwer

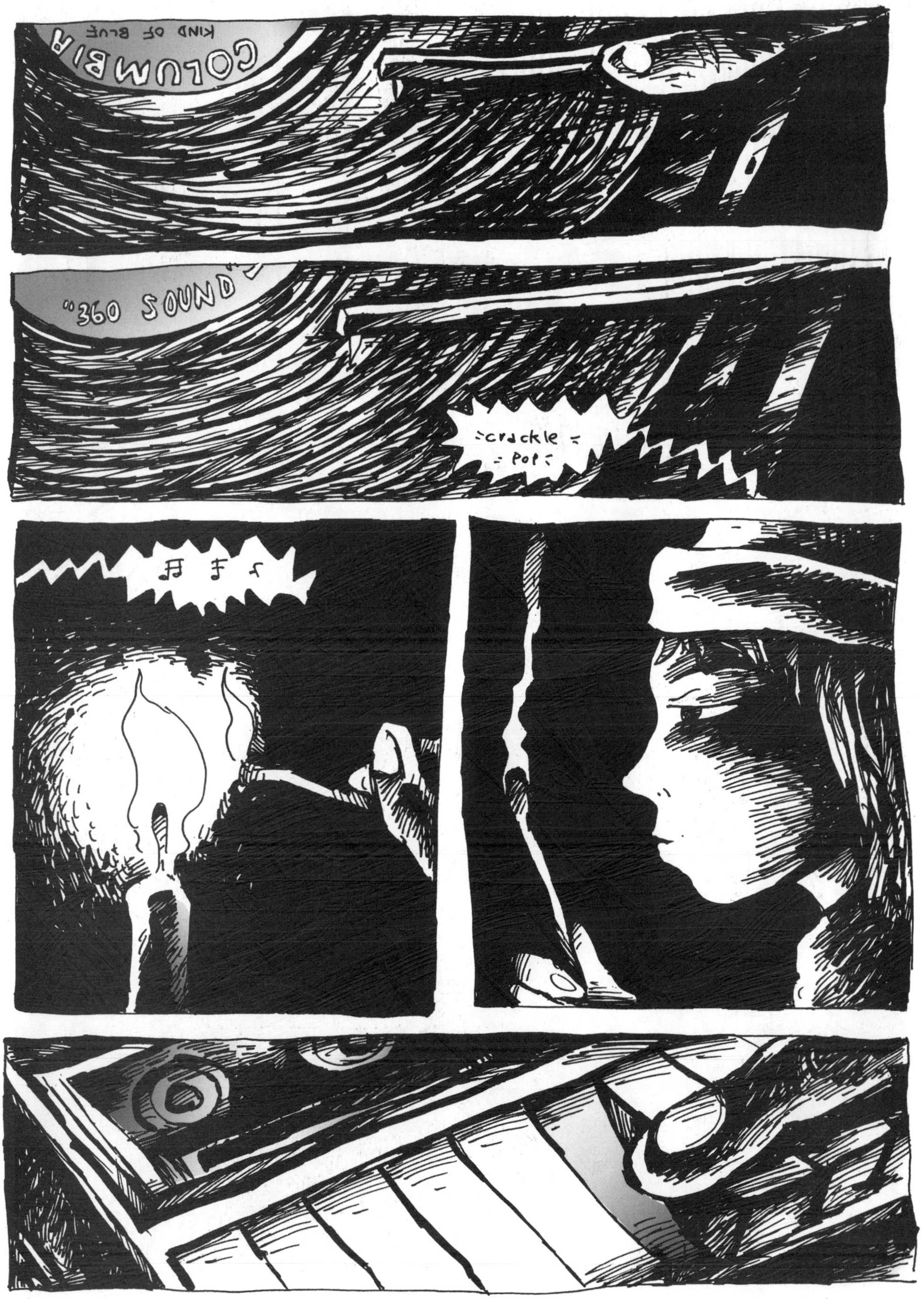
COLUMBIA
KIND OF BLUE
"360 SOUND"
crackle
pop

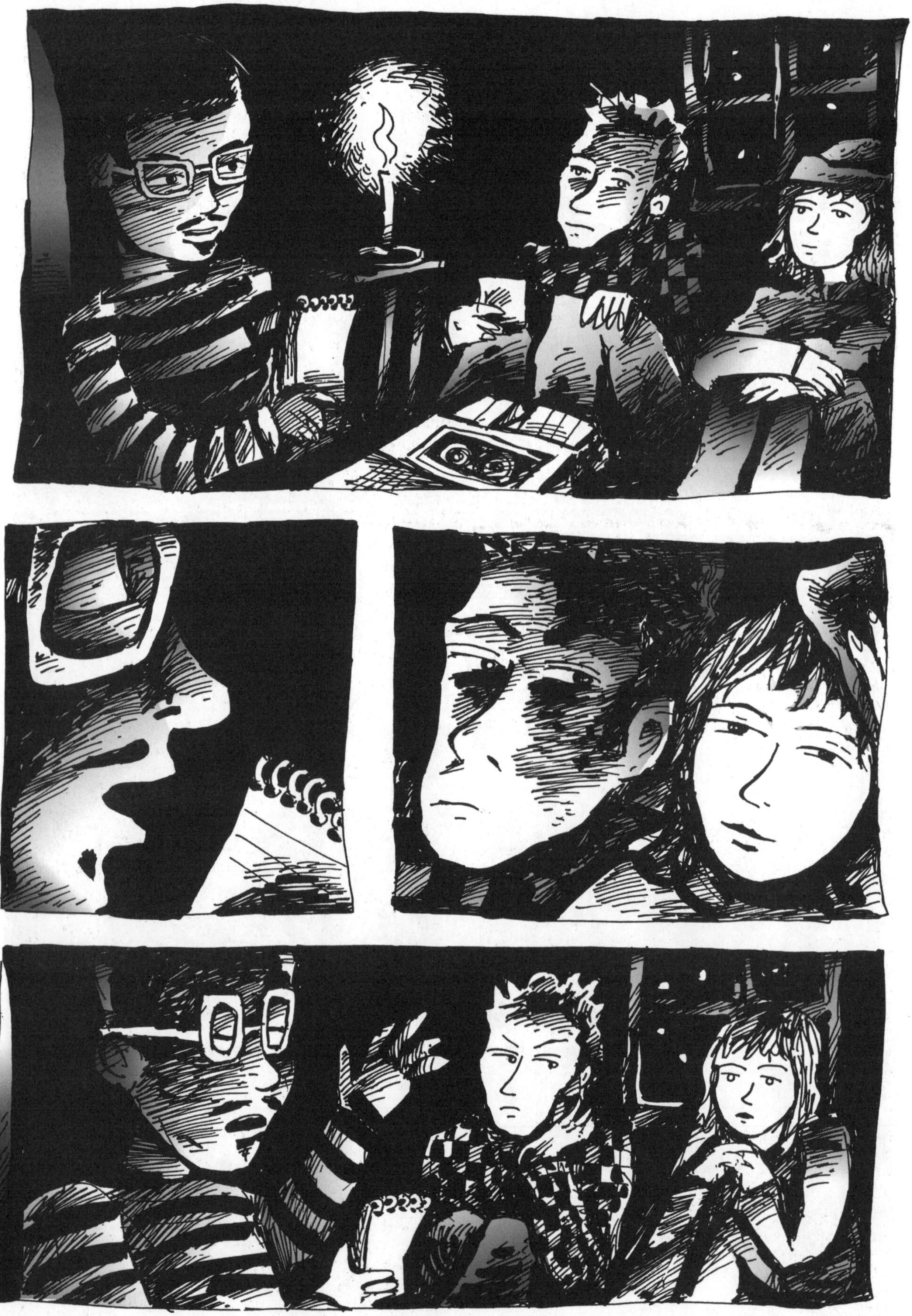

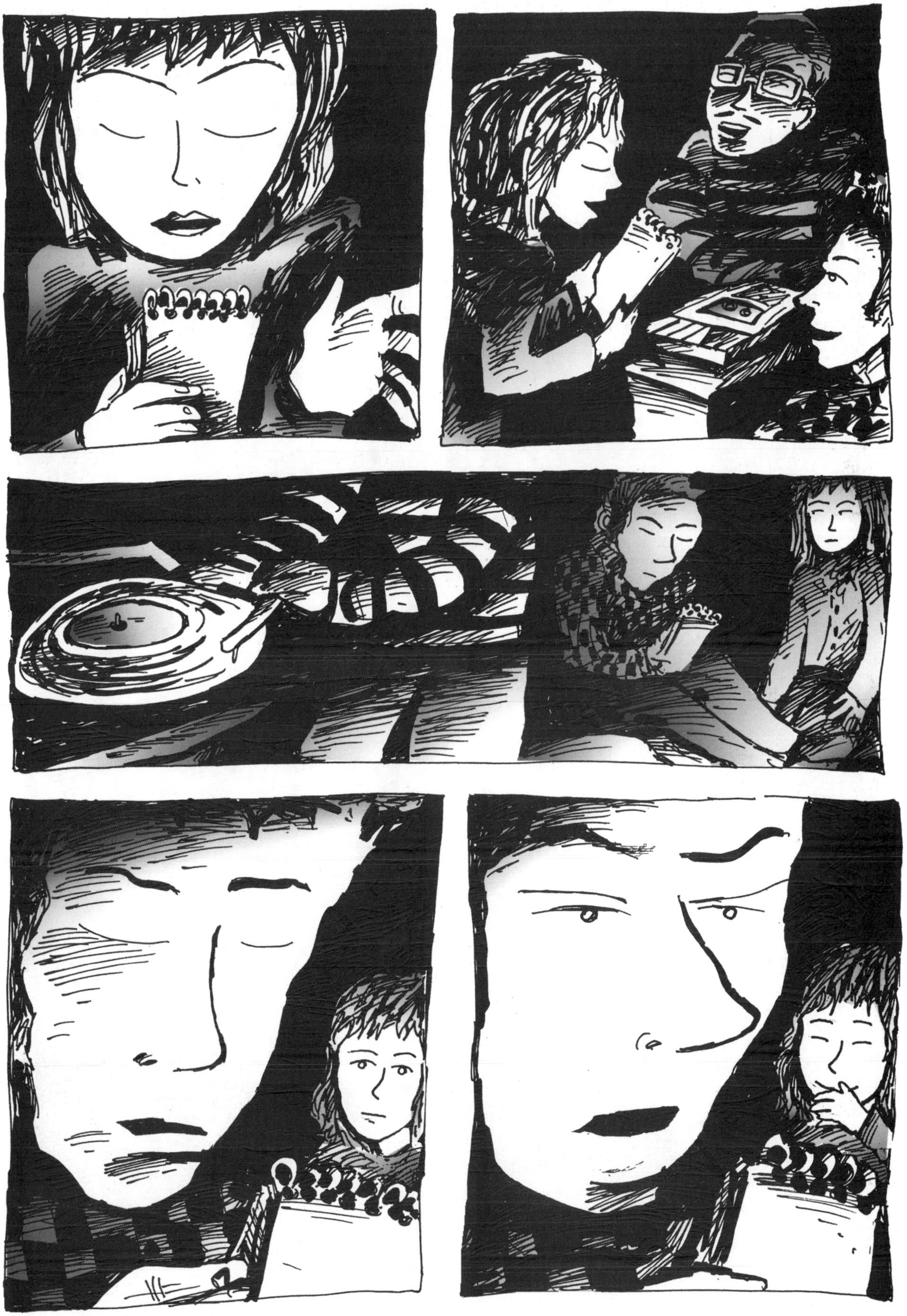

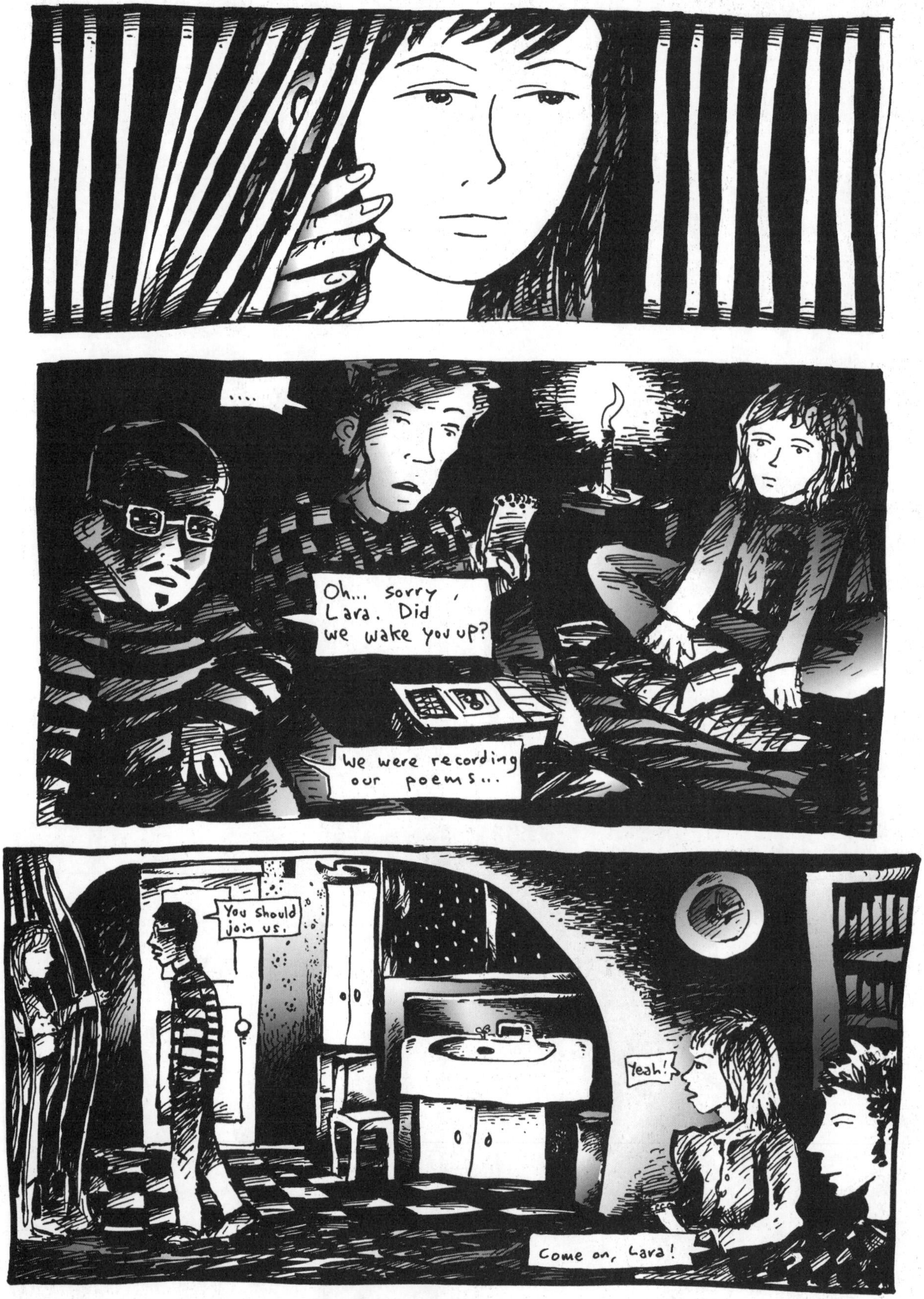
....
Oh... sorry, Lara. Did we wake you up?
We were recording our poems...
You should join us.
Yeah!
Come on, Lara!

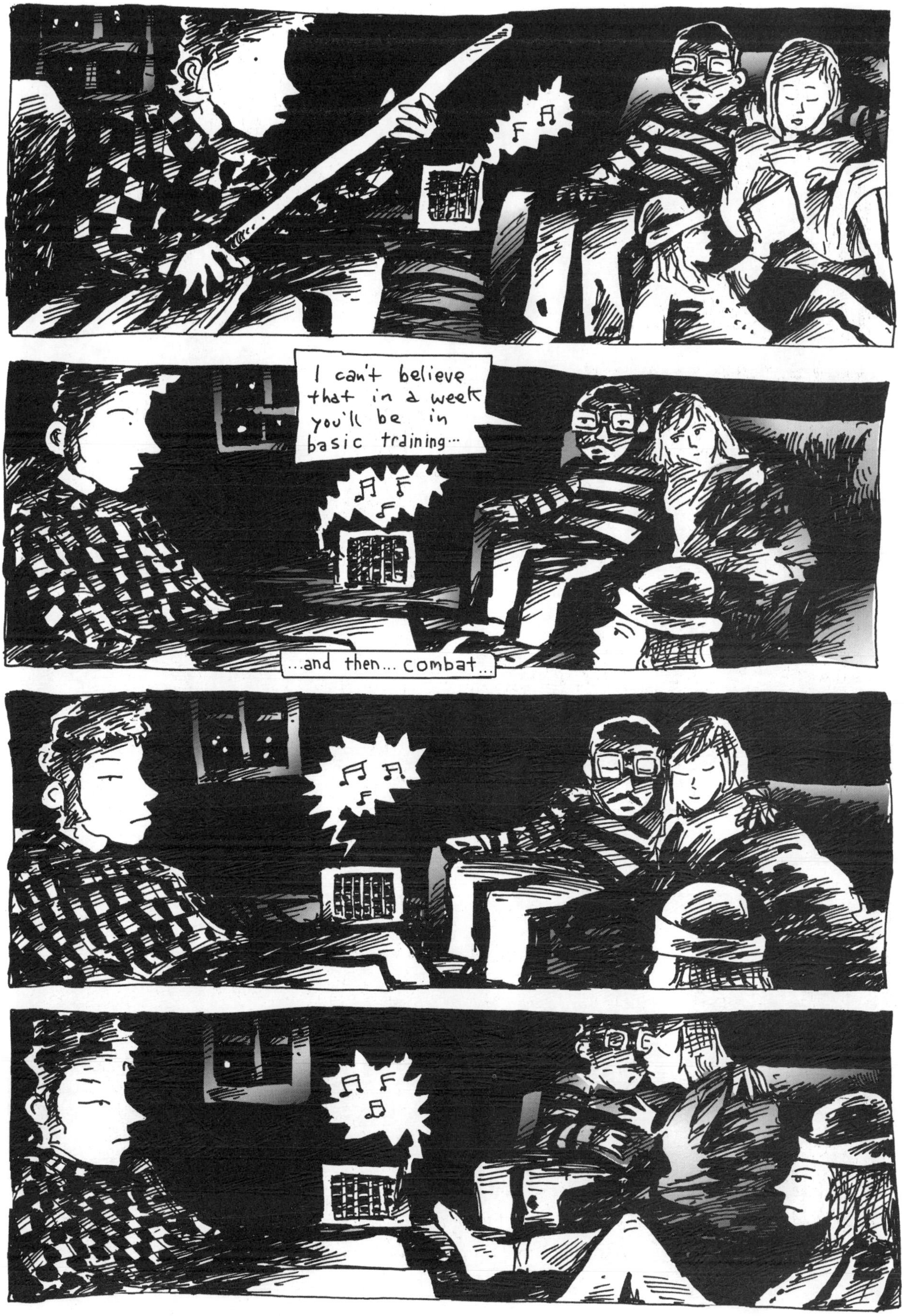
I can't believe that in a week you'll be in basic training...
...and then... combat...

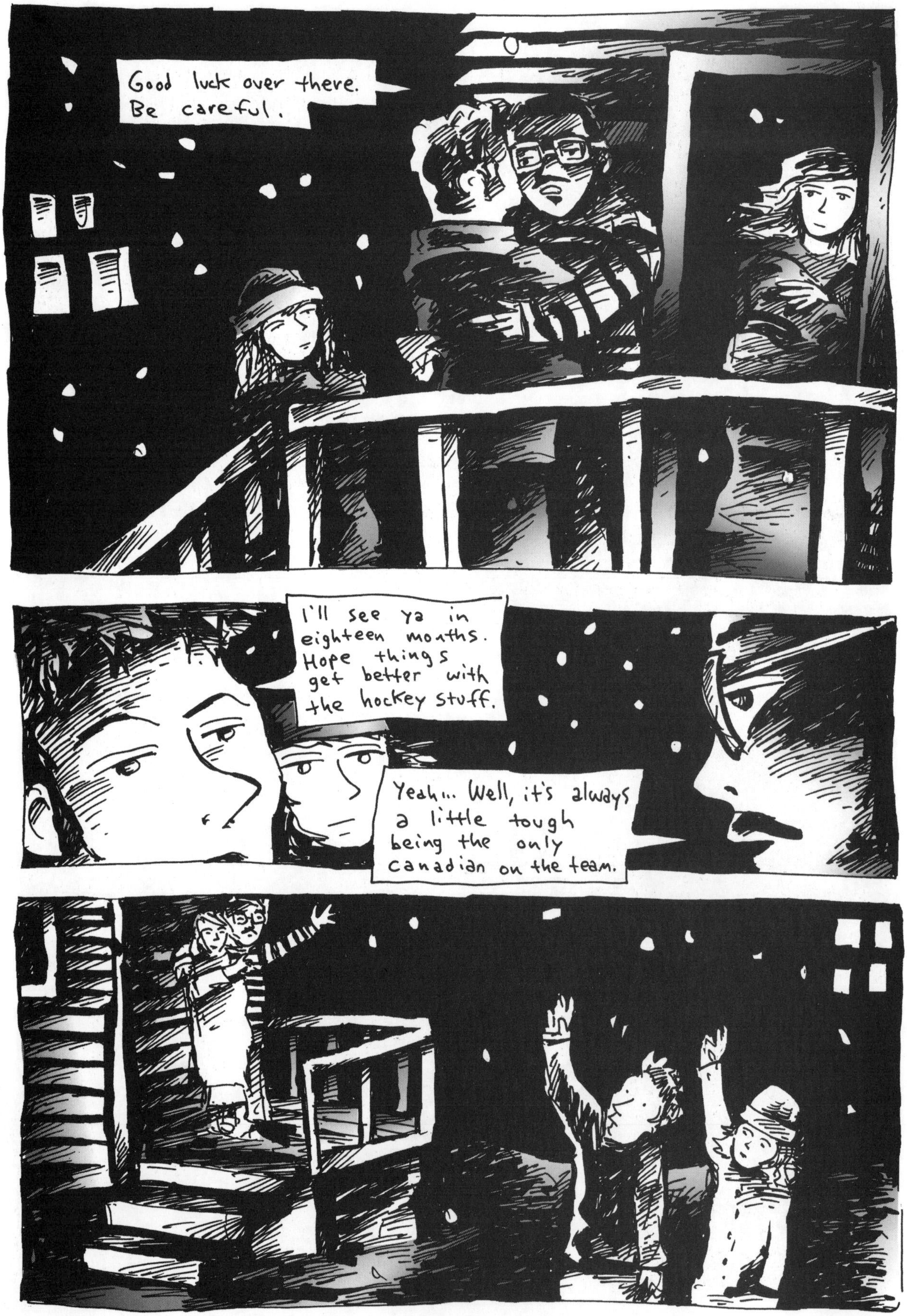
Good luck over there. Be careful.
I'll see ya in eighteen months. Hope things get better with the hockey stuff.
Yeah... Well, it's always a little tough being the only canadian on the team.

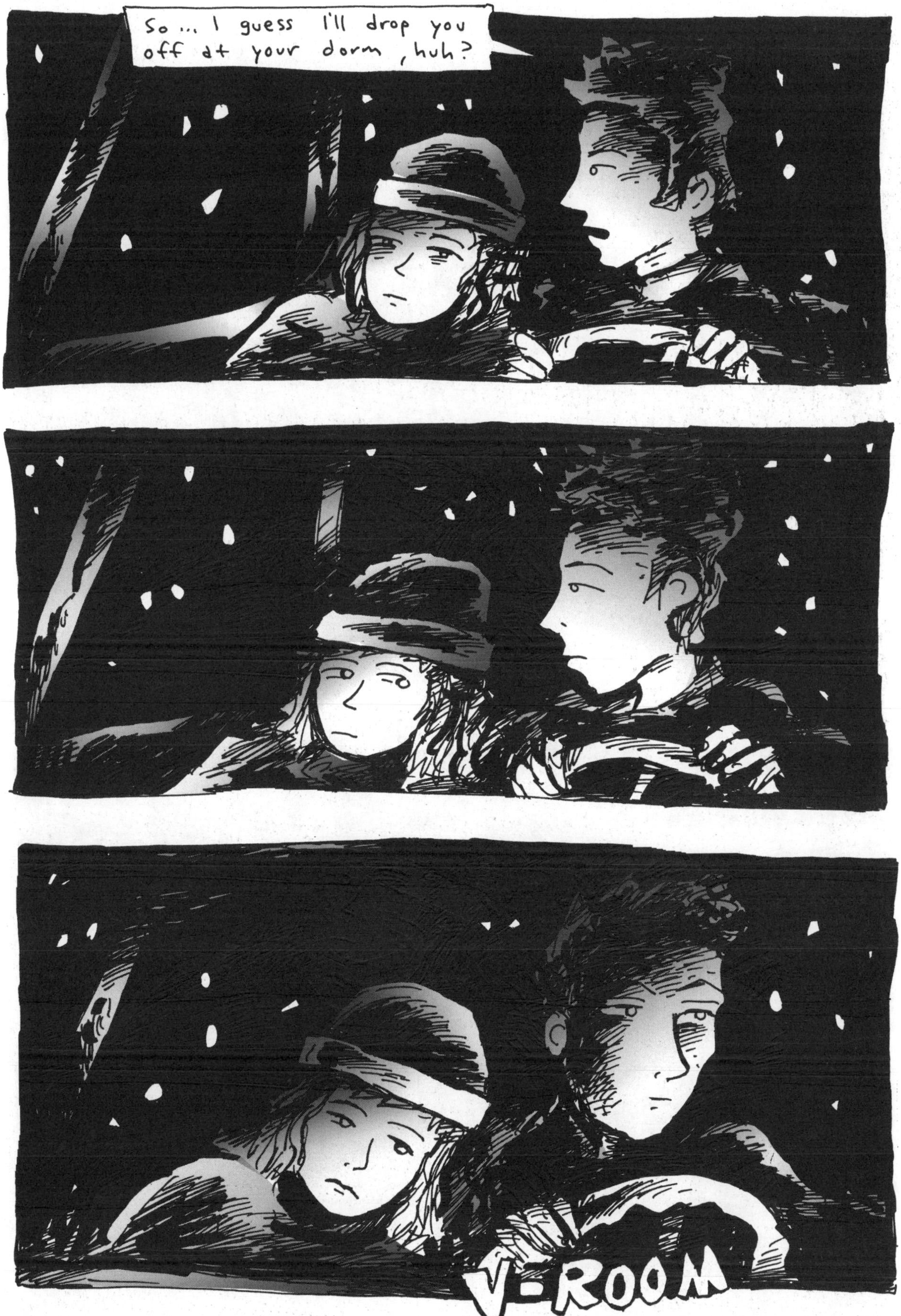
So... I guess I'll drop you off at your dorm, huh?
V-ROOM

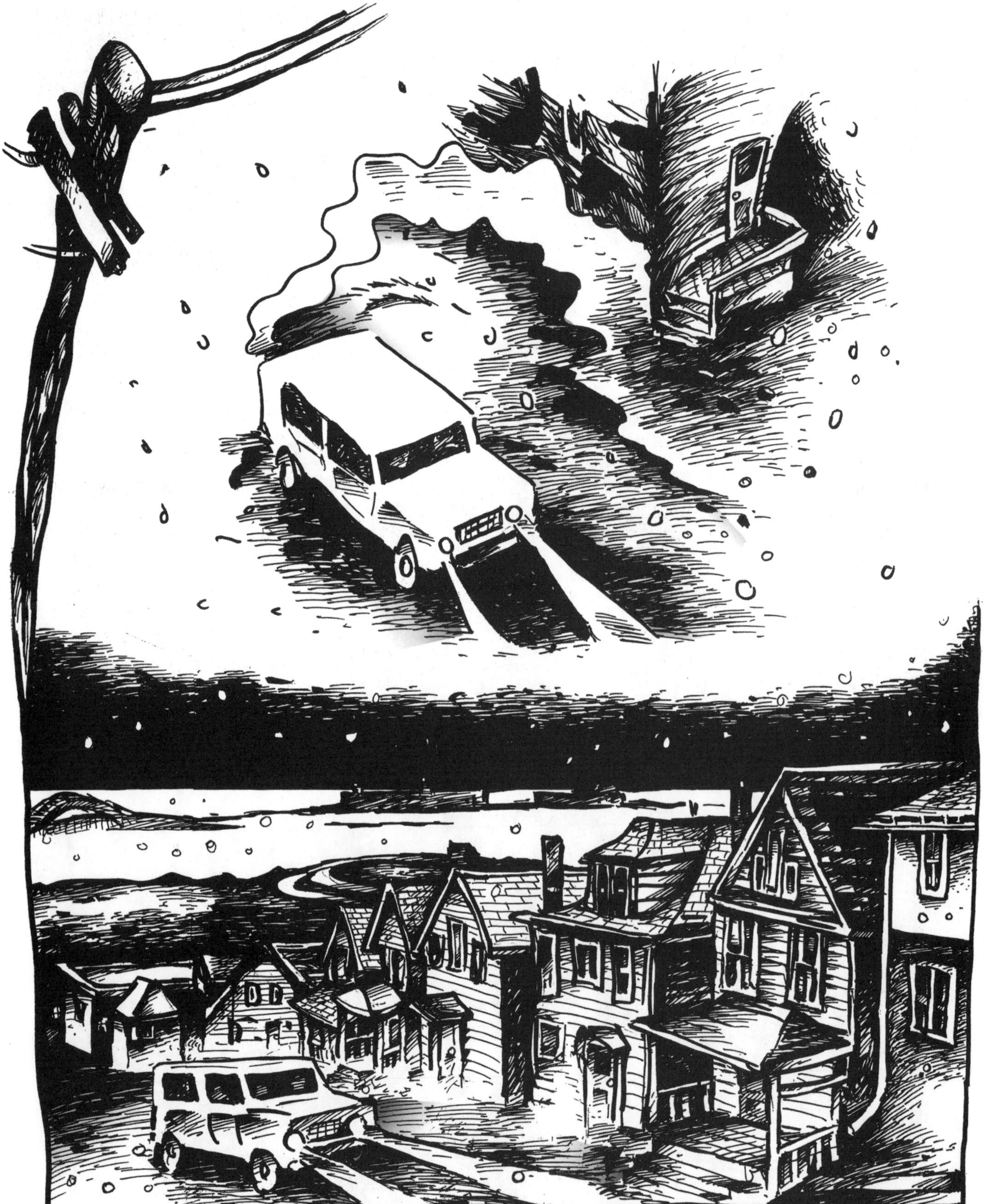

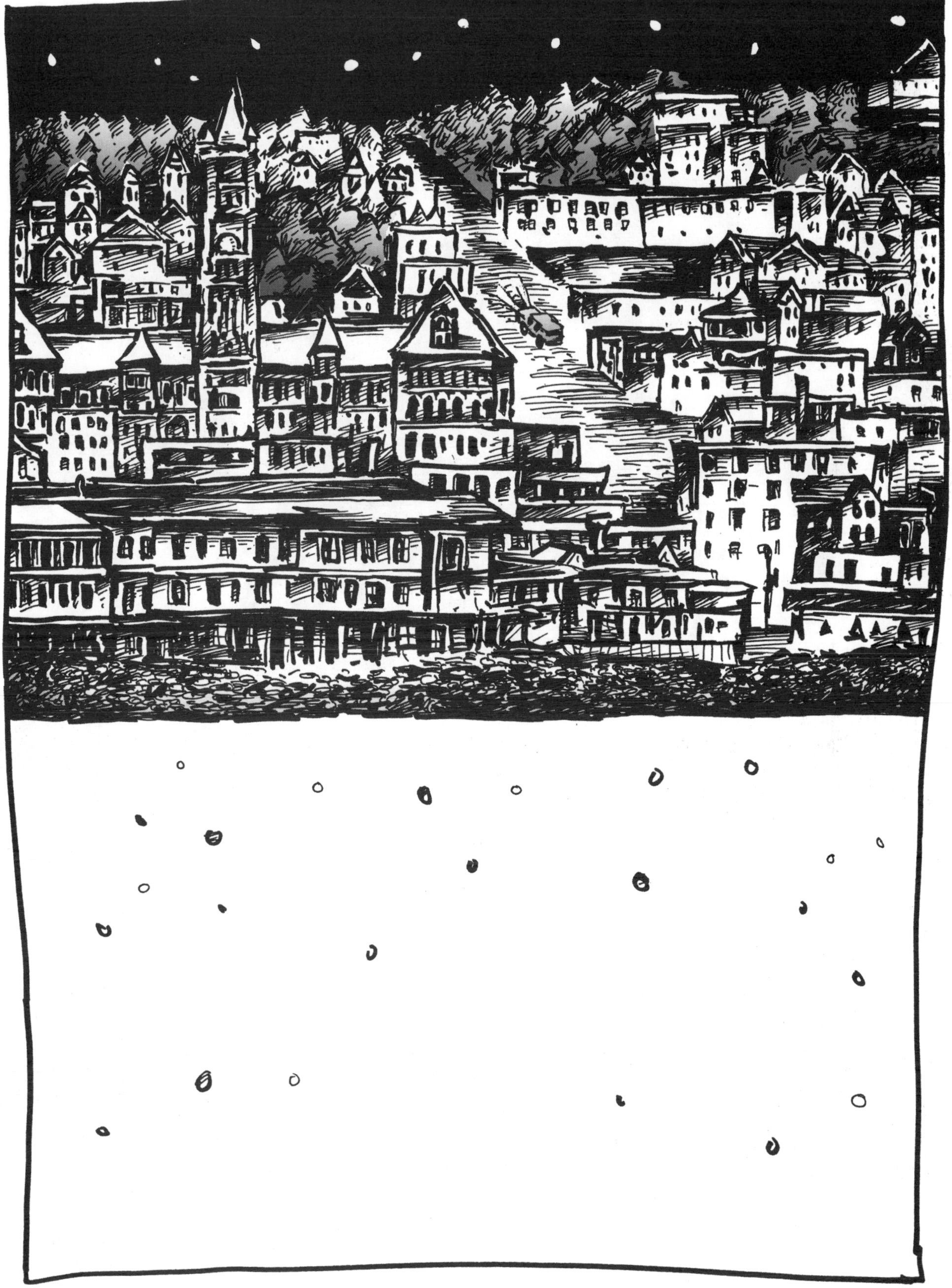

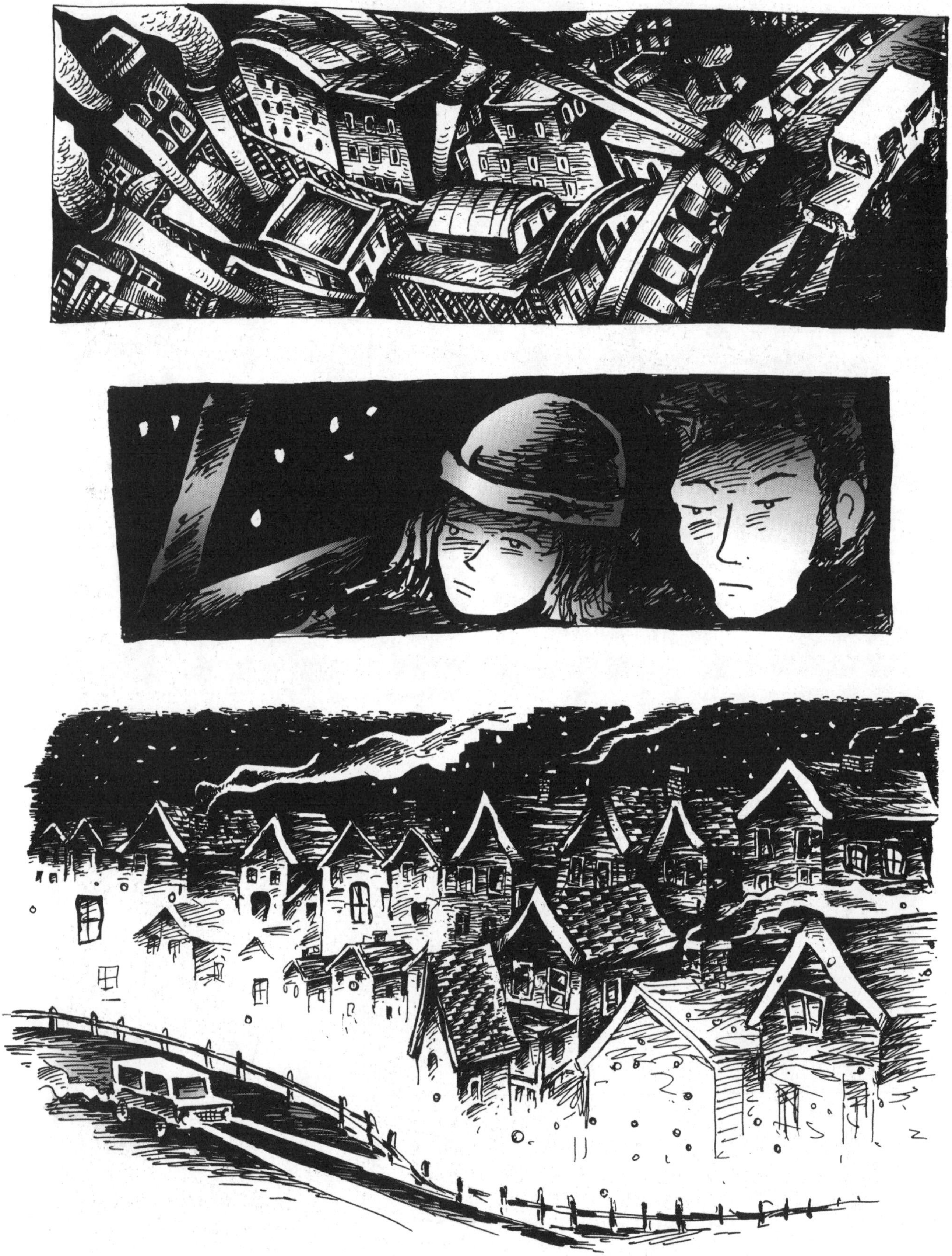

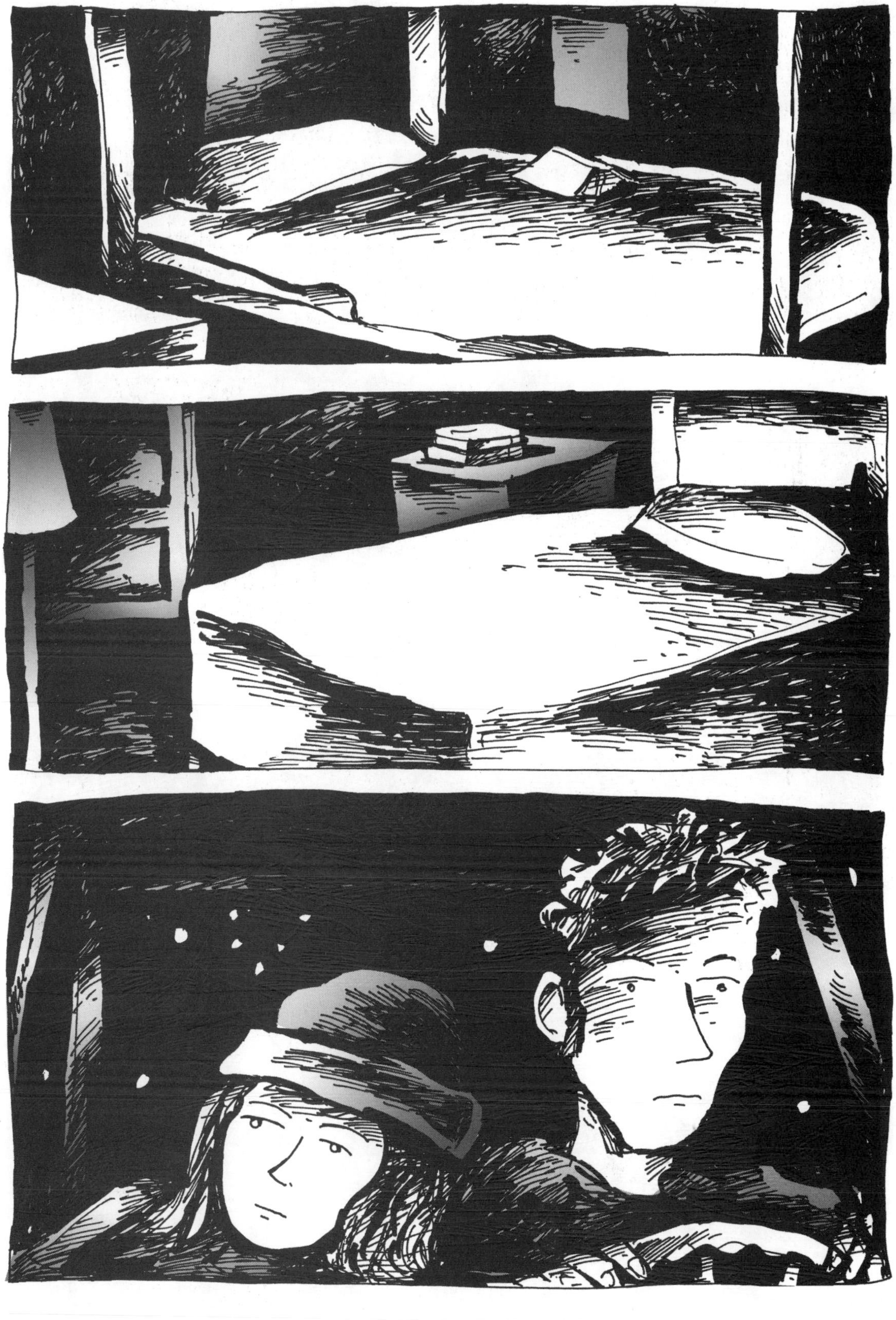

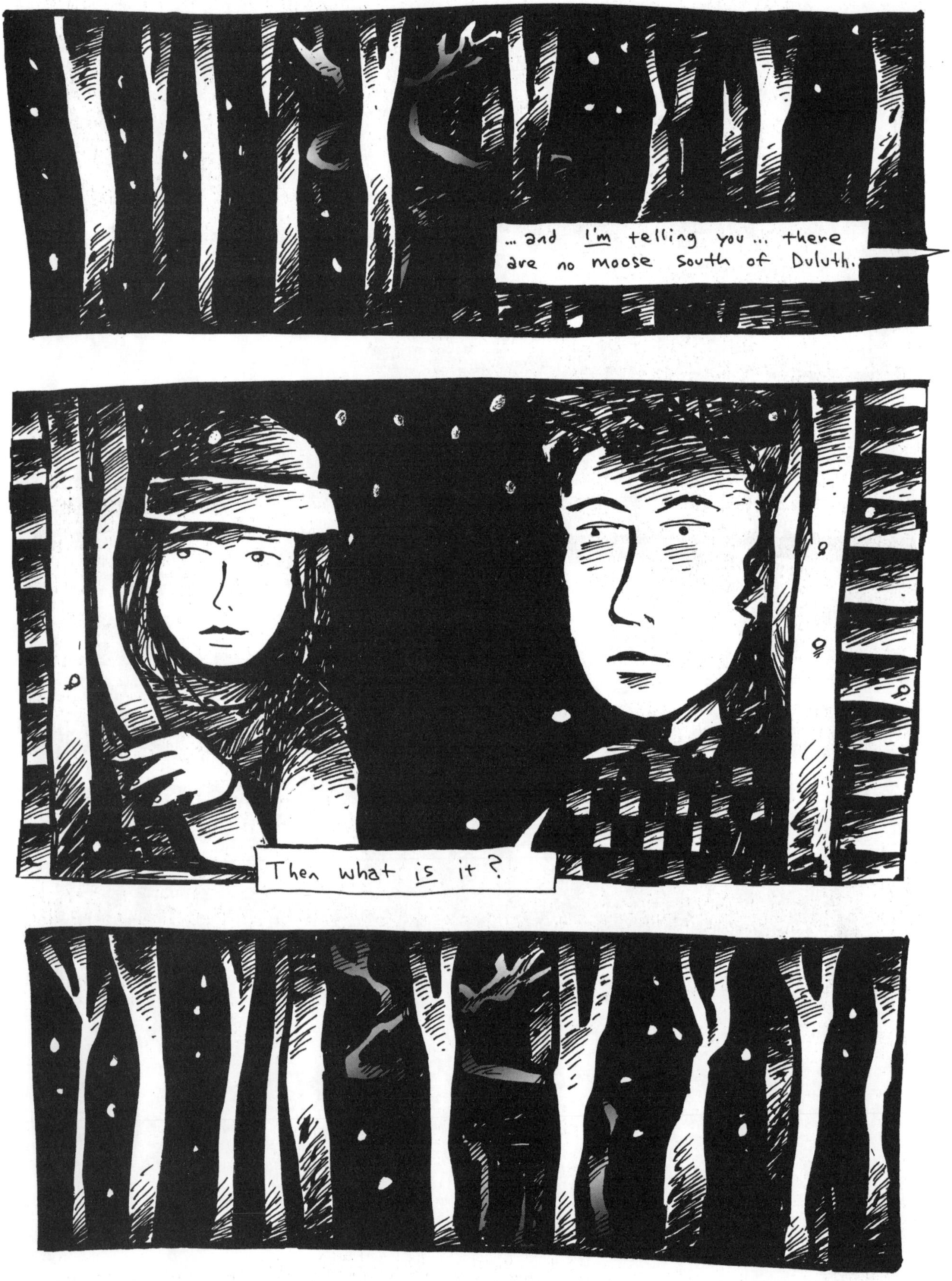
... and I'm telling you ... there are no moose south of Duluth.
Then what is it?

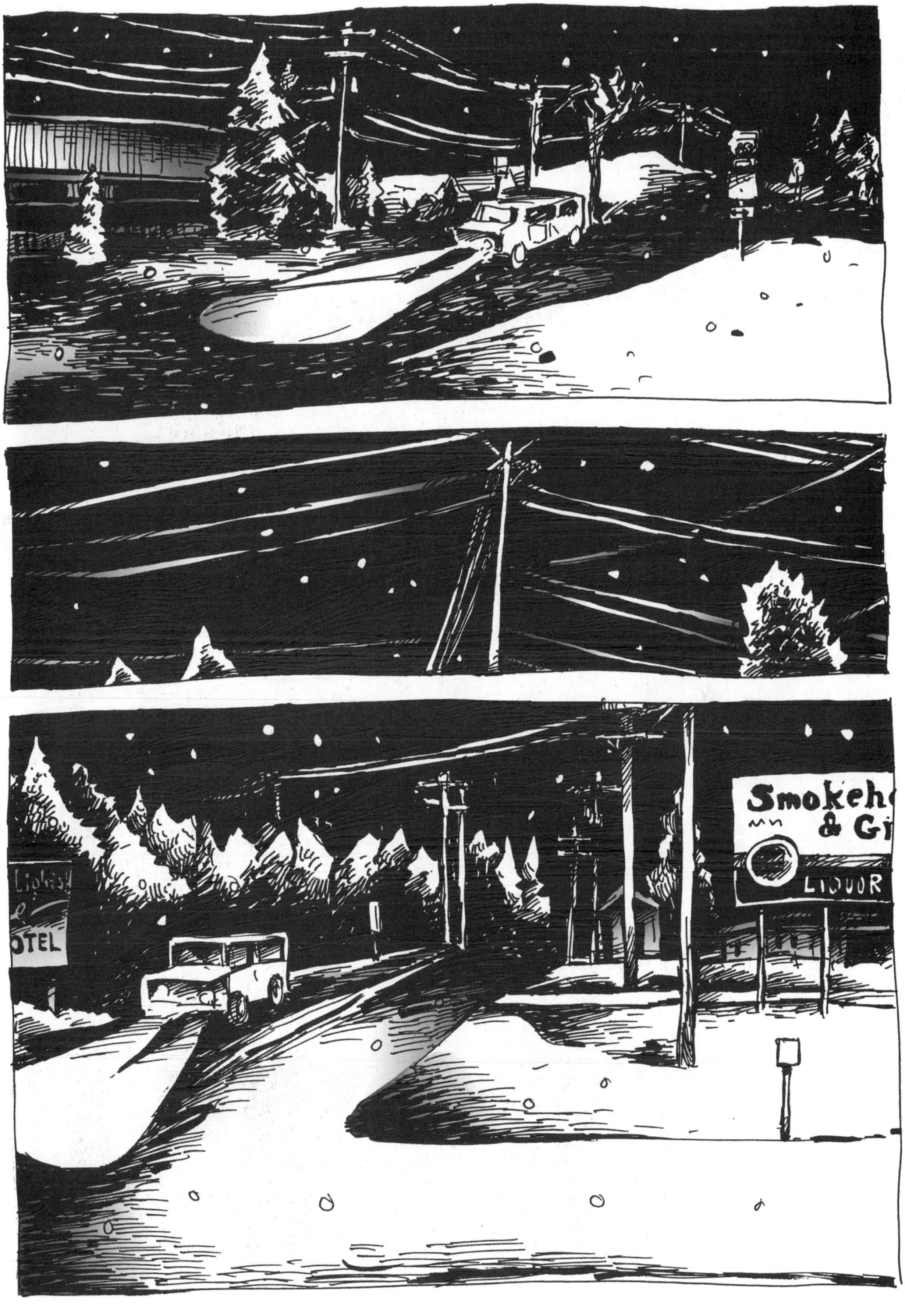
Smokeh
& G
LIQUOR
OTEL

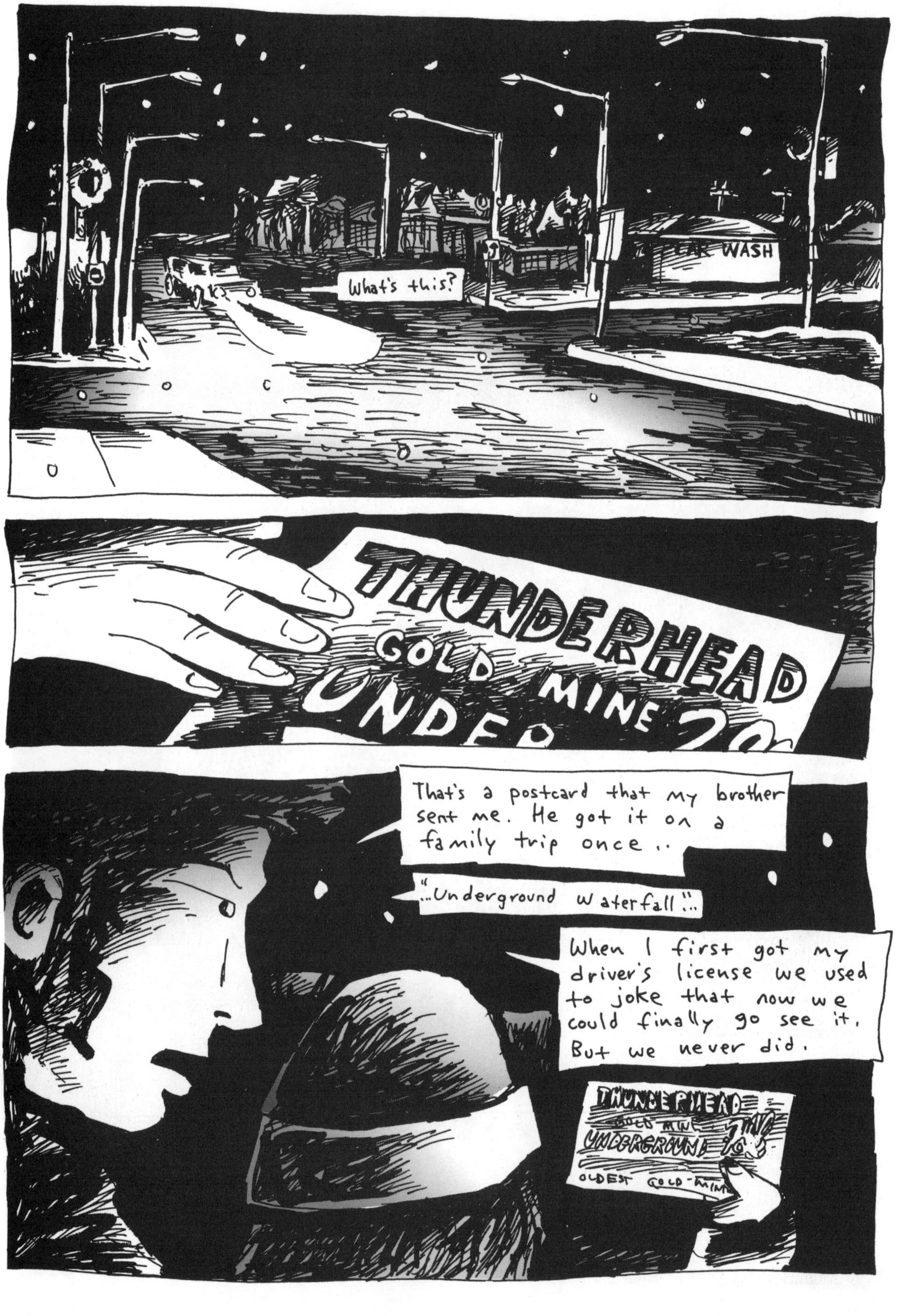
CAR WASH
What's this?
THUNDERHEAD
GOLD MINE
That's a postcard that my brother sent me. He got it on a family trip once..
"...Underground waterfall"...
When I first got my driver's license we used to joke that now we could finally go see it. But we never did.

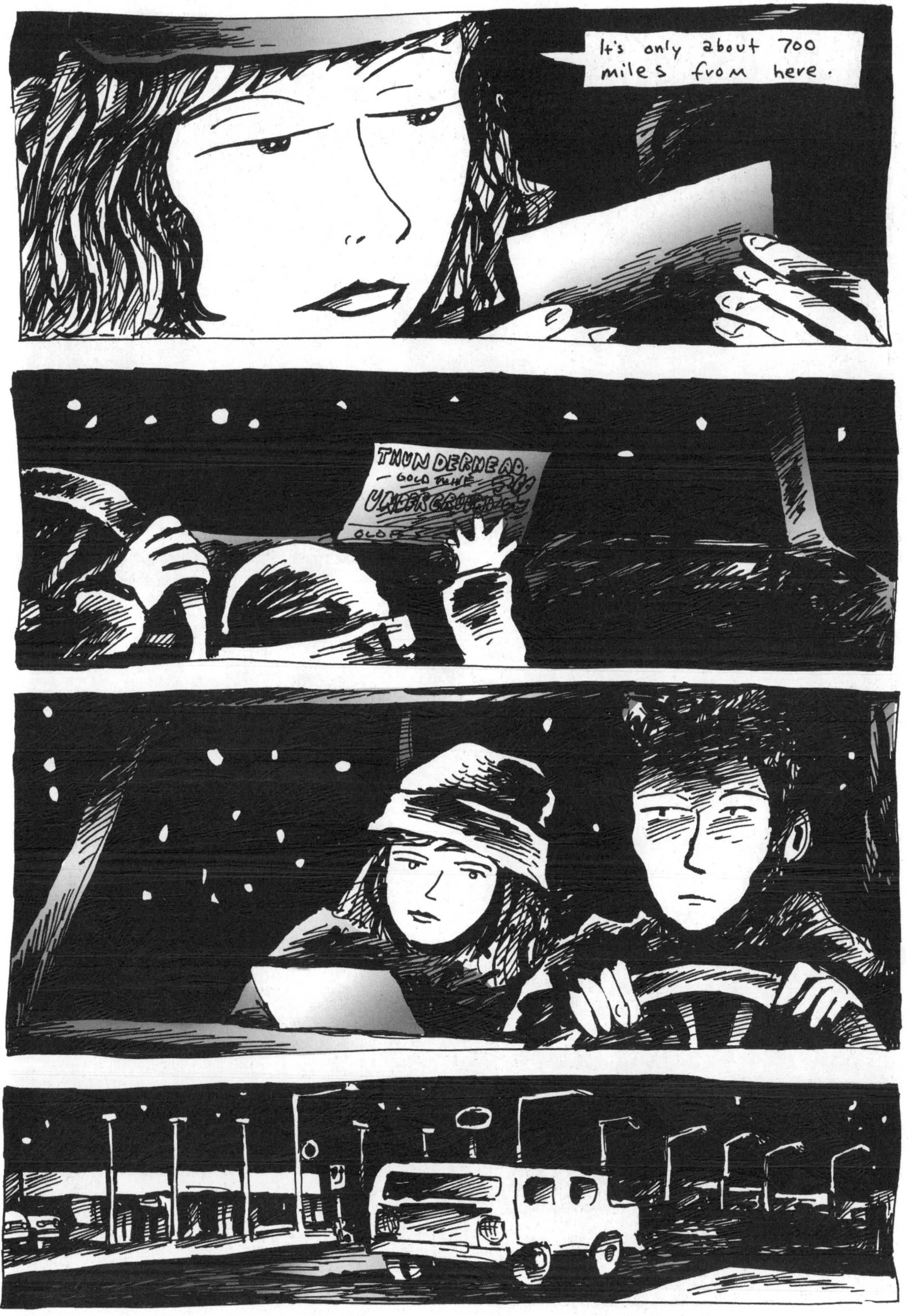
It's only about 700 miles from here.
THUNDERHEAD

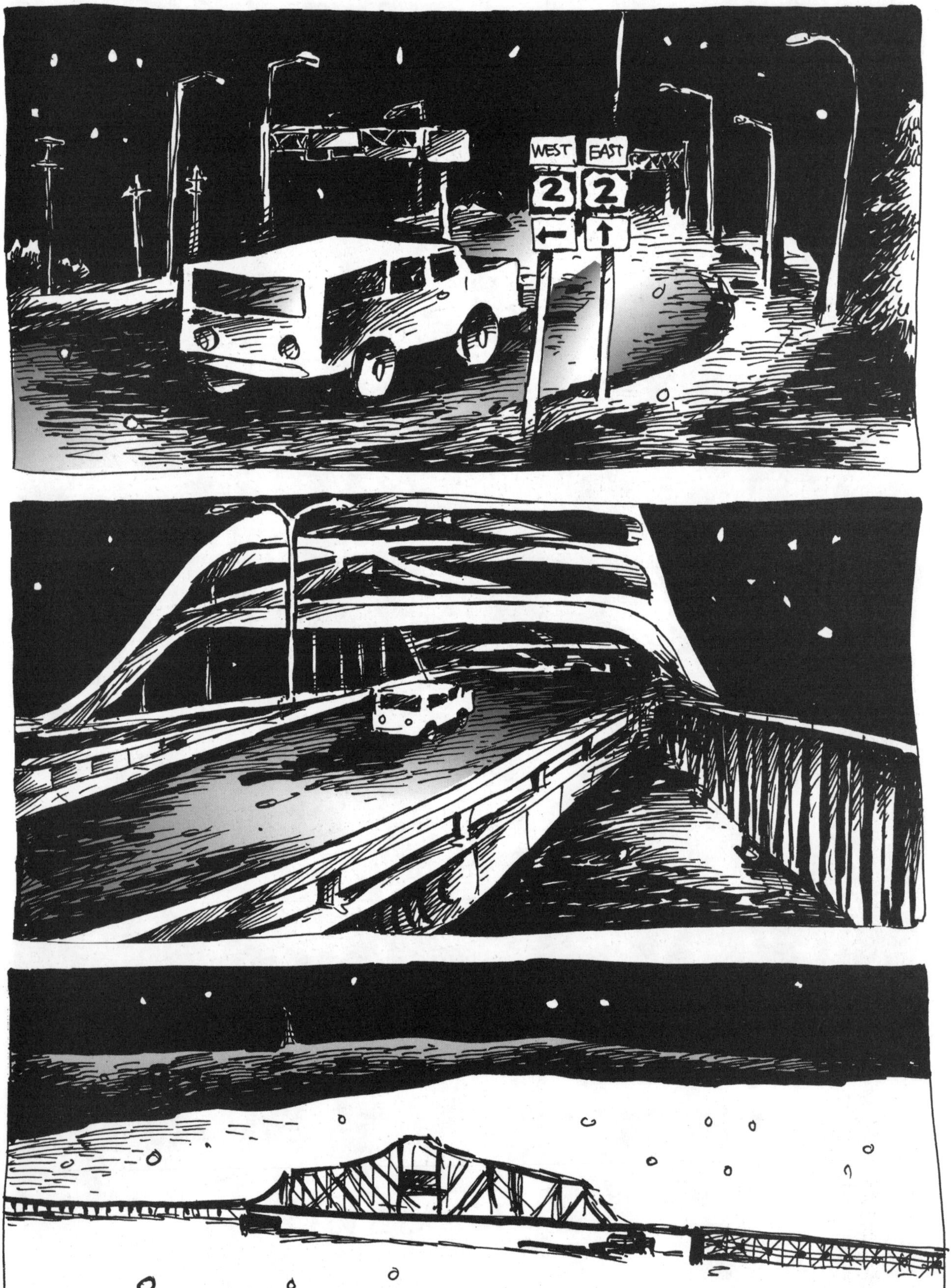
WEST
2
EAST
2

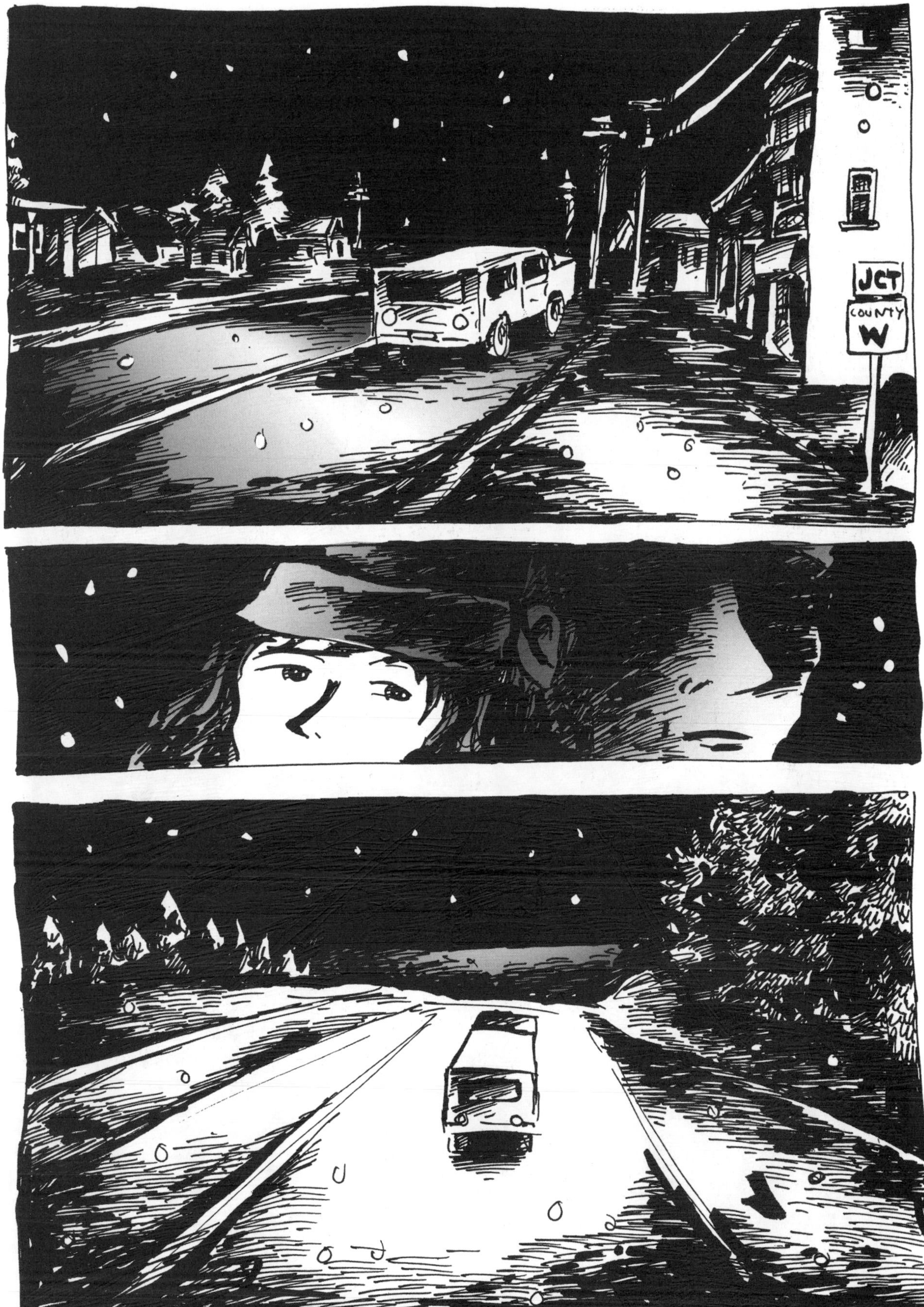
JCT
COUNTY
W

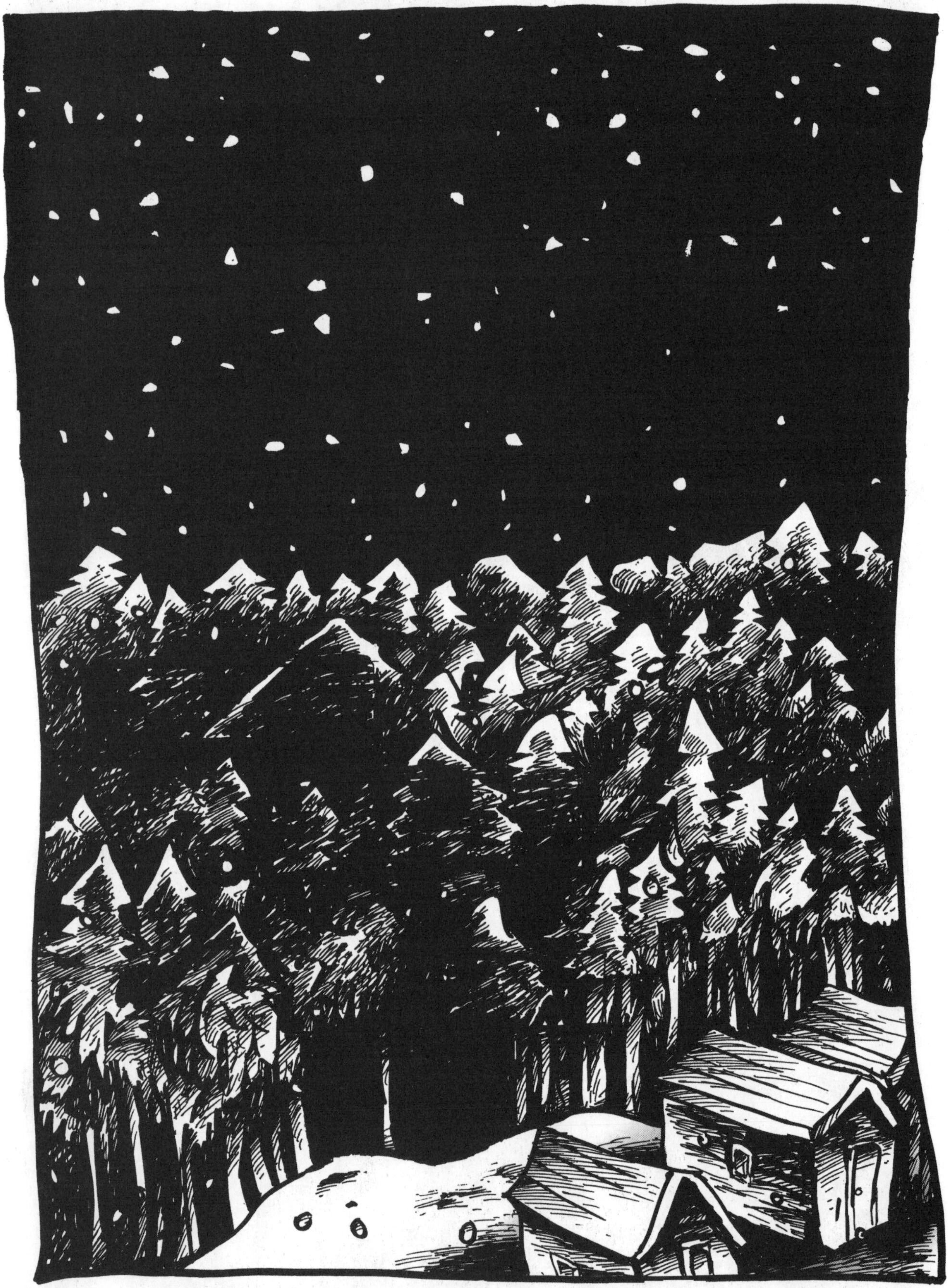

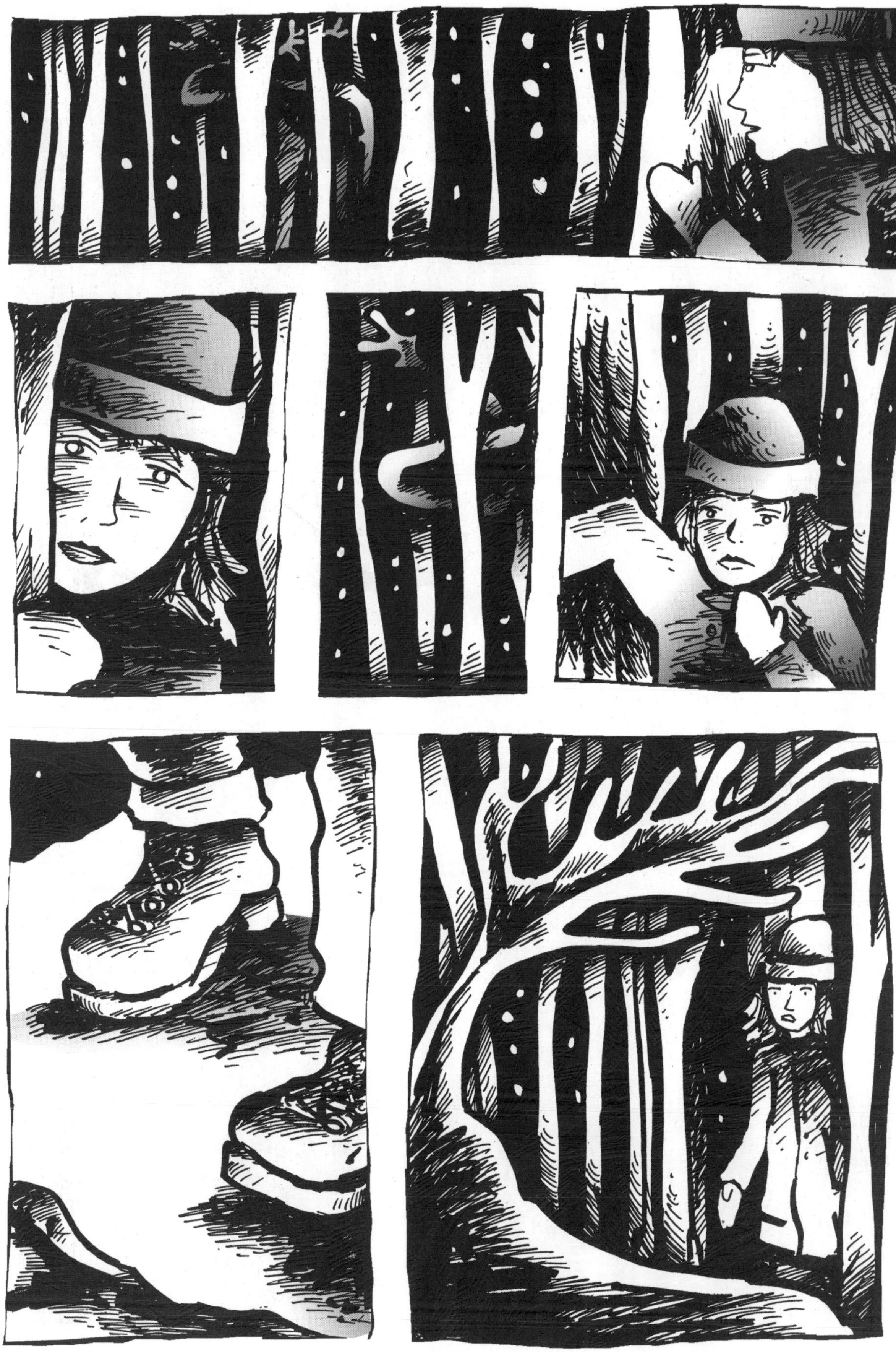

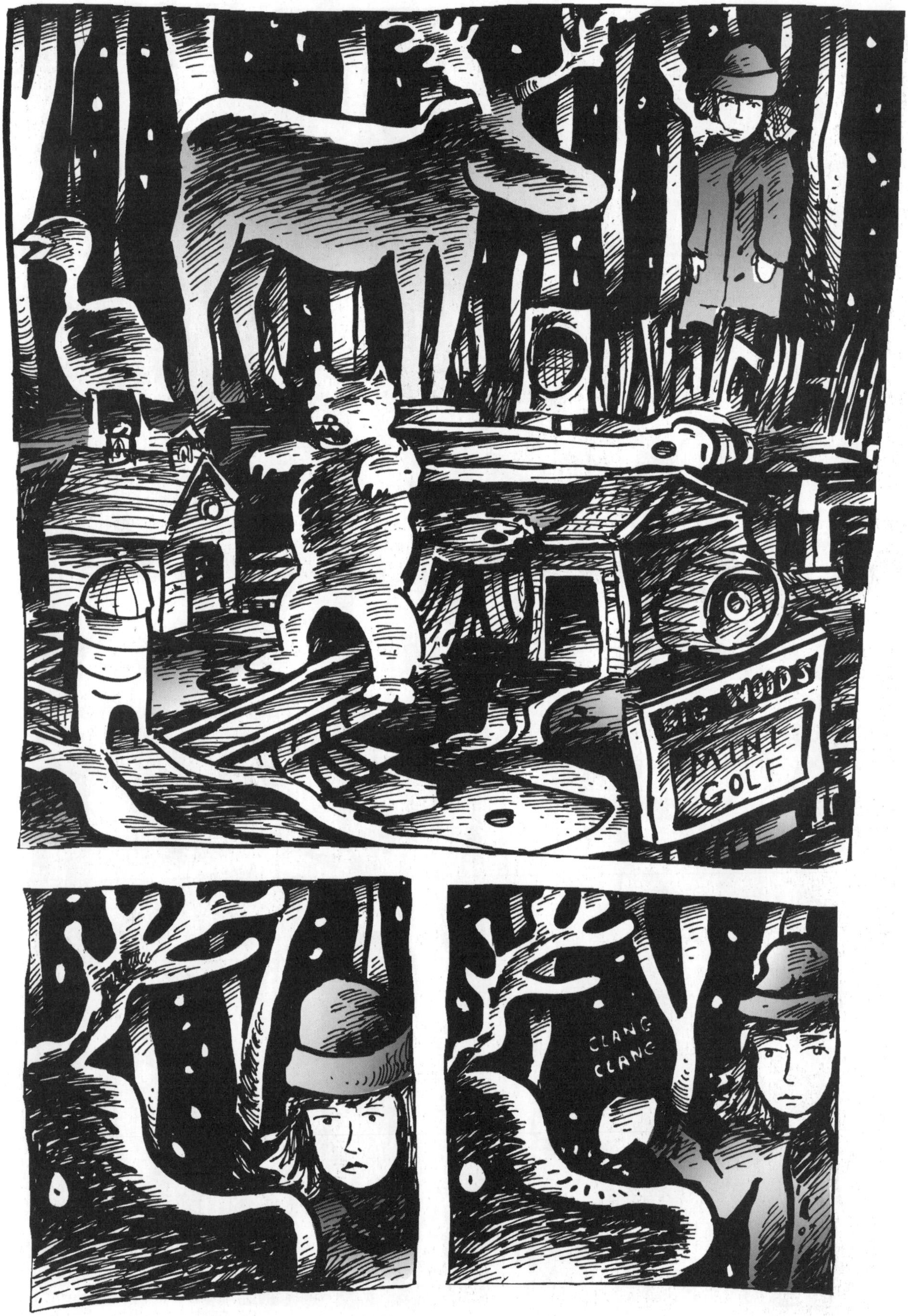
BIG WOODS
MINI GOLF
CLANG
CLANG

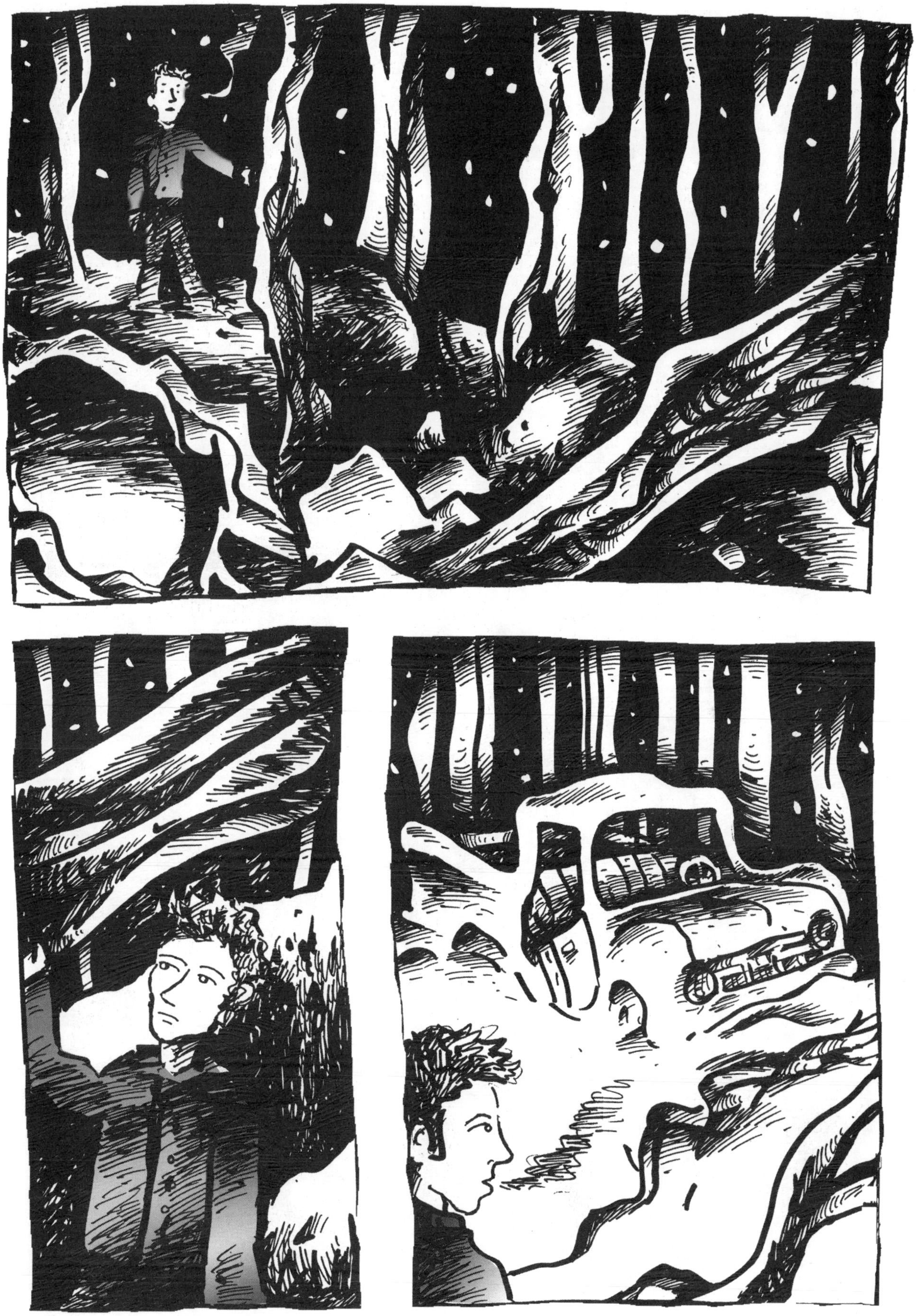

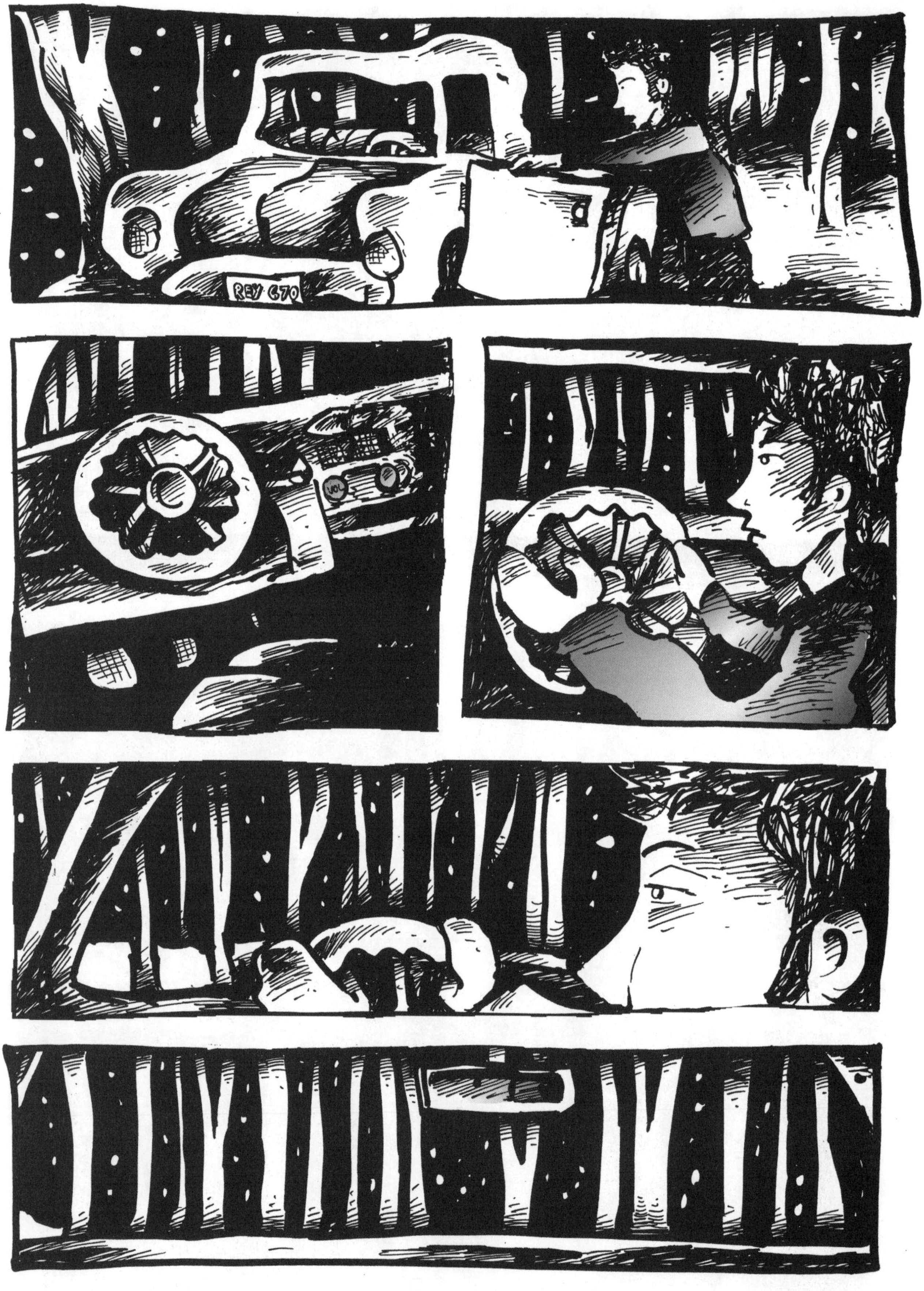
REY 670
VOL

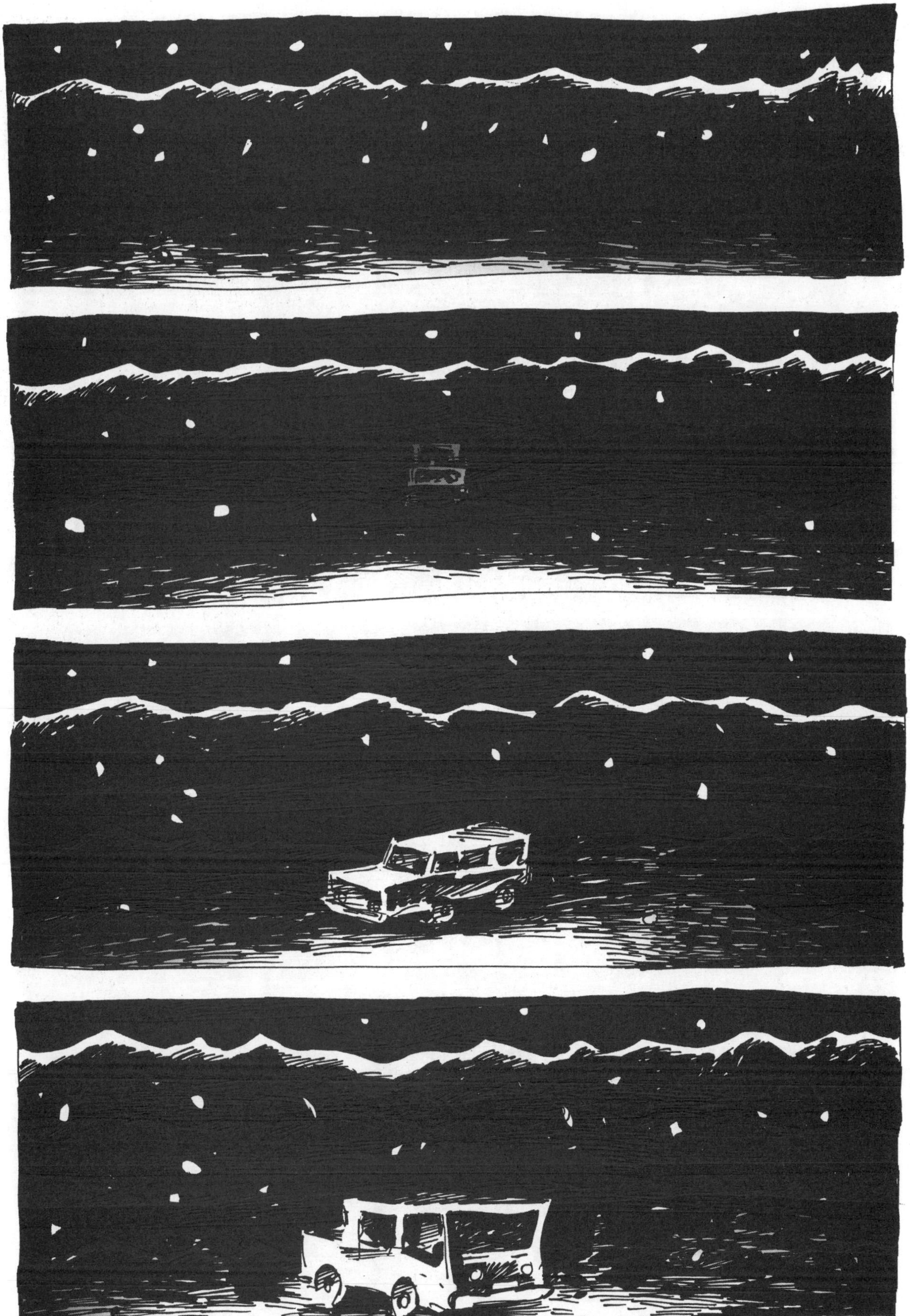

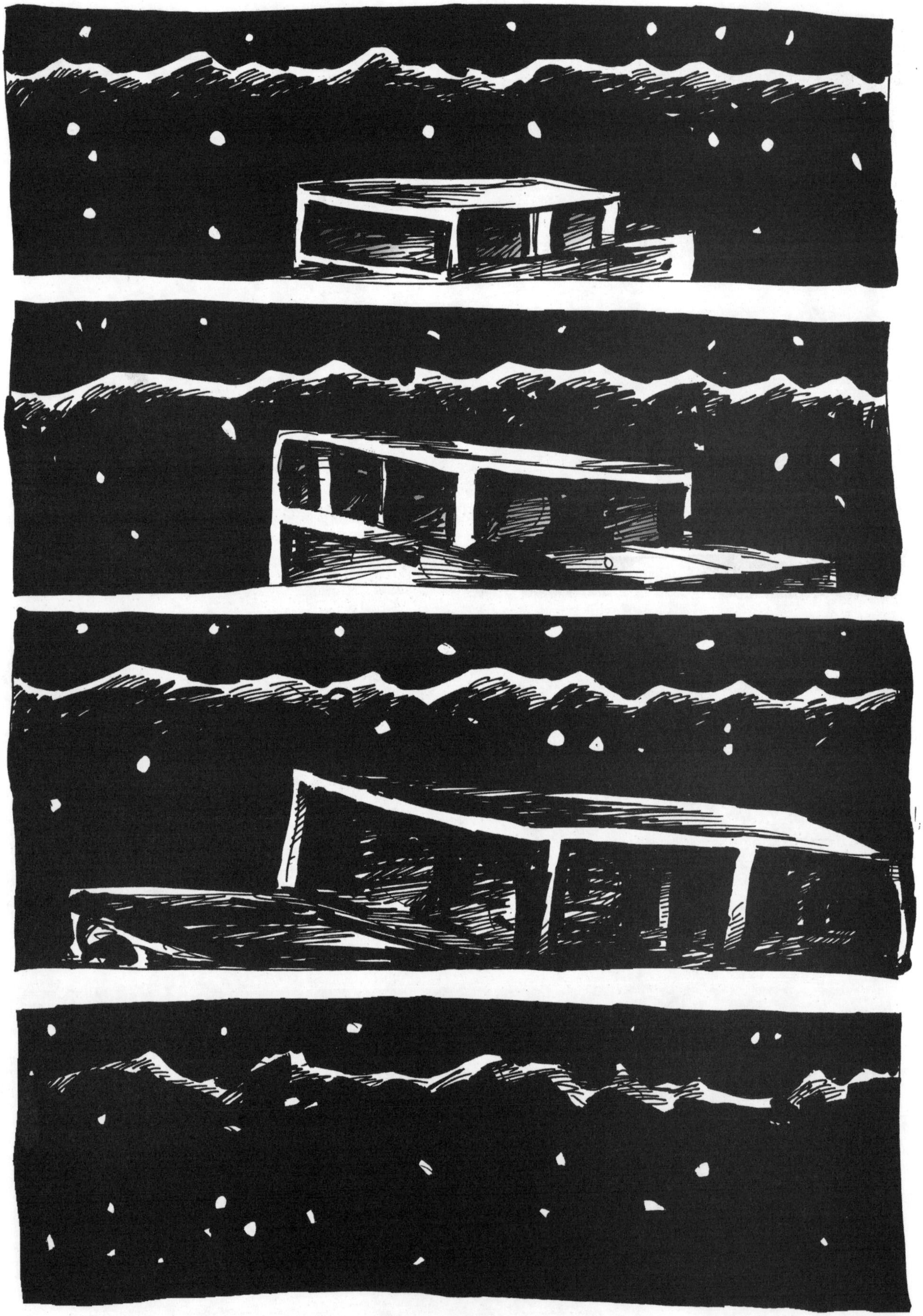

Screeee

RRRRRRR

RRRRR

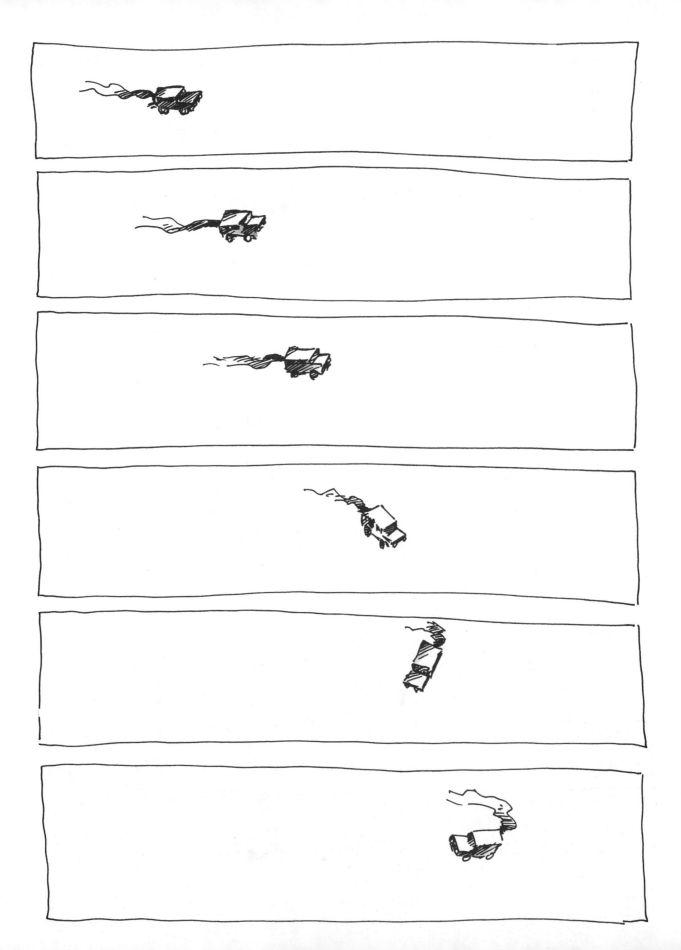

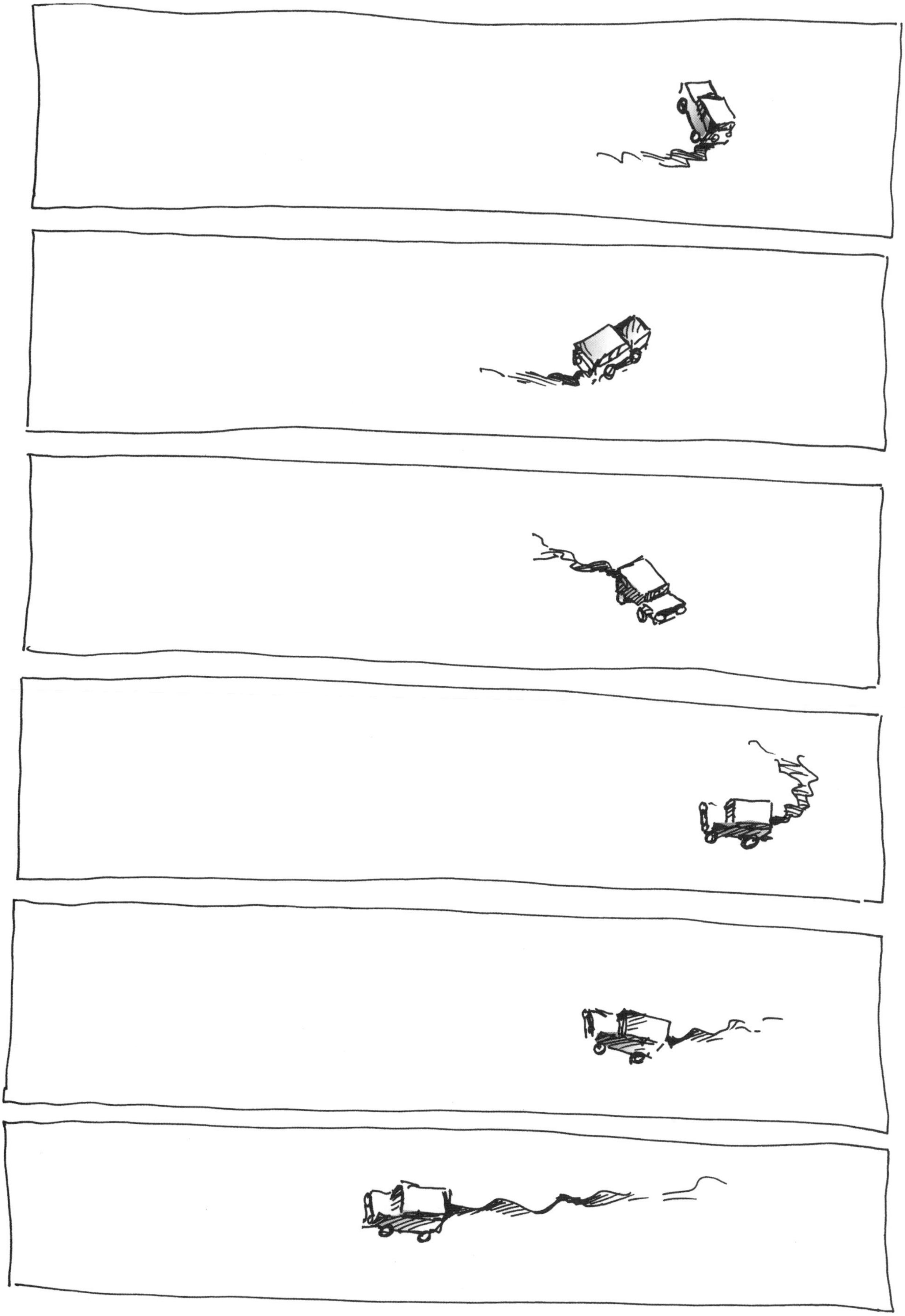

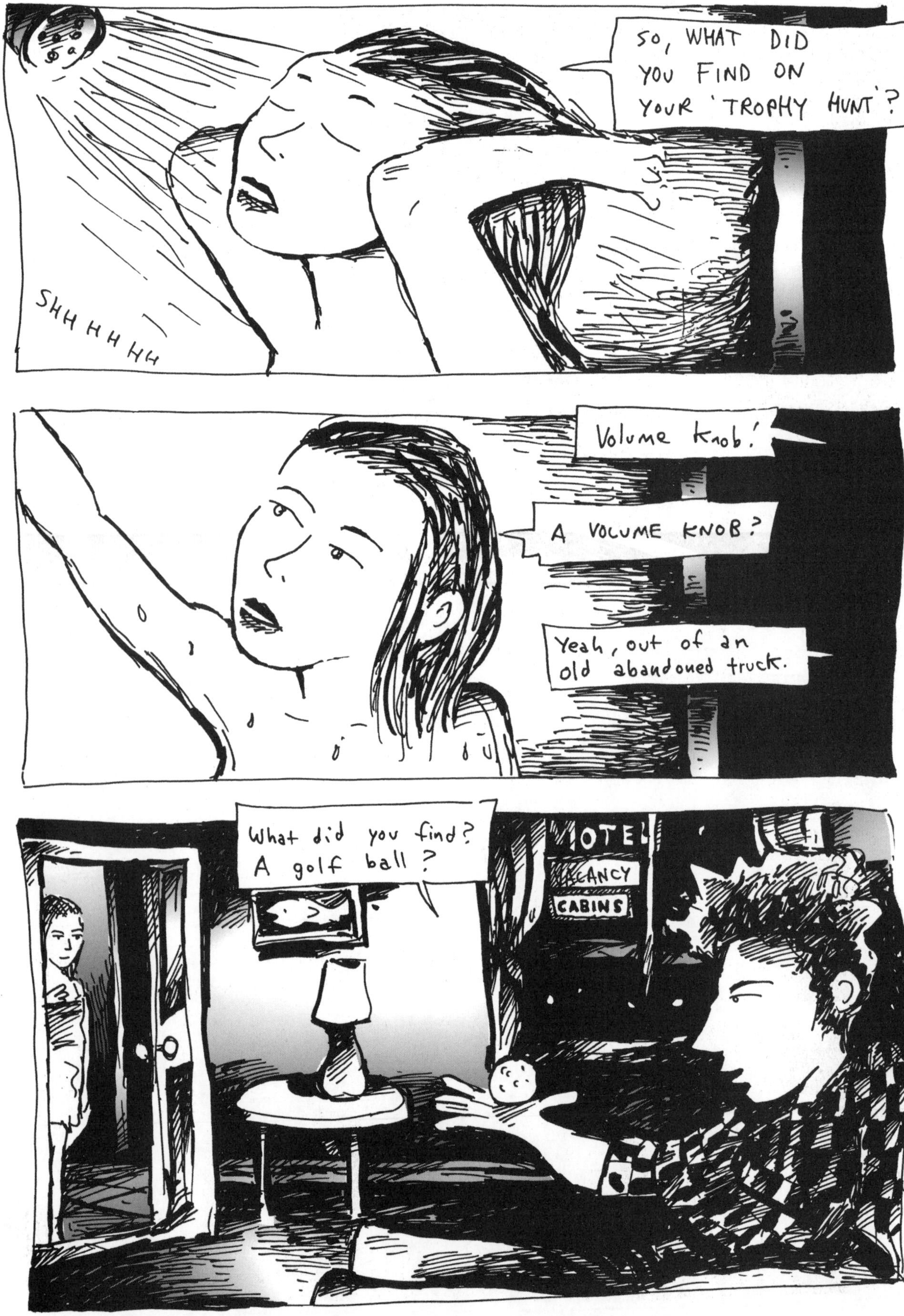

SO, WHAT DID YOU FIND ON YOUR 'TROPHY HUNT'?
SHHHHHH
Volume knob!
A VOLUME KNOB?
Yeah, out of an old abandoned truck.
What did you find? A golf ball?
MOTEL
VACANCY
CABINS

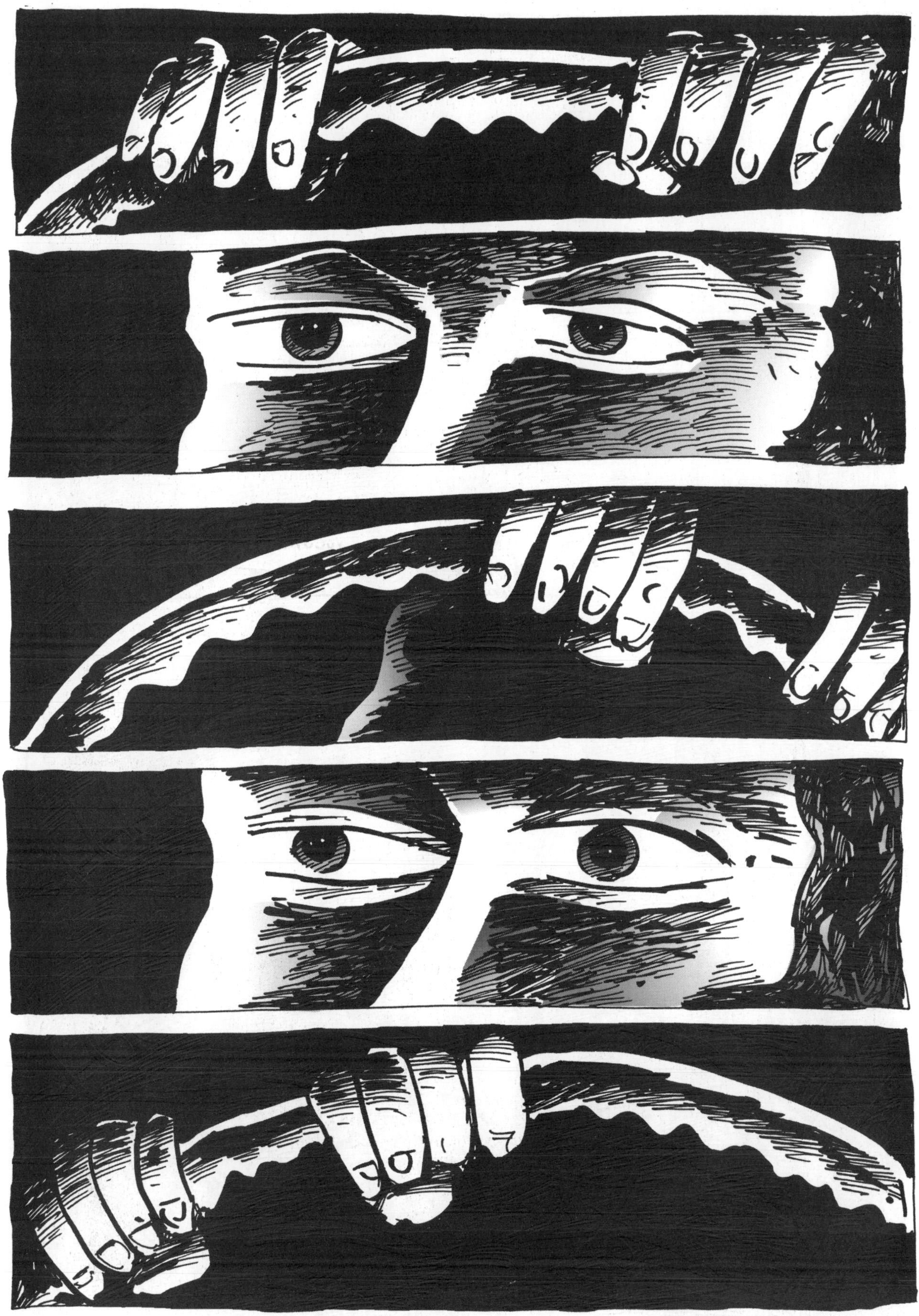

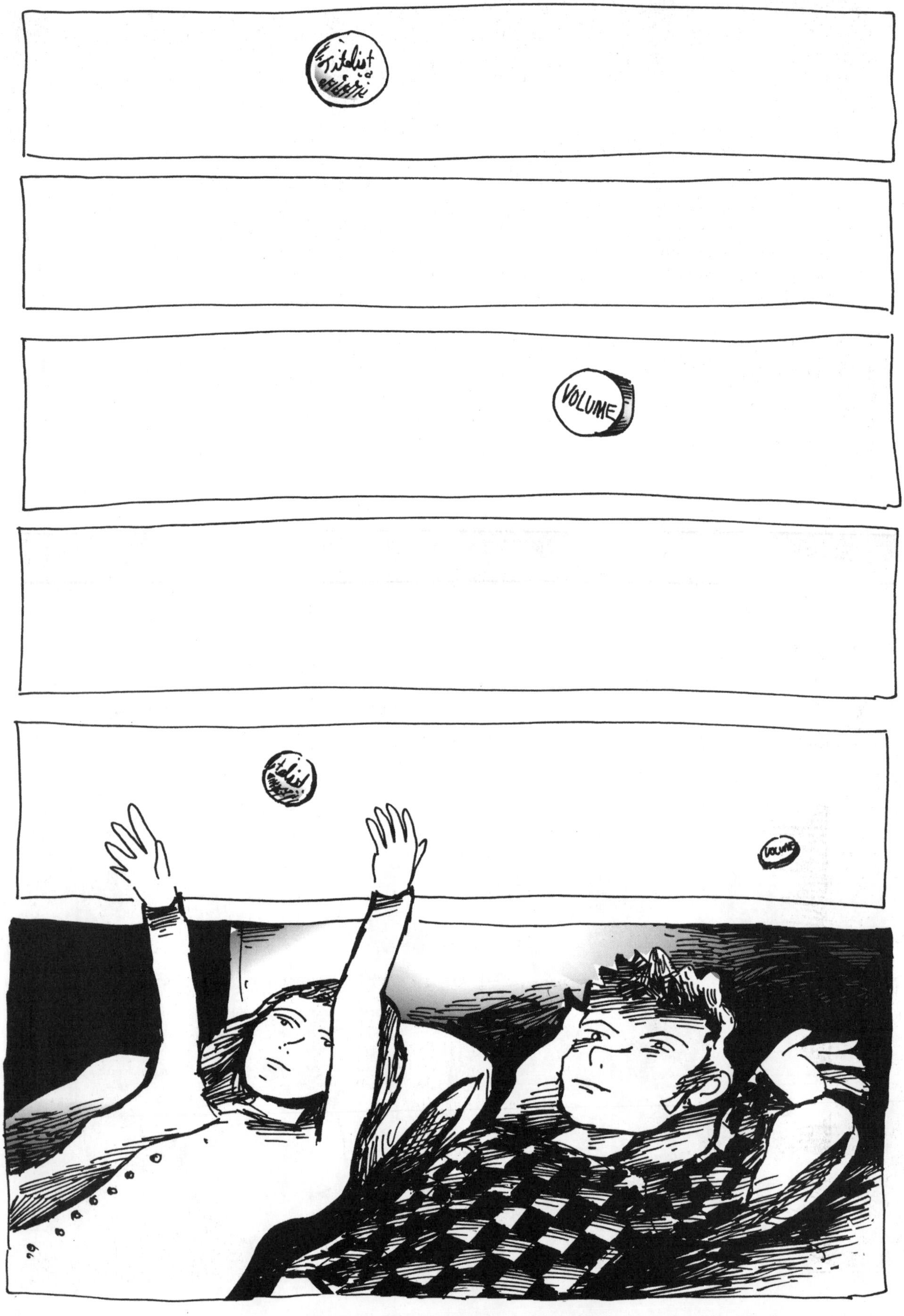
VOLUME
VOLUME

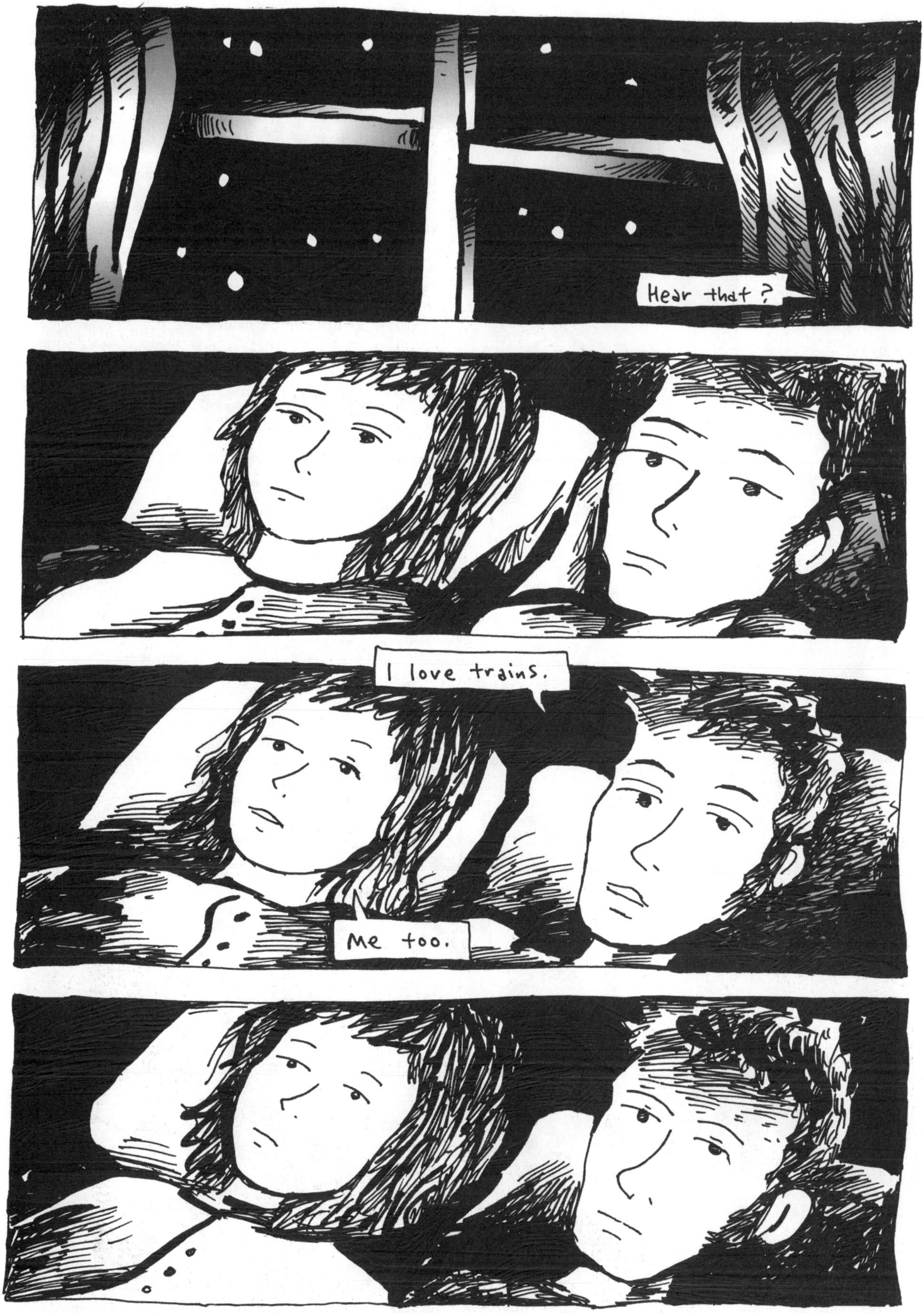
Hear that?
I love trains.
Me too.

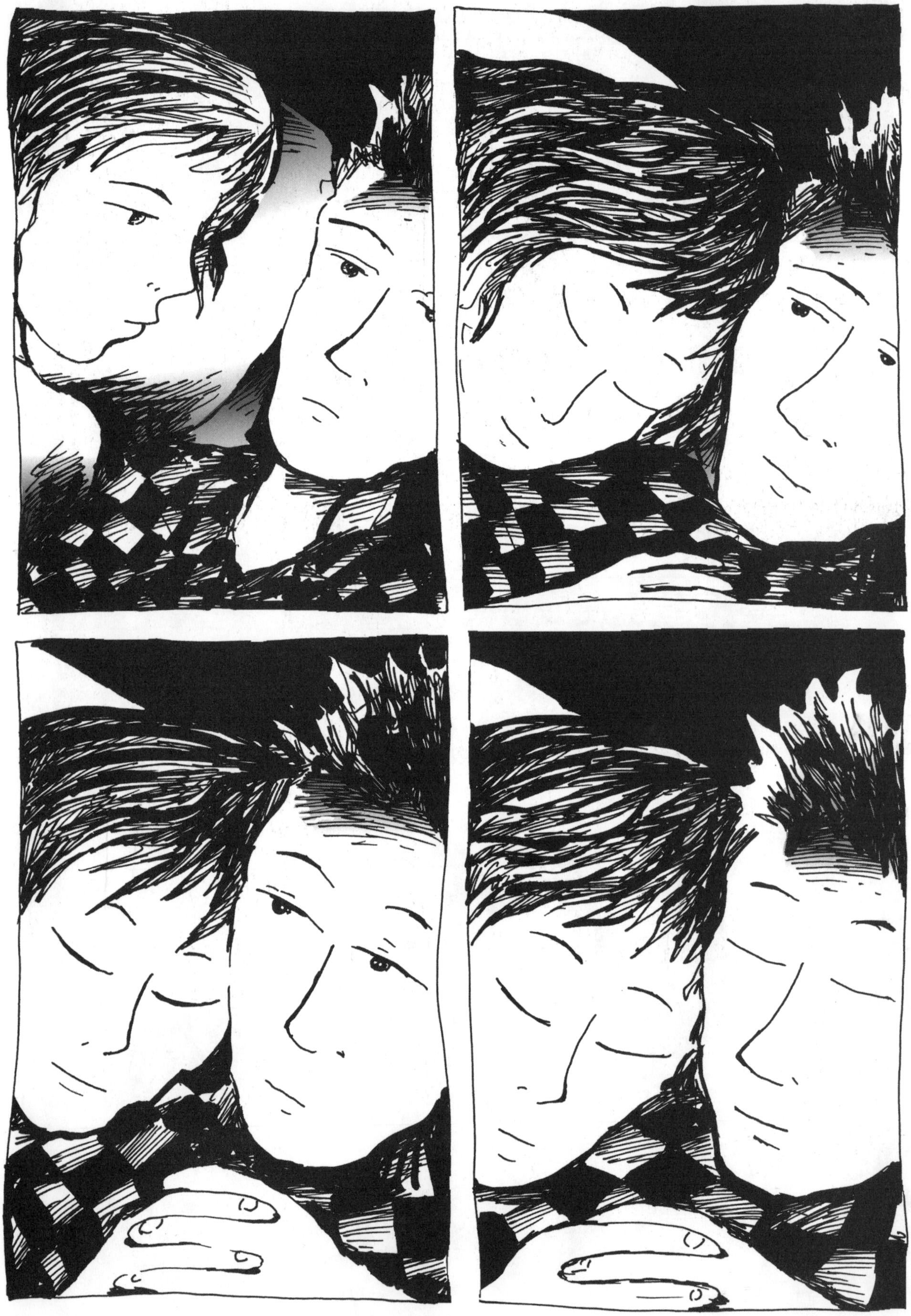

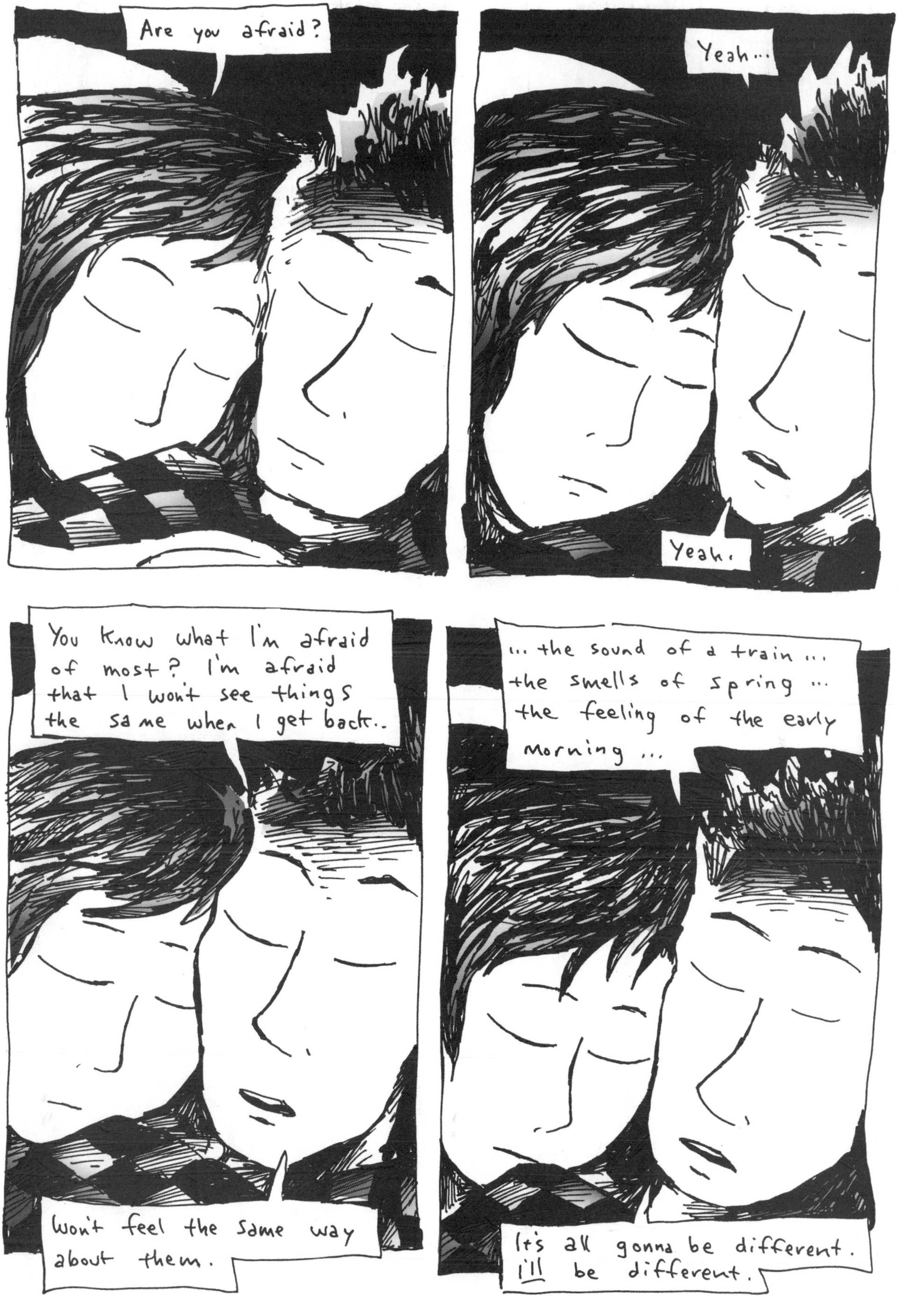
Are you afraid?
Yeah...
Yeah.
You know what I'm afraid of most? I'm afraid that I won't see things the same when I get back..
won't feel the same way about them.
... the sound of a train ... the smells of spring ... the feeling of the early morning ...
It's all gonna be different. I'll be different.

I wish...

...I wish that I was a kid again.

I wish that this was all just a dream.

Tomorrow morning I'd wake up with nothing more to do but run around the ravines by my house...

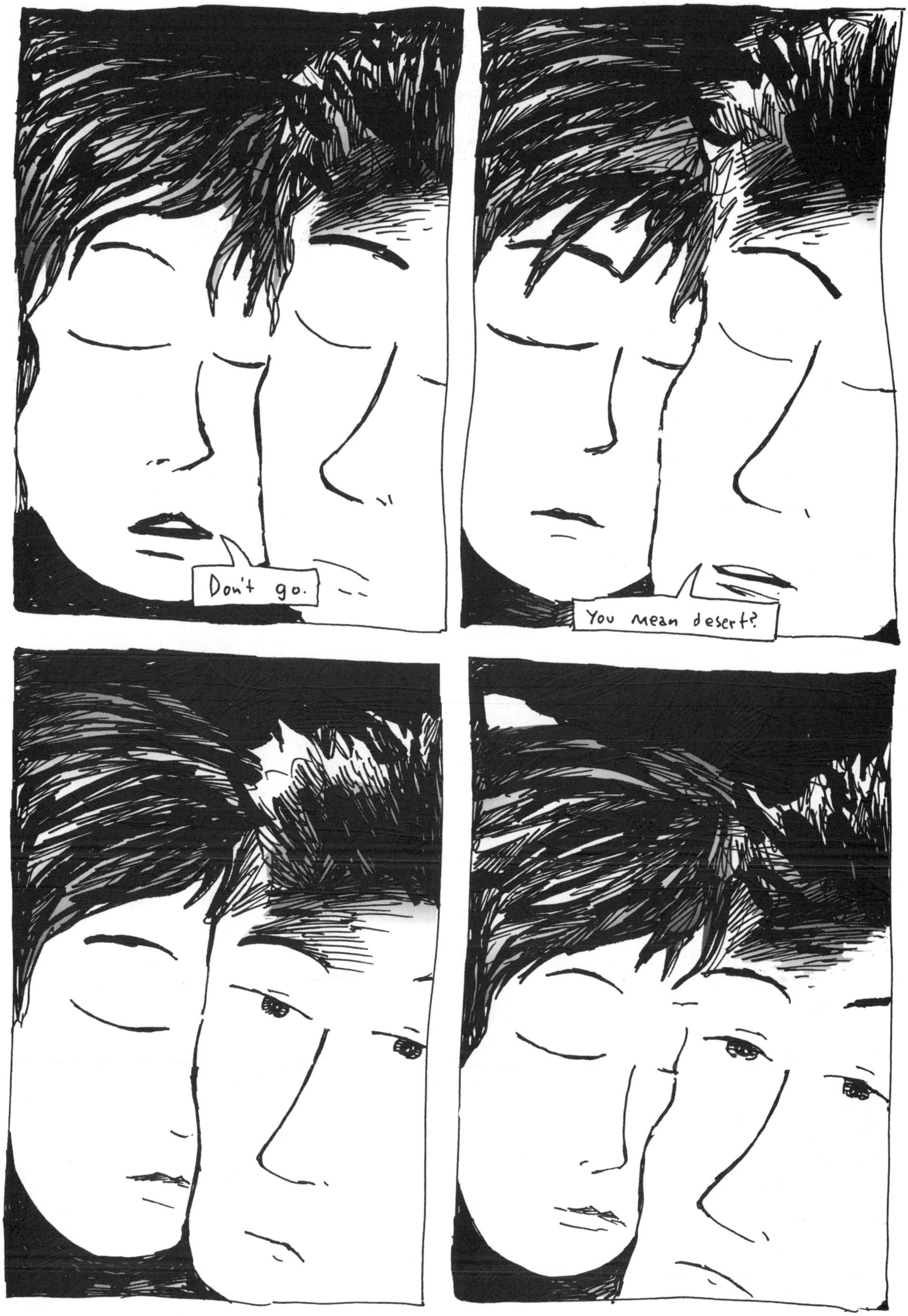
Don't go.
You mean desert?

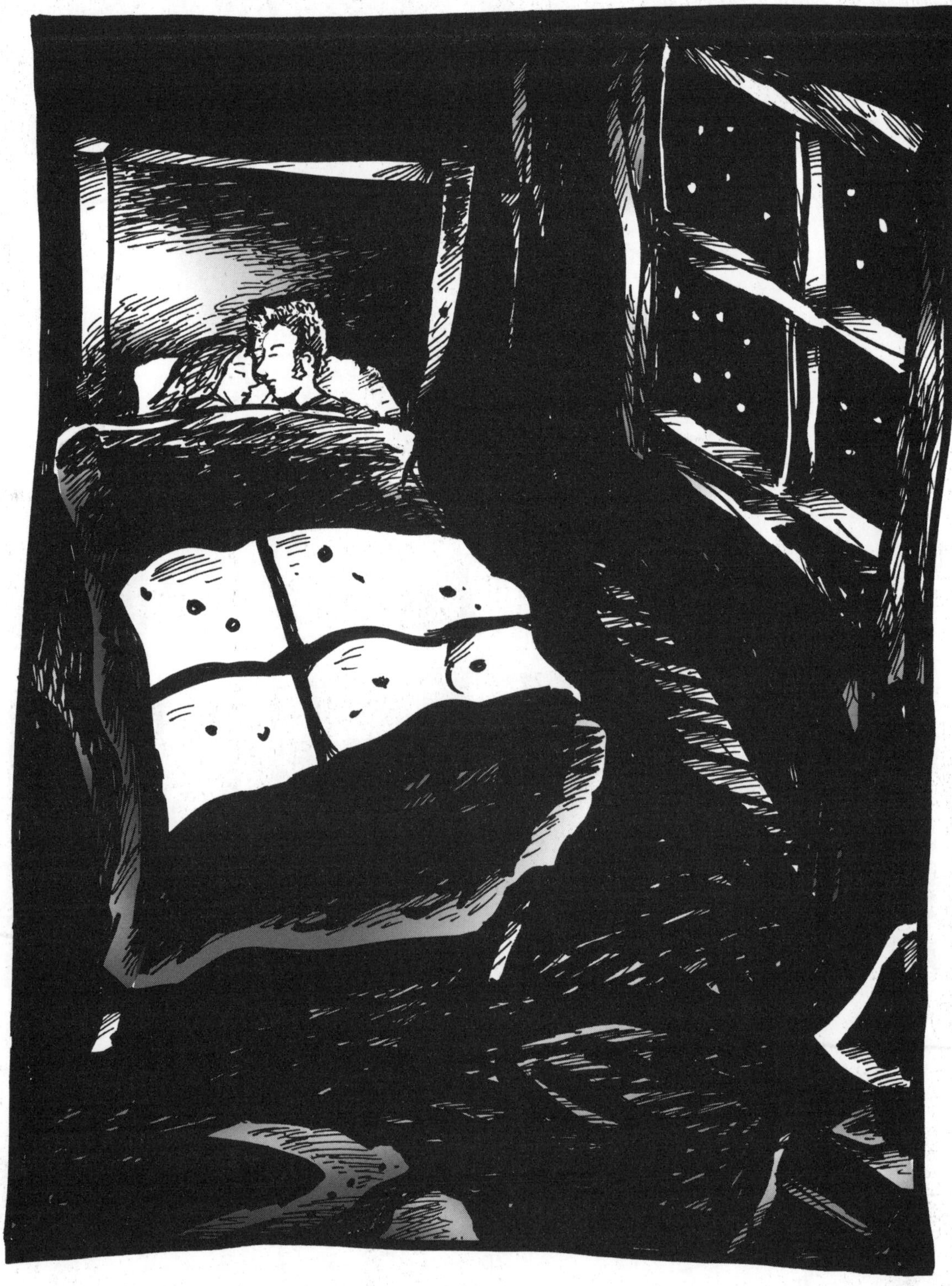

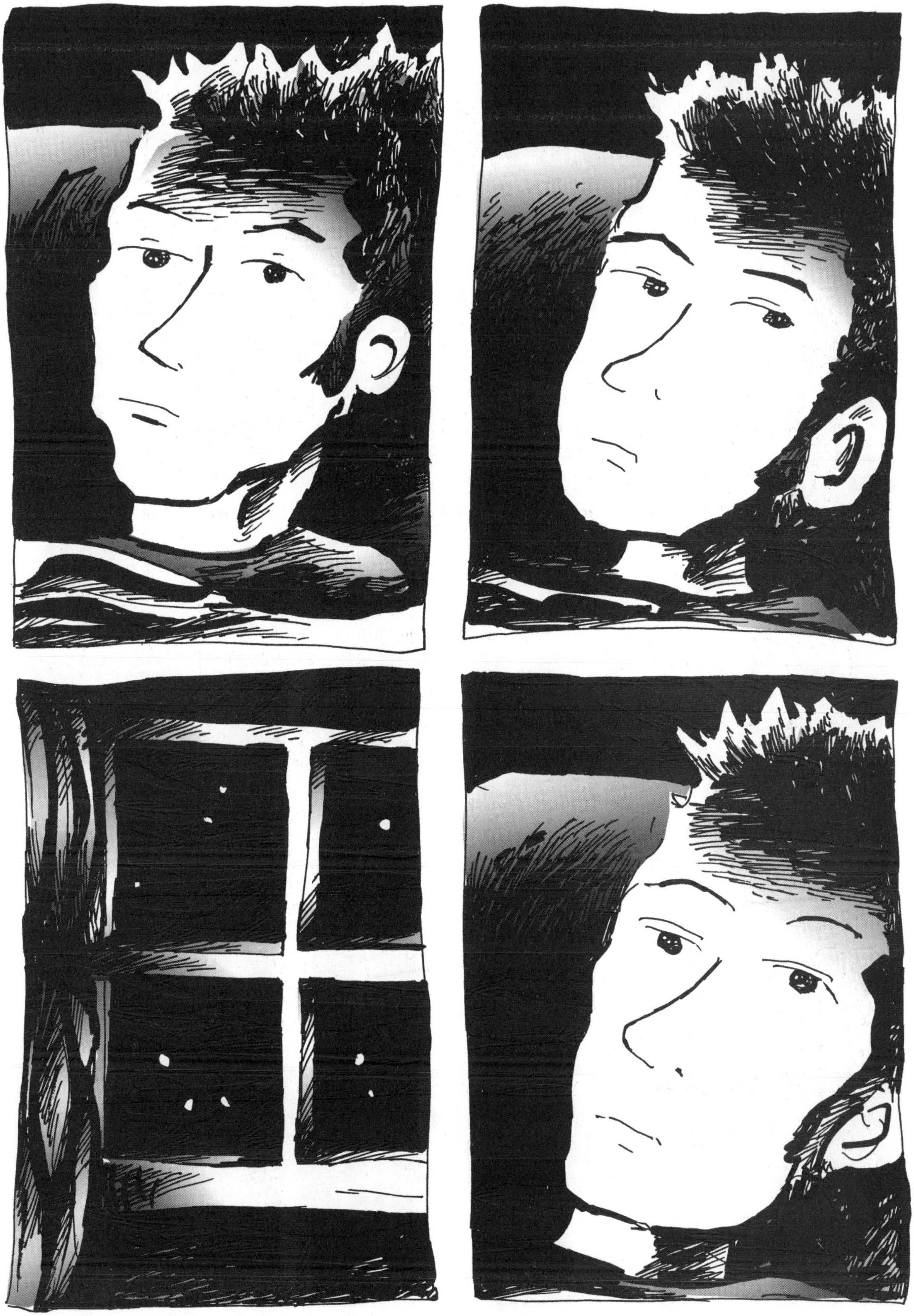

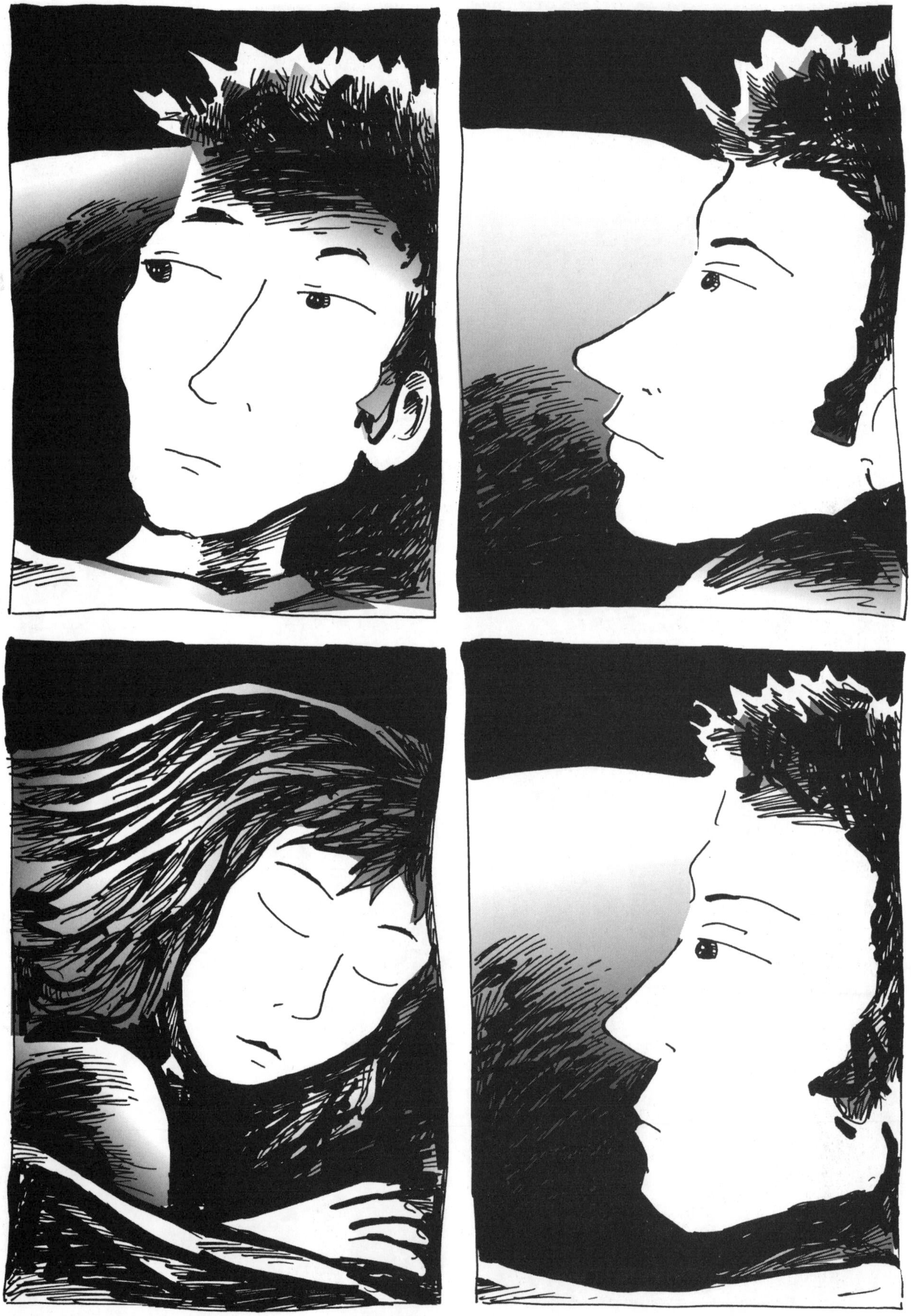

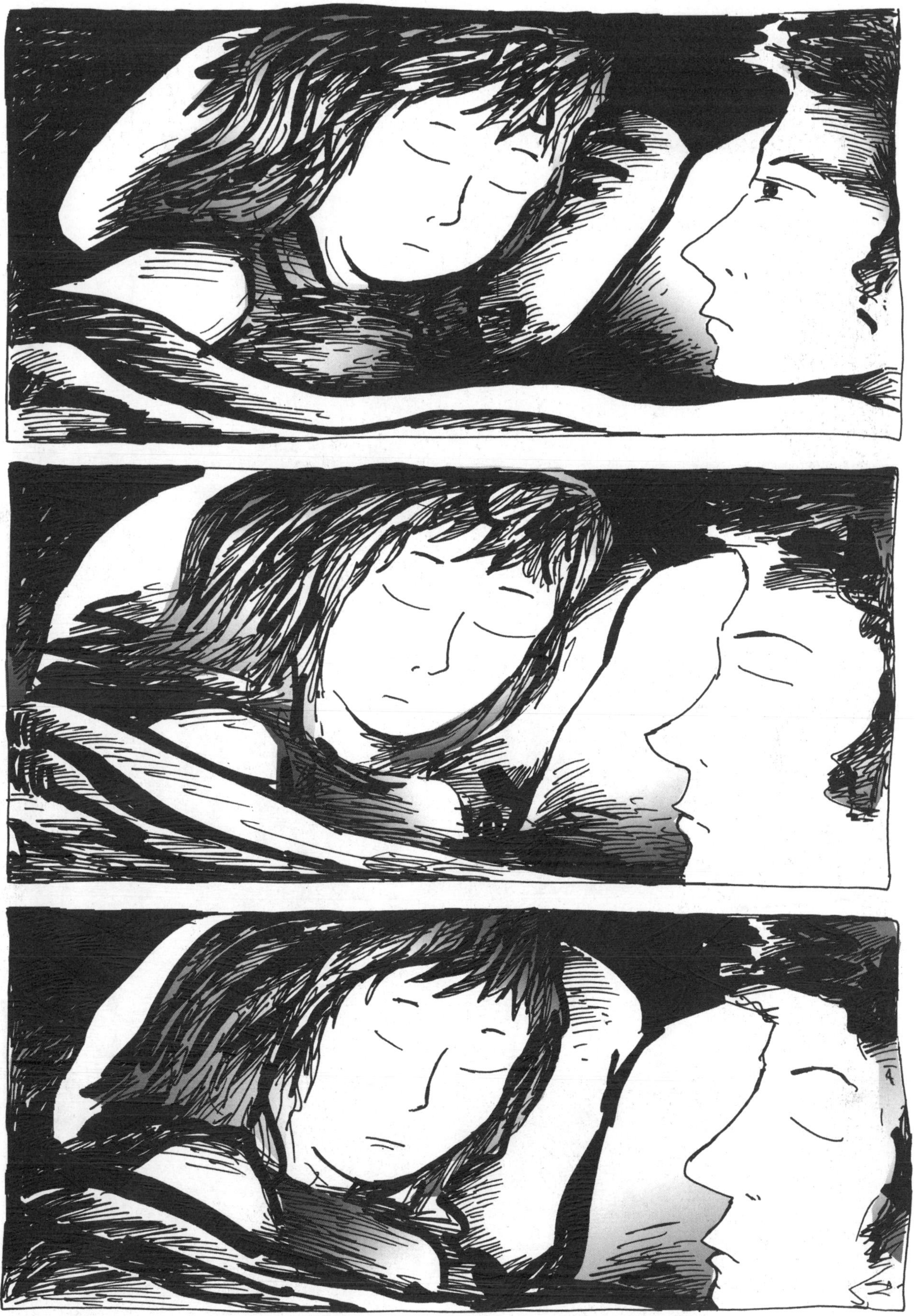

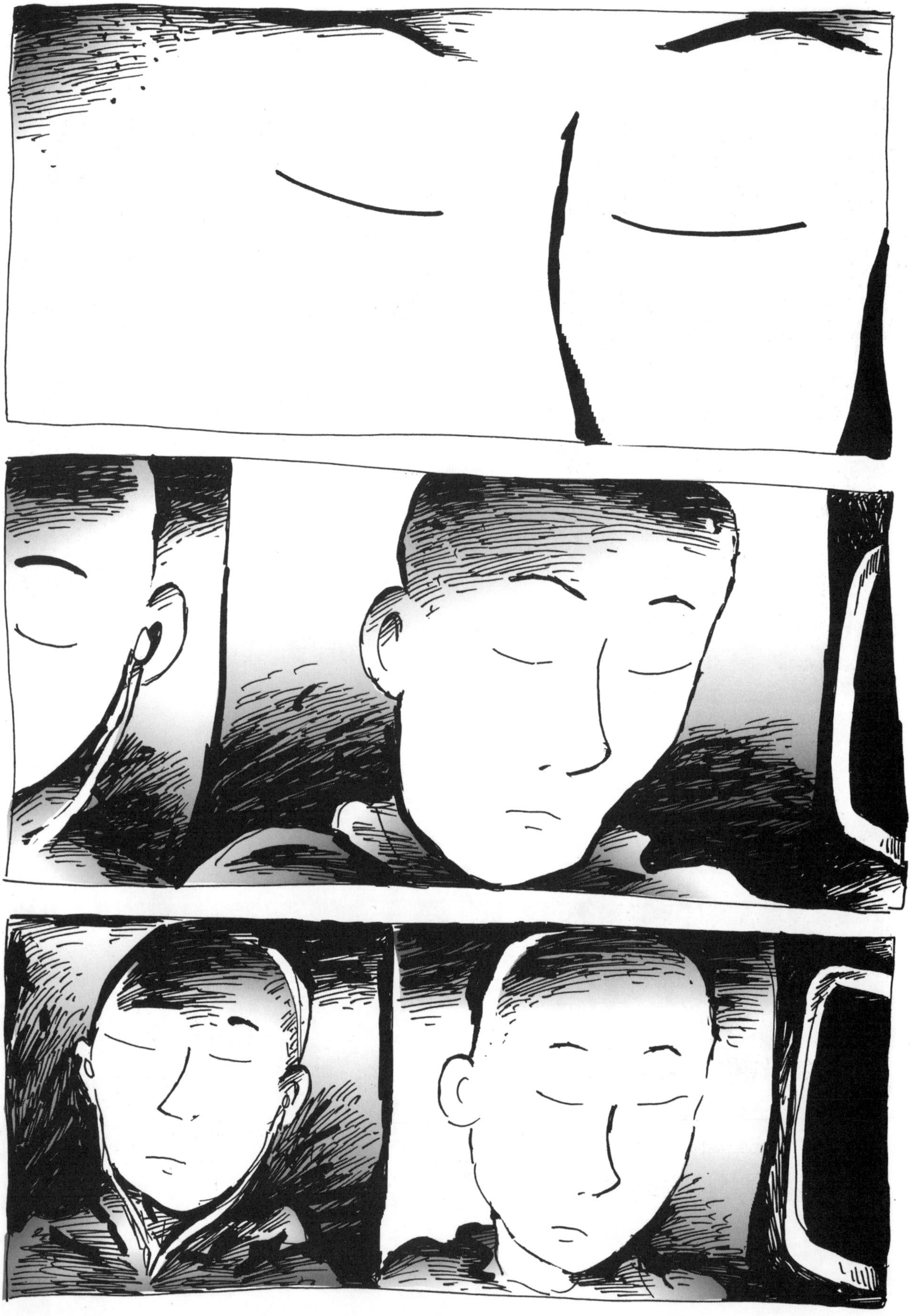

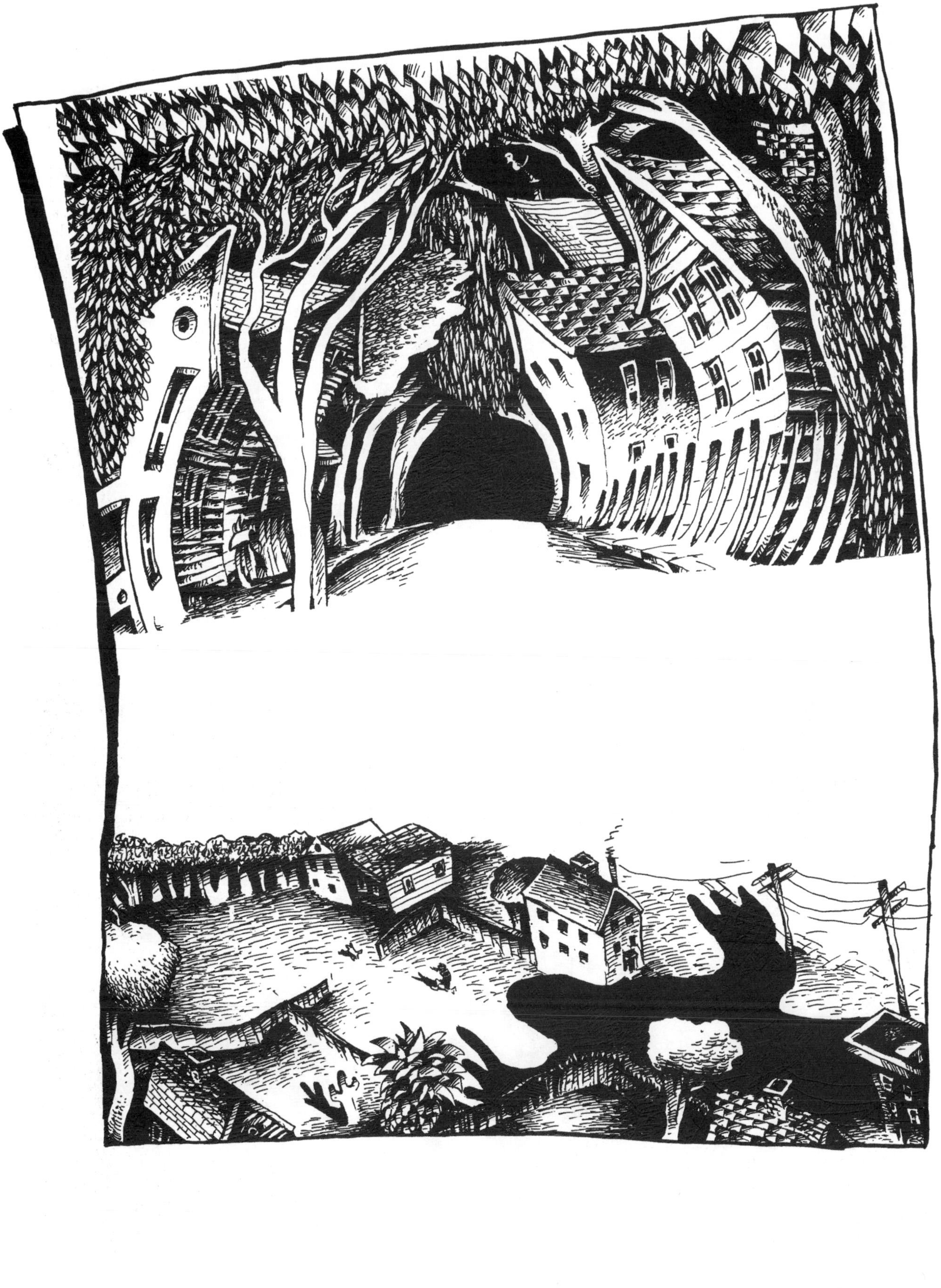

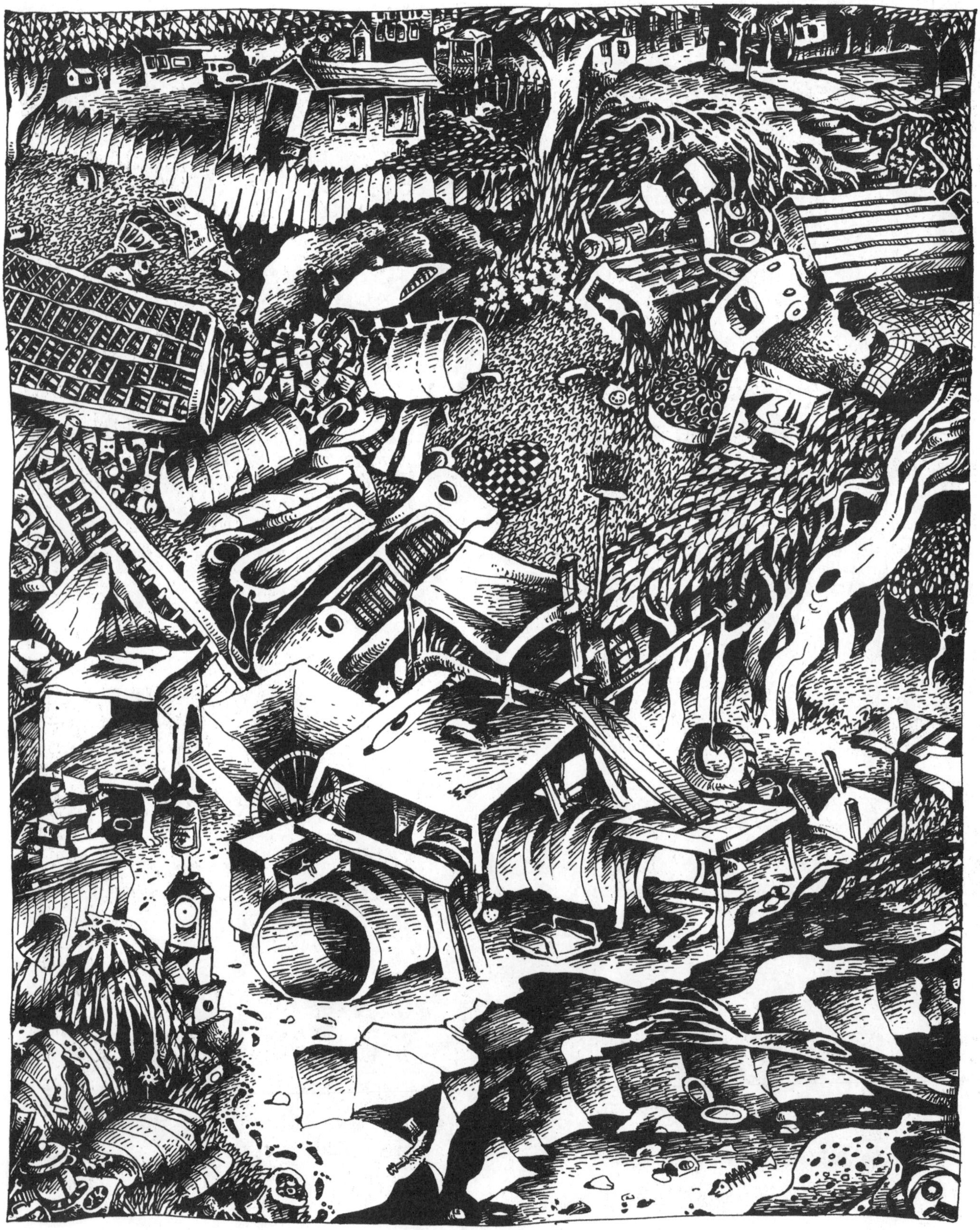

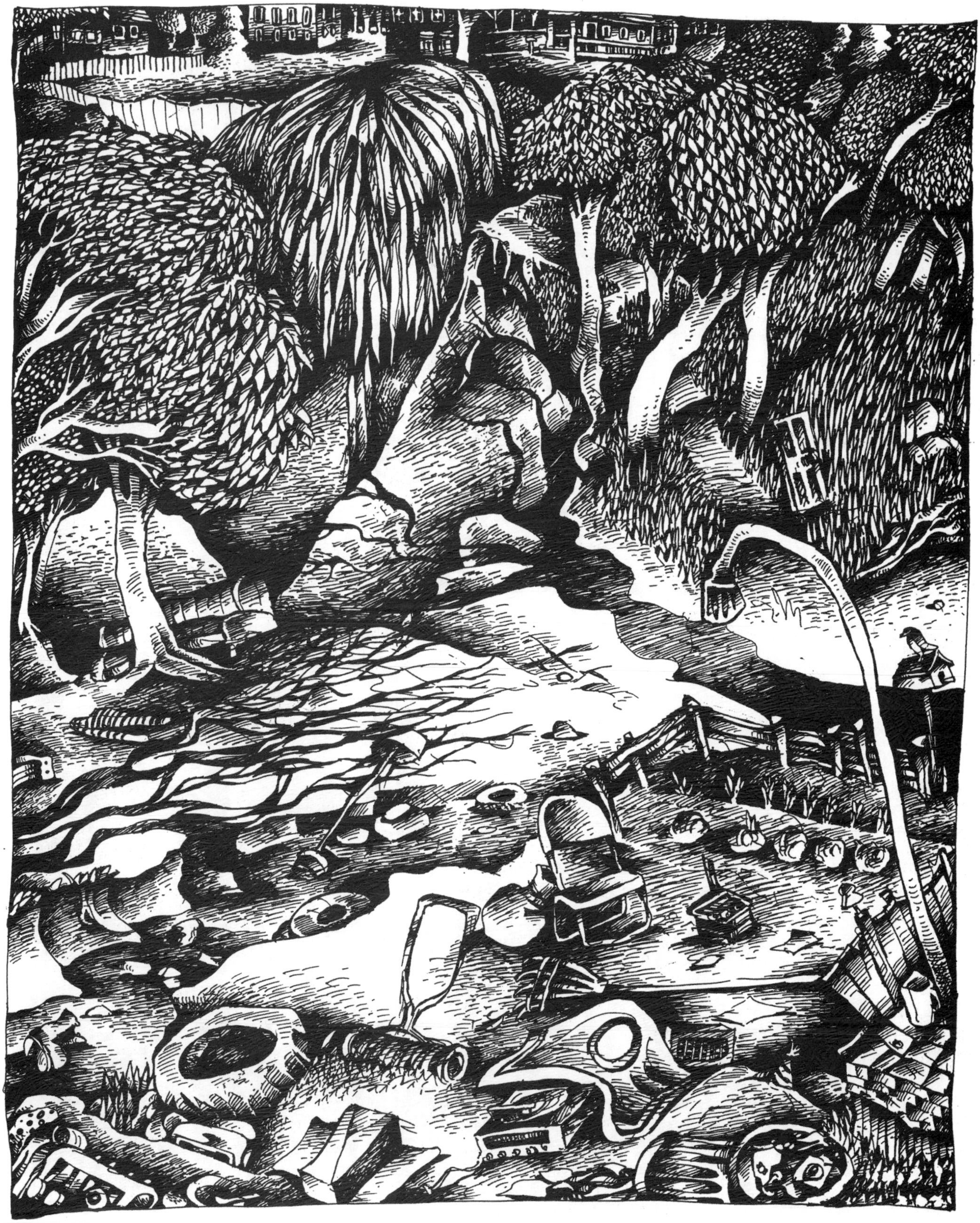

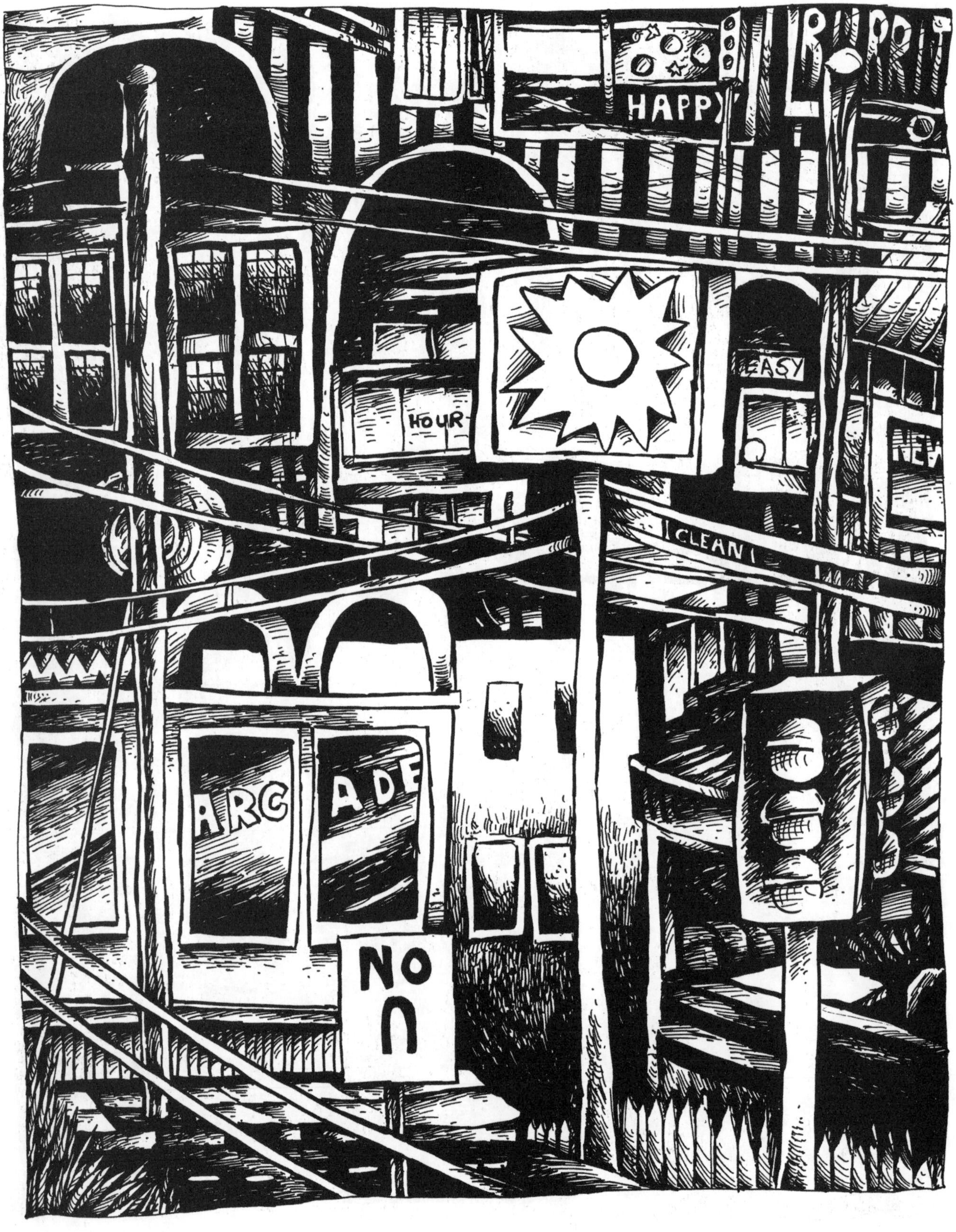
HAPPY
HOUR
EASY
CLEAN
ARC ADE
NO

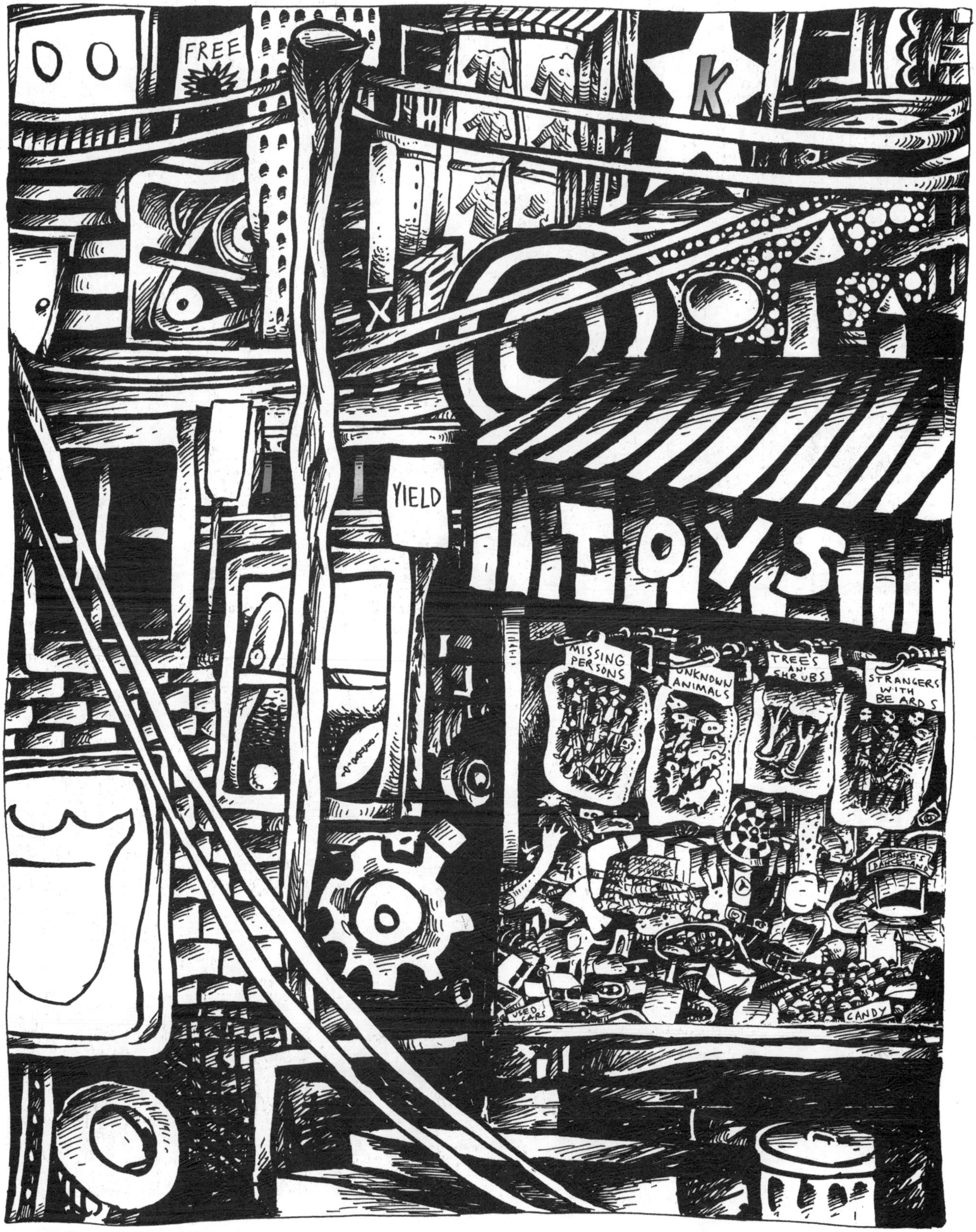

FREE
YIELD
TOYS
MISSING PERSONS
UNKNOWN ANIMALS
TREES AN' SHRUBS
STRANGERS WITH BEARDS
USED CARS
CANDY

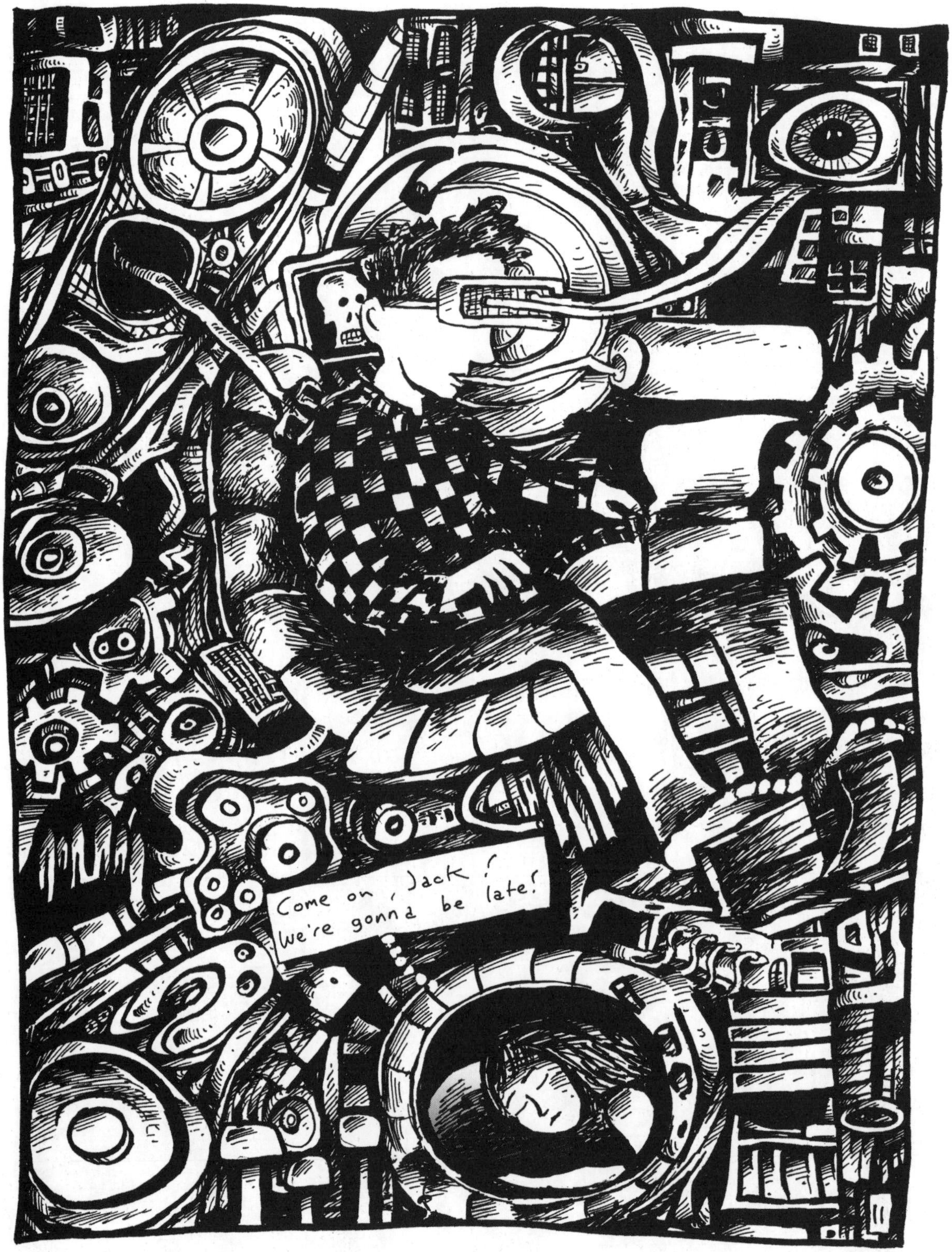
Come on, Jack! We're gonna be late!

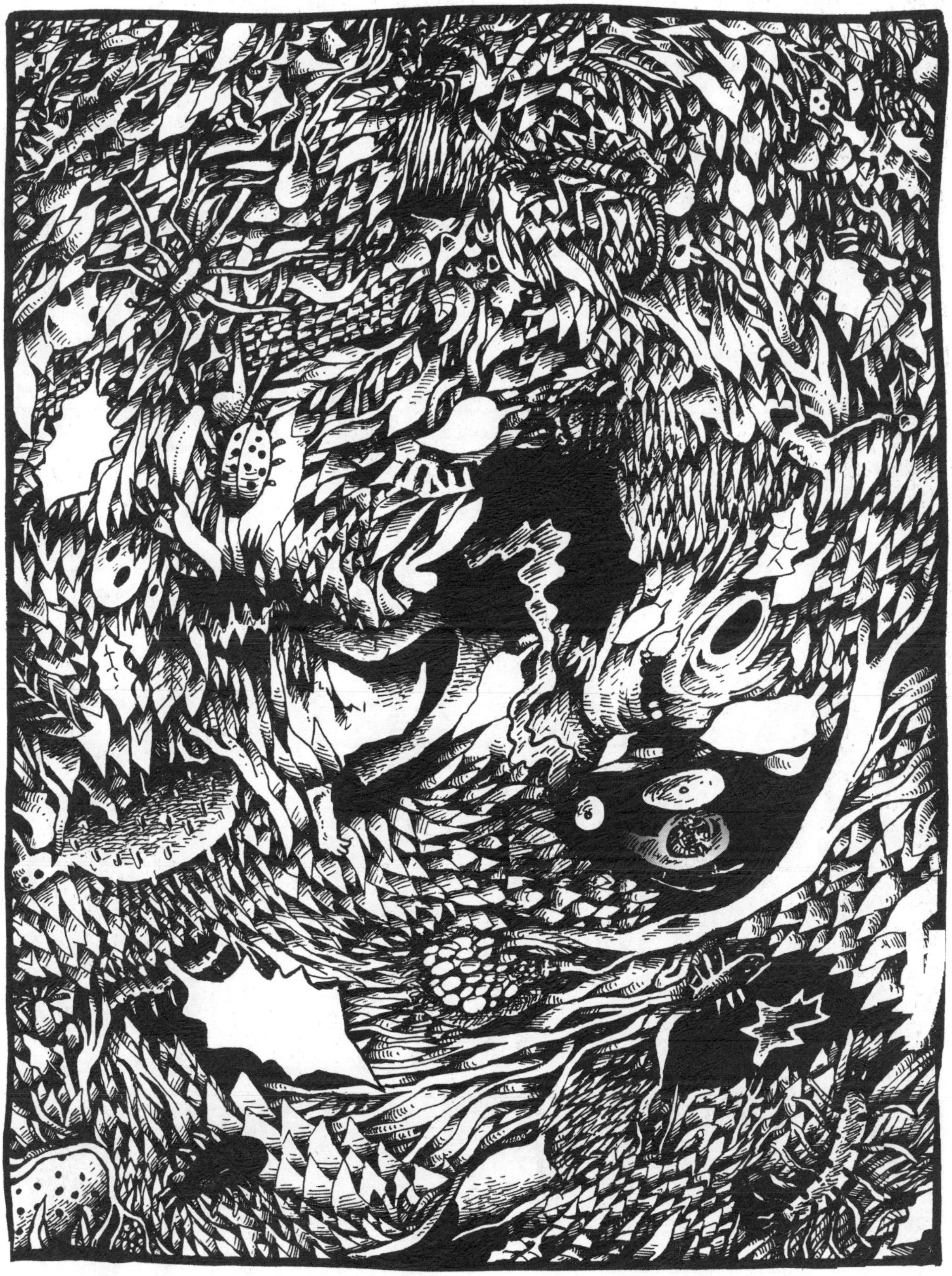

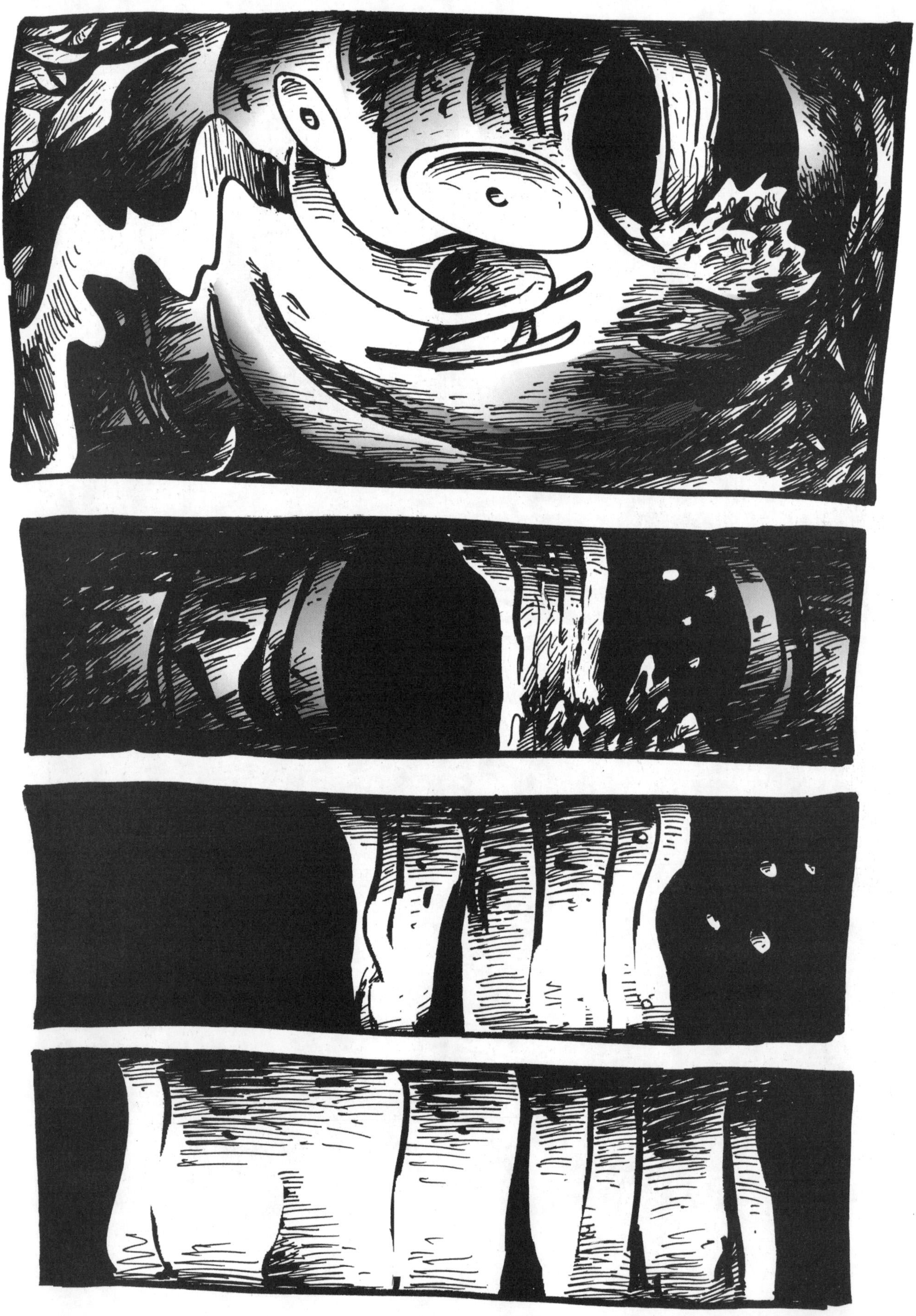

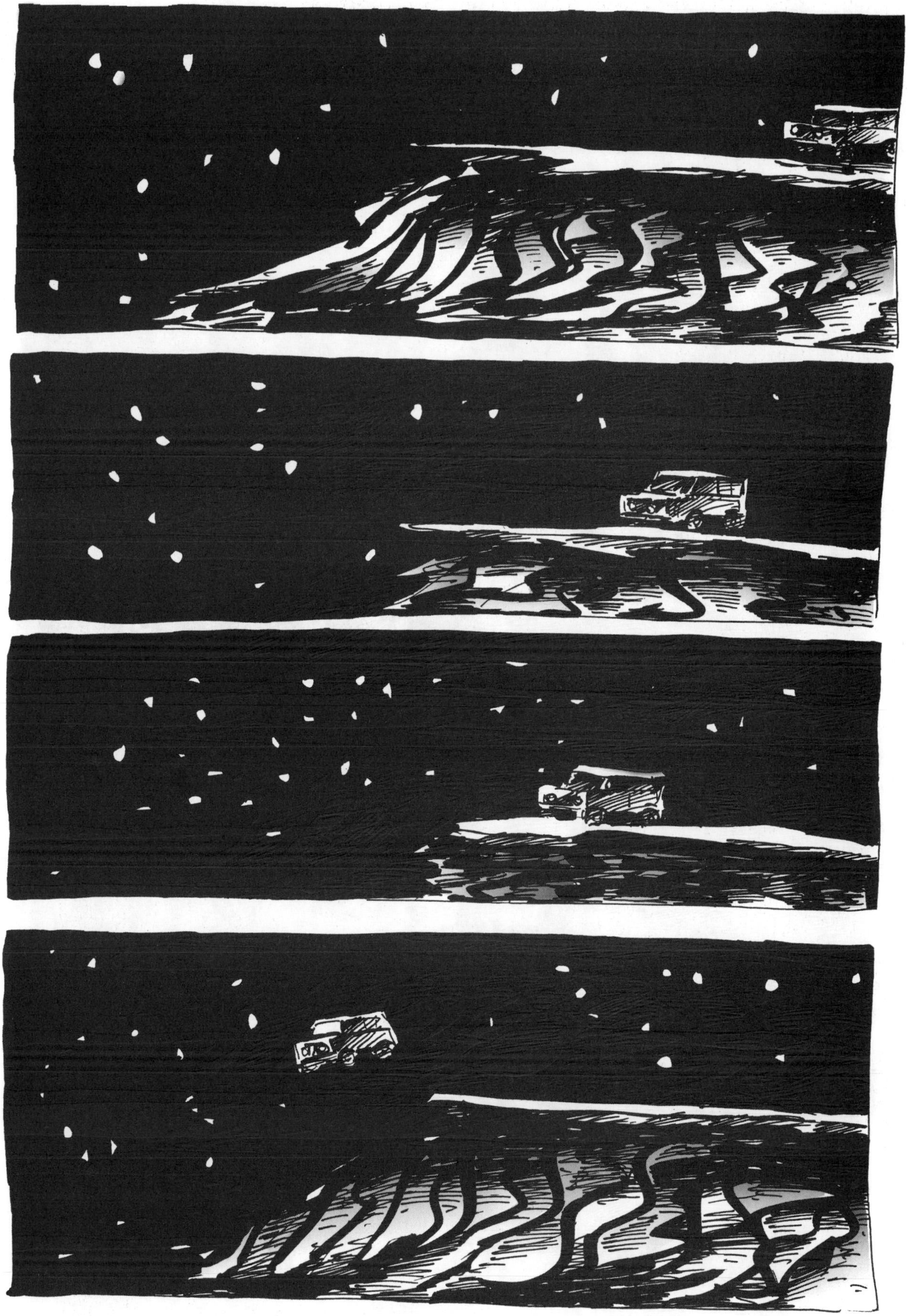

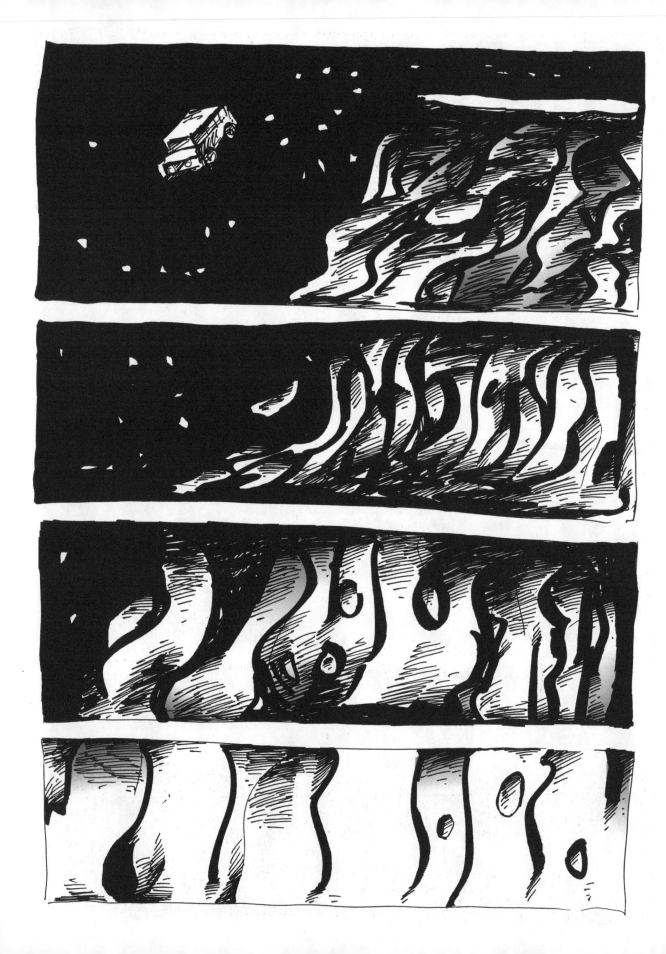

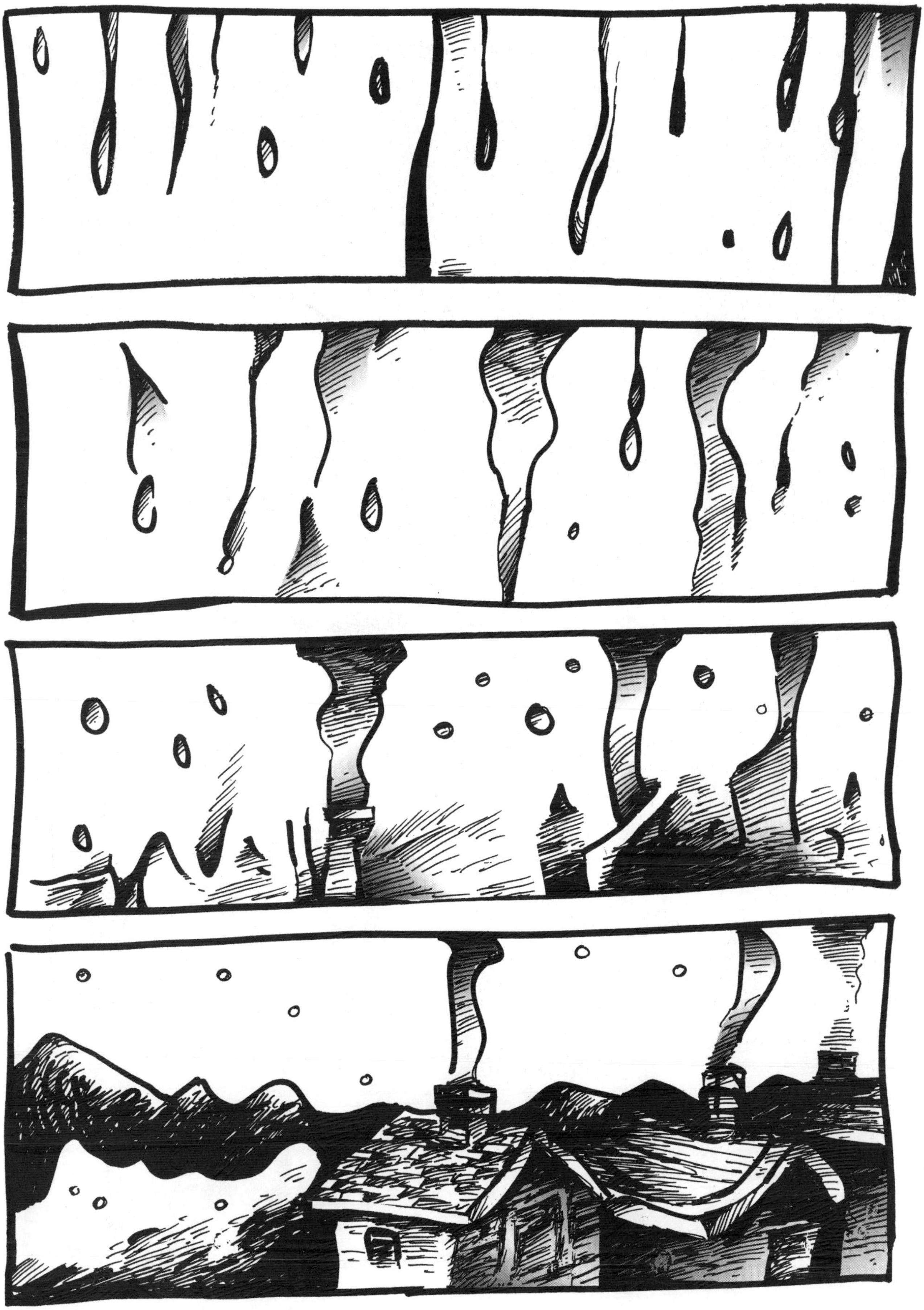

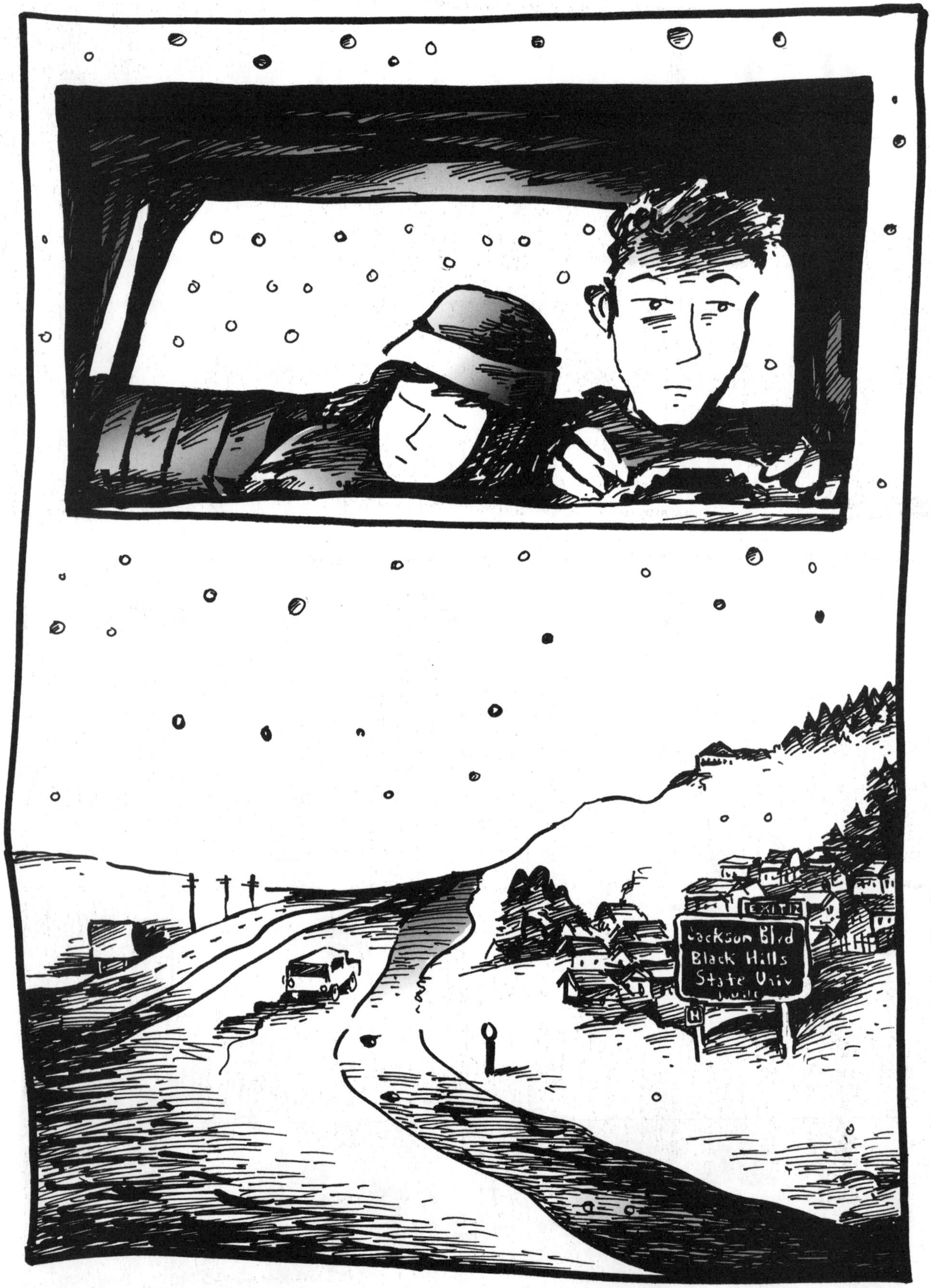
EXIT
Jackson Blvd
Black Hills
State Univ
H

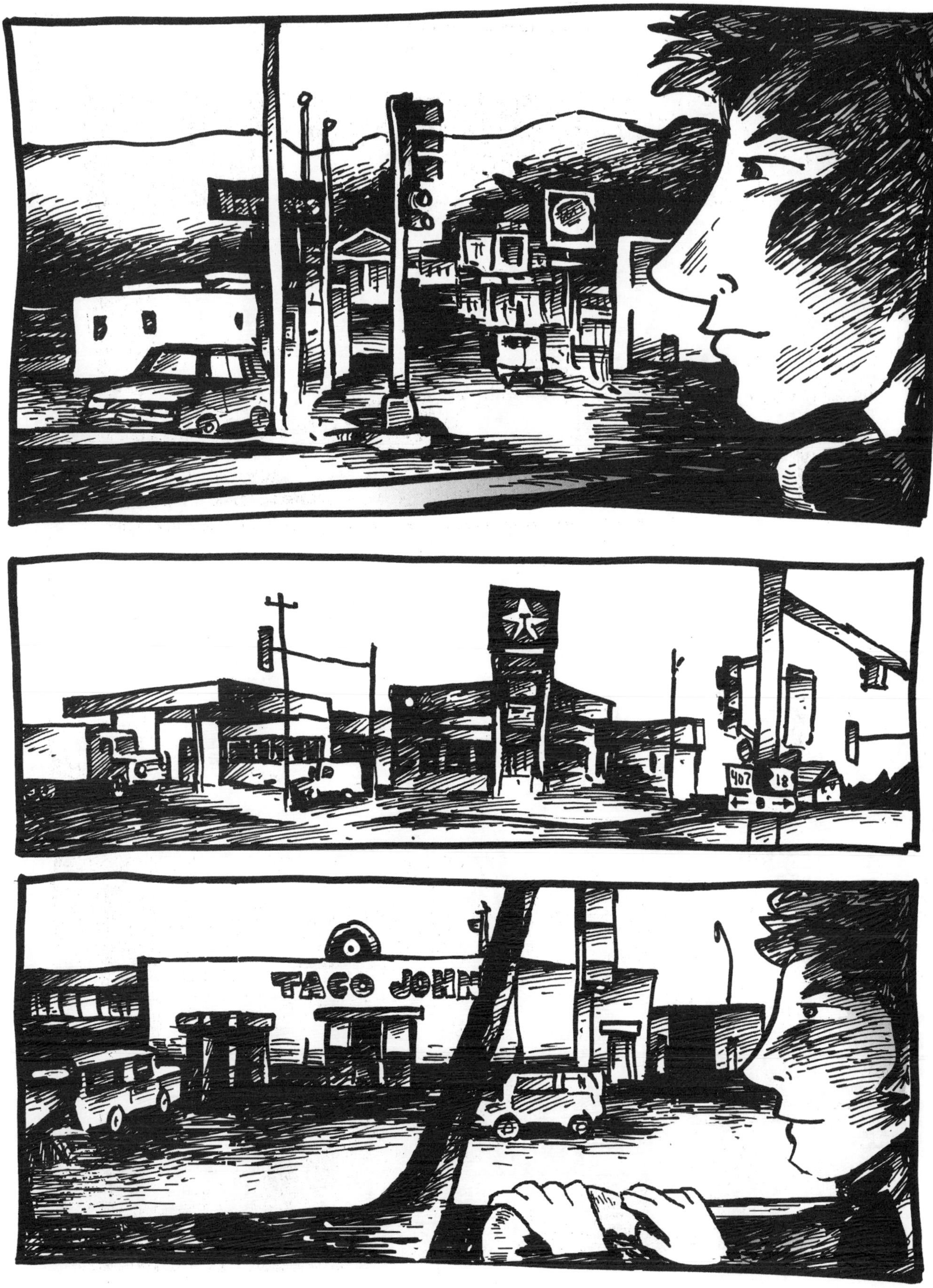
407
18
TACO JOHN

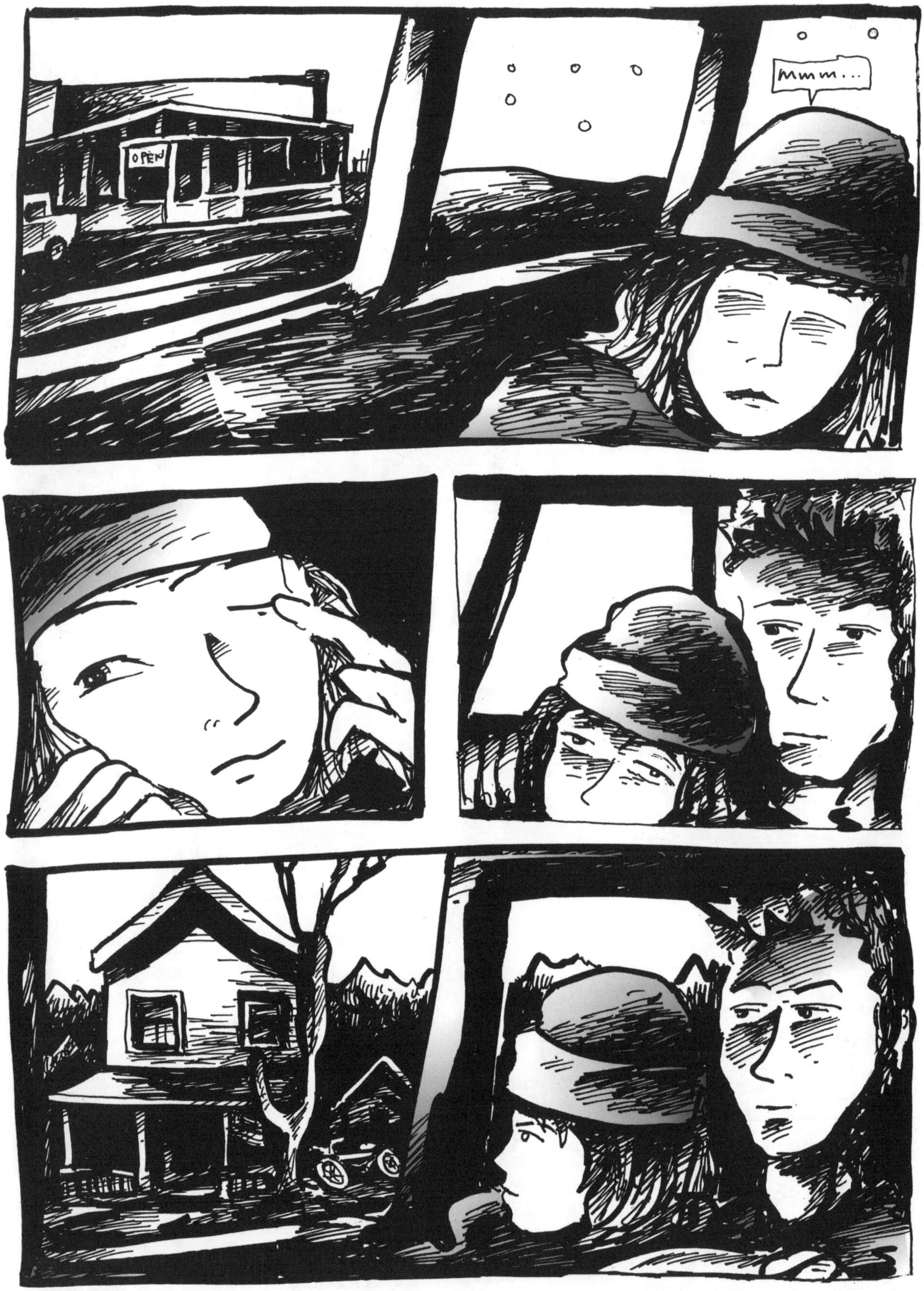
OPEN
Mmm...

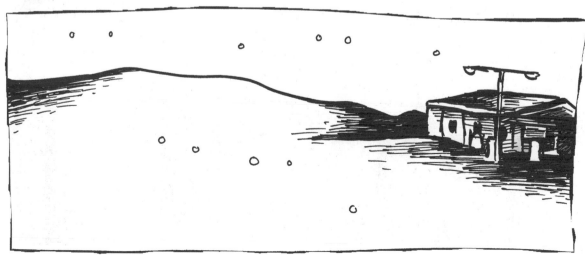

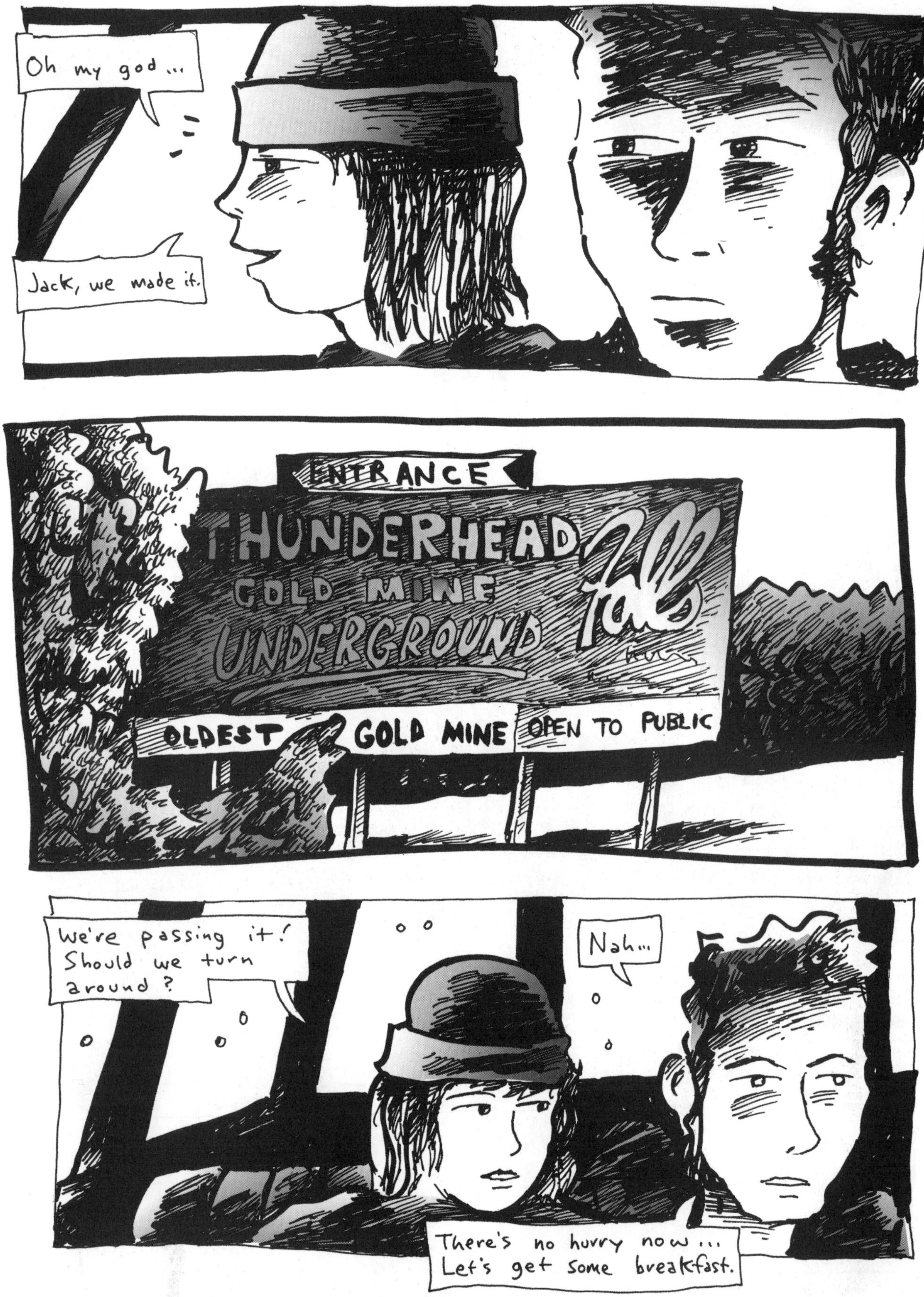
Oh my god...
Jack, we made it.
ENTRANCE
THUNDERHEAD
GOLD MINE
UNDERGROUND
OLDEST GOLD MINE OPEN TO PUBLIC
We're passing it! Should we turn around?
Nah...
There's no hurry now... Let's get some breakfast.

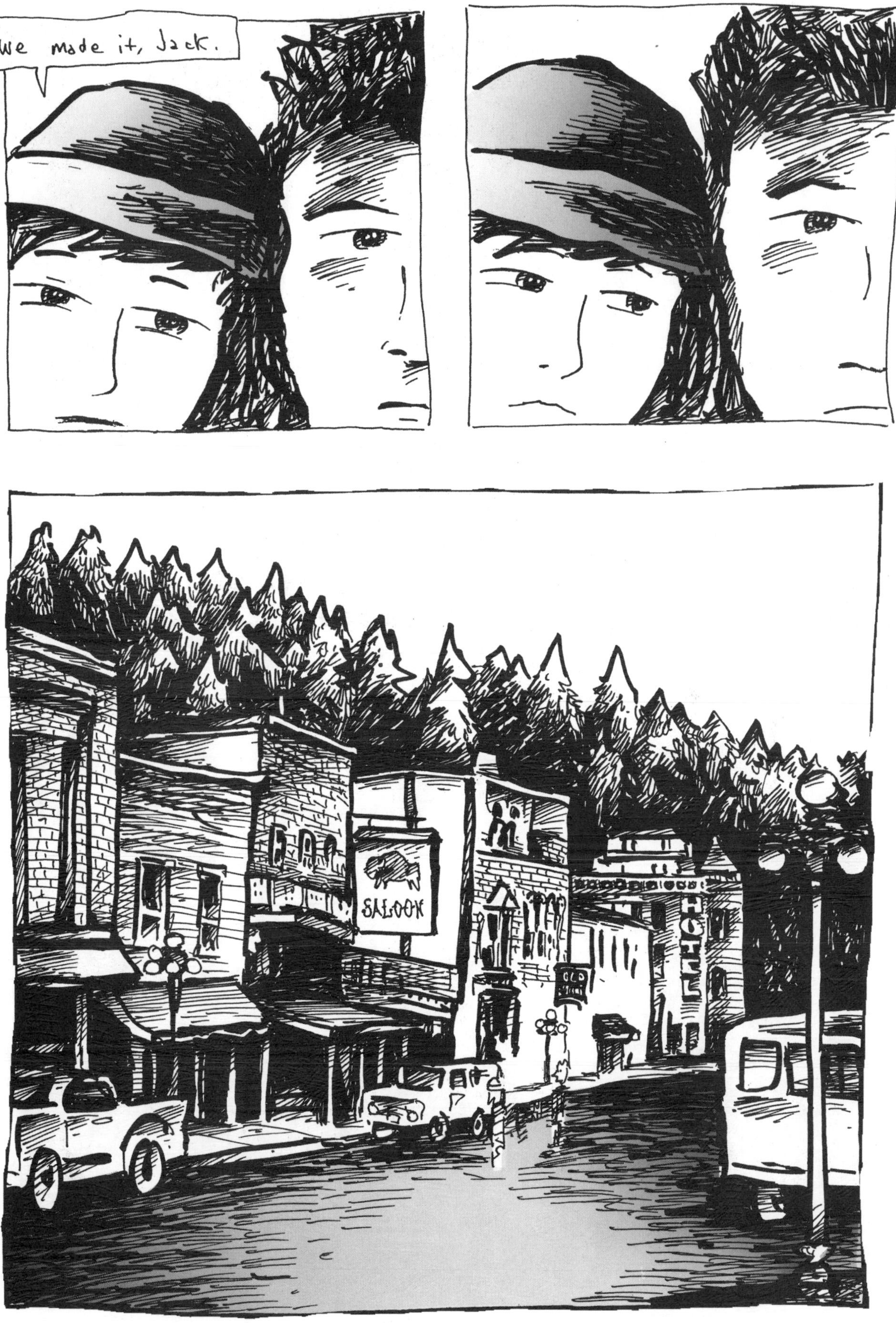
We made it, Jack.
SALOON
HOTEL

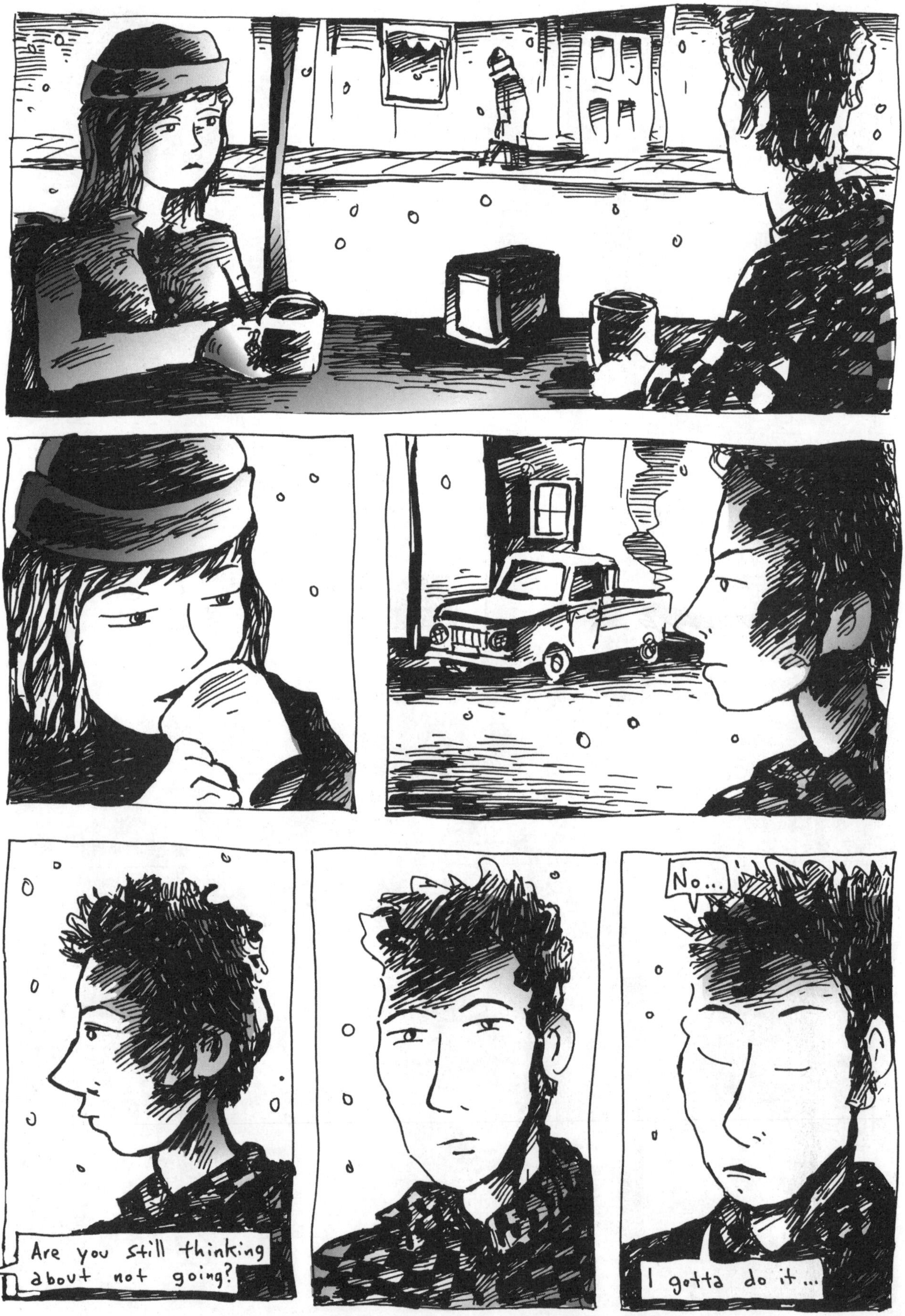
Are you still thinking about not going?
No...
I gotta do it...

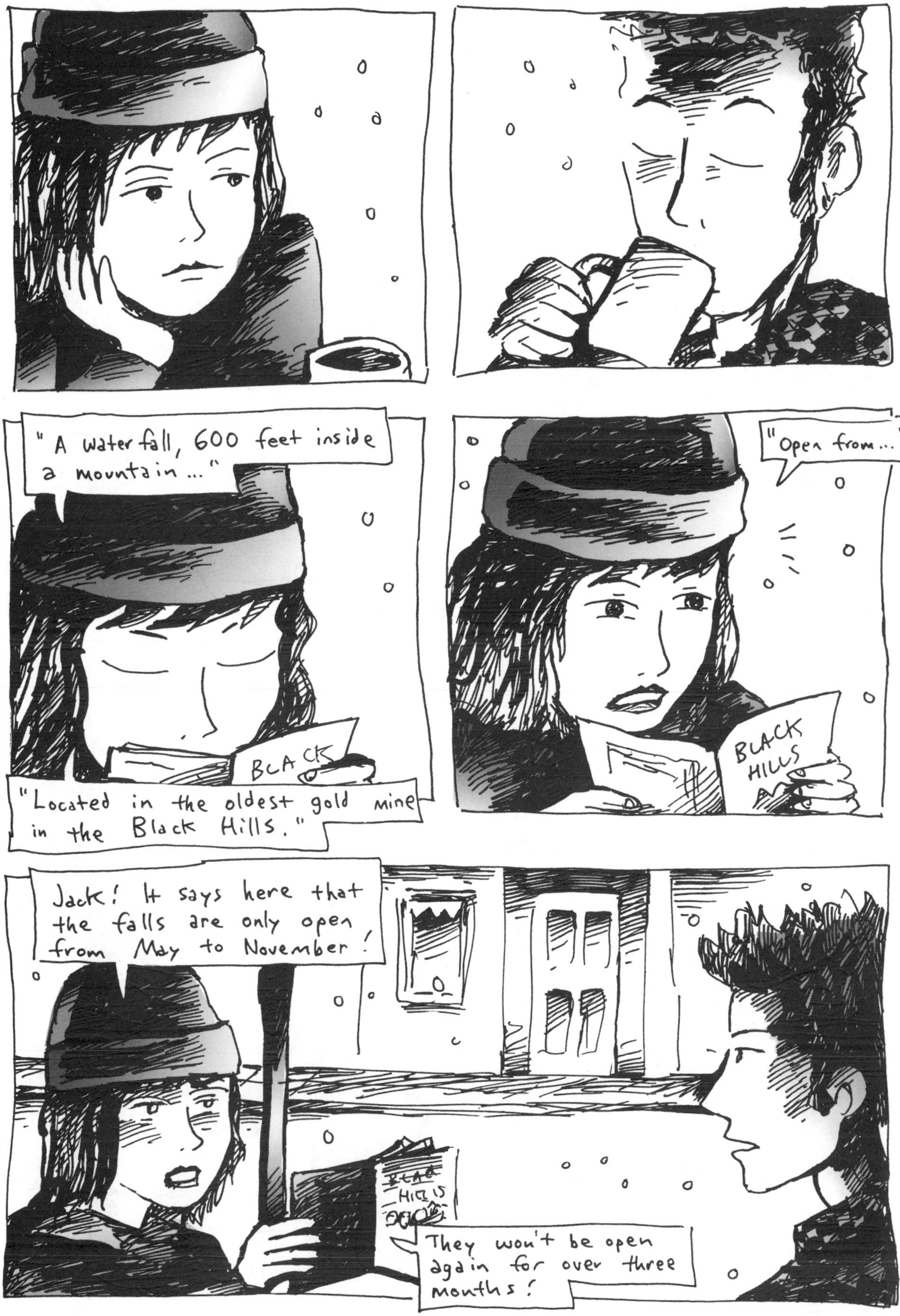
"A waterfall, 600 feet inside a mountain..."
BLACK
"Located in the oldest gold mine in the Black Hills."
"Open from..."
BLACK HILLS
Jack! It says here that the falls are only open from May to November!
BLACK HILLS
They won't be open again for over three months!

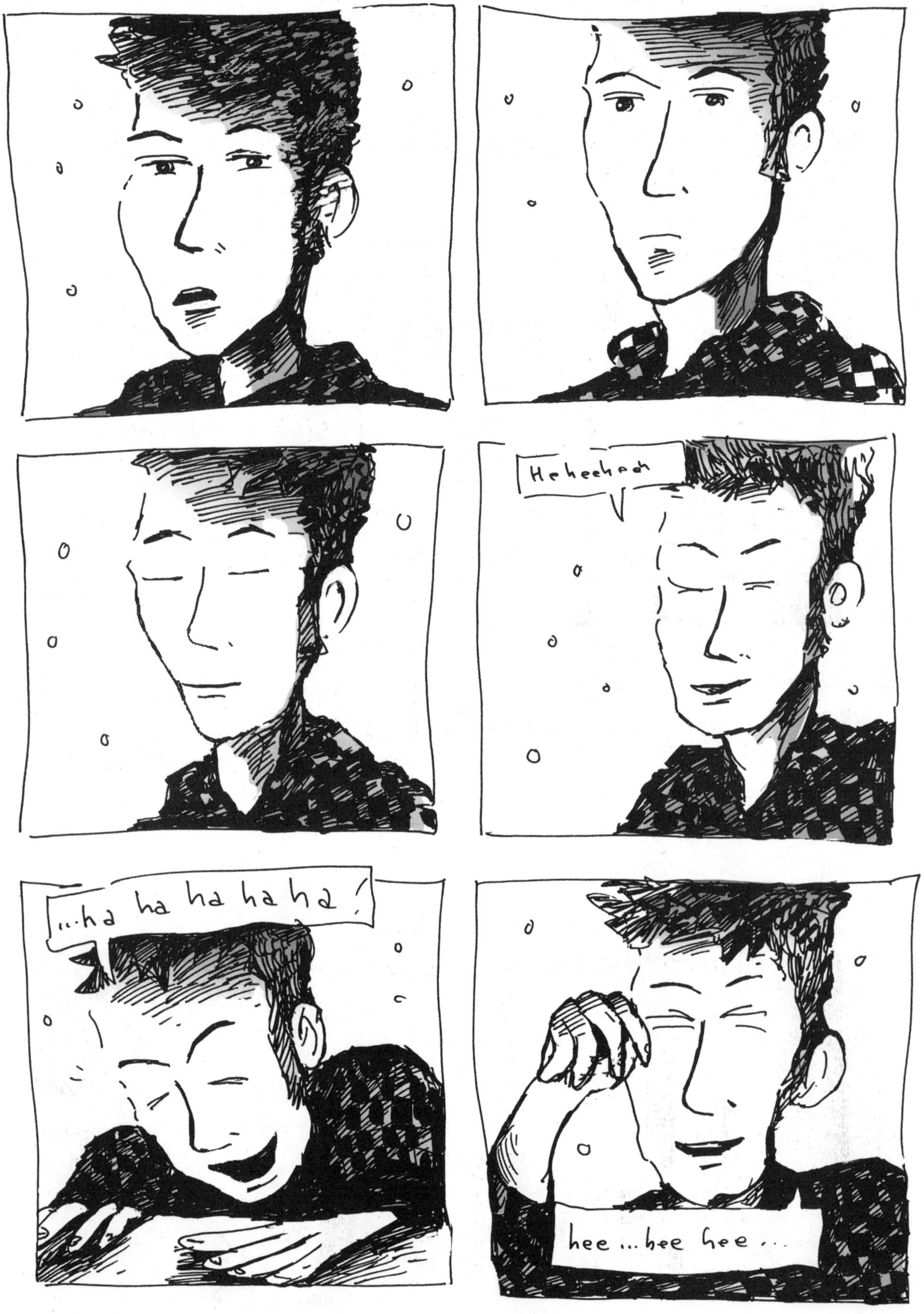
Heheeheeh
...ha ha ha ha ha!
hee ... hee hee ...

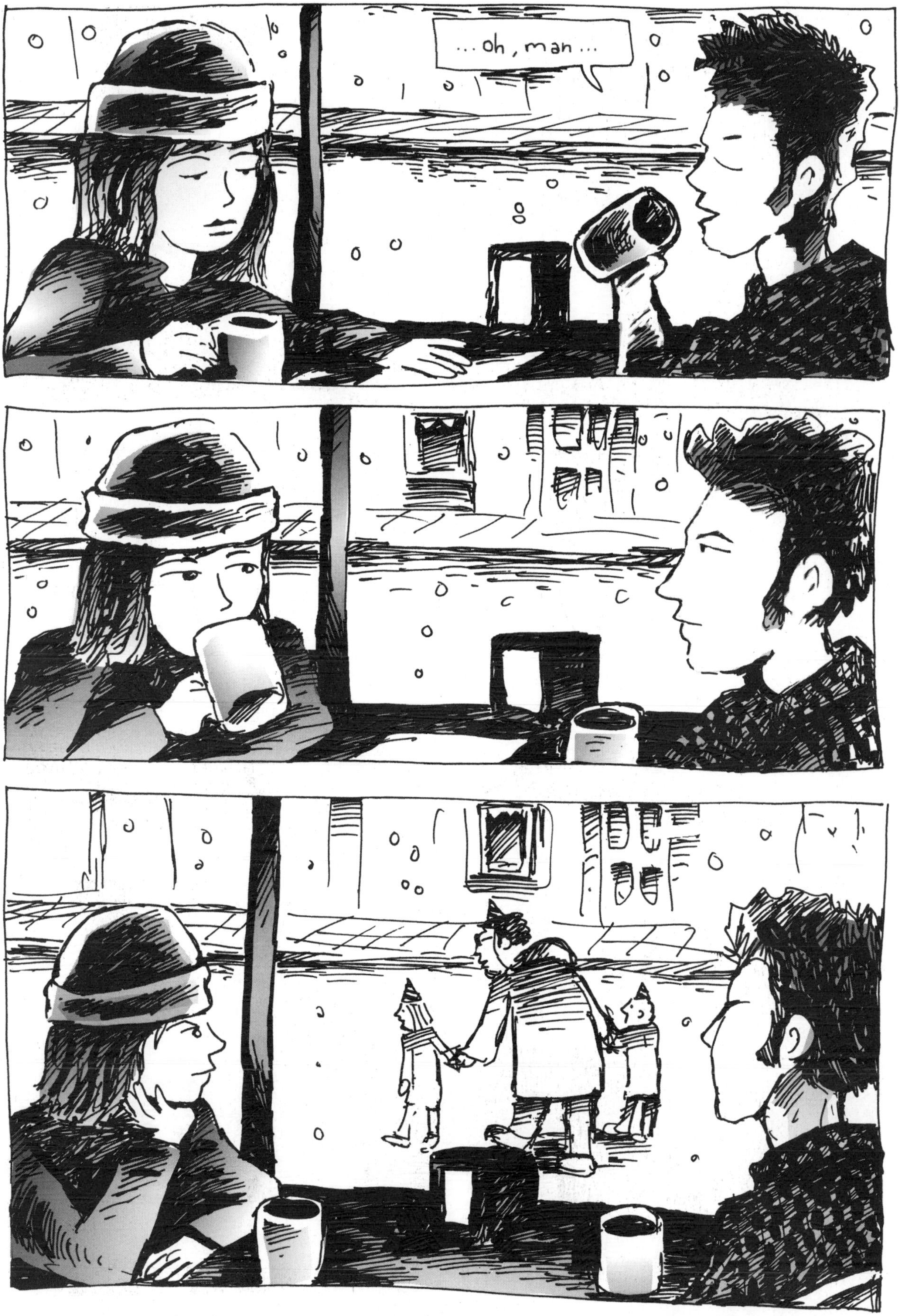
...oh, man...